D0836833

Marrakech
day BY day™
1st Edition

by Kerry Christiani

WILEY

A John Wiley and Sons, Ltd, Publication

Contents

15 Favorite Moments 1

1 The Best Full-Day Tours 5
The Best in One Day 6
The Best in Two Days 10
The Best in Three Days 14

2 The Best Special-Interest Tours 17
Magical Marrakech 18
Arts & Crafts 24
Urban Escape Acts 30
Celebrity Marrakech 36
Architectural Elements 42

3 The Best Neighborhood Walks 47
Central Souks & Around 48
Kasbah, Mellah & Around 54
Jemaa el Fna & Around 60
North of Souks & Mouassine 64
Ville Nouvelle 72

4 The Best Shopping 79
Shopping Best Bets 80
Marrakech Shopping A to Z 86

5 The Great Outdoors 95
Best Outdoor Pursuits 96
Green Marrakech 100

6 The Best Dining 103
Dining Best Bets 104
Marrakech Dining A to Z 110

7 The Best Nightlife 119
Nightlife Best Bets 120
Marrakech Nightlife A to Z 124

8 The Best Arts & Entertainment 129
Arts & Entertainment Best Bets 130
Arts & Entertainment A to Z 133

9 The Best Lodging 135
Lodging Best Bets 136
Marrakech Lodging A to Z 140

**10 The Best Day Trips &
Excursions 147**
Essaouira 148
Where to Stay 154
Where to Dine 155
Ourika Valley & Oukaïmeden 156

The Savvy Traveler 159
Before You Go 160
Getting There 162
Getting Around 163
Fast Facts 164
Marrakech: A Brief History 168
Marrakech Culture Savvy 169
Useful Phrases & Menu Terms 170
Toll-Free Numbers & Websites 173

Index 174

Copyright © 2010 John Wiley & Sons Ltd, The Atrium, Southern Gate,
Chichester, West Sussex PO19 8SQ, England
Telephone (+44) 1243 779777
Email (for orders and customer service enquiries): cs-books@wiley.co.uk.
Visit our Home Page on www.wiley.com

UK Publisher: Sally Smith
Executive Project Editor: Daniel Mersey
Commissioning Editor: Mark Henshall
Development Editor: Jill Emeny
Project Editor: Hannah Clement
Photo Research: Jill Emeny
Cartography: SY Cartography

Wiley also publishes its books in a variety of electronic formats. Some
content that appears in print may not be available in electronic books.

British Library Cataloguing in Publication Data
A catalogue record for this book is available from the British Library

ISBN: 978-0-470-71711-0

Typeset by Wiley Indianapolis Composition Services
Printed and bound in China by RR Donnelley

5 4 3 2 1

A Note from the Editorial Director

Organizing your time. That's what this guide is all about.

Other guides give you long lists of things to see and do and then expect you to fit the pieces together. The Day by Day guides are different. These guides tell you the best of everything, and then they show you how to see it *in the smartest, most time-efficient way.* Our authors have designed detailed itineraries organized by time, neighborhood, or special interest. And each tour comes with a bulleted map that takes you from stop to stop.

Hoping to be spellbound by the magic and madness of Jemaa el Fna, haggle in the souks amongst the carpenters and ironworkers with a mint tea or stay in a romantic riad? Looking to gaze in awe at Marrakech's iconic landmark Koutoubia Minaret, be pummelled into relaxation at a local hammam or savor a tagine? Whatever your interest or schedule, the Day by Days give you the smartest routes to follow. Not only do we take you to the top attractions, hotels, and restaurants, but we also help you access those special moments that locals get to experience—those "finds" that turn tourists into travelers.

The Day by Days are also your top choice if you're looking for one complete guide for all your travel needs. The best hotels and restaurants for every budget, the greatest shopping values, the wildest nightlife—it's all here.

Why should you trust our judgment? Because our authors personally visit each place they write about. They're an independent lot who say what they think and would never include places they wouldn't recommend to their best friends. They're also open to suggestions from readers. If you'd like to contact them, please send your comments our way at feedback@frommers.com, and we'll pass them on.

Enjoy your Day by Day guide—the most helpful travel companion you can buy. And have the trip of a lifetime.

Warm regards,

Kelly Regan, Editorial Director
Frommer's Travel Guides

About the Author

Born in the UK and based in Germany, **Kerry Christiani** is a travel writer with a masters degree in languages. Her travels in more than 40 countries have inspired some 15 guidebooks as well as print and online features for publishers including BBC Olive, Mandarin Oriental and Whatsonwhen. Marrakech's joyous people and labyrinthine souks never cease to amaze her. Dodging carpet-laden donkeys, discovering *savon noir* secrets in the hammams and watching the sun set over the Atlas Mountains were memorable moments in writing this guide. Kerry is also the author of Frommer's *Berlin Day by Day*.

About the Photographer

Andy Christiani is a travel photographer based in Germany's Black Forest, represented online by www.alamy.com. His photography has appeared worldwide in magazines, newspapers and travel guides. He also illustrated Frommer's *Berlin Day by Day*.

Acknowledgments

A big thank you to my husband, Andy Christiani, for his souk navigation skills and inspiring photography. Enormous thanks to Authentic Morocco for their first-rate guided tours to Essaouira and the Ourika Valley. *Shukran bezzef* (many thanks) to the Marrakchi people for the heartfelt hospitality we experienced while researching this guide. Special thanks to Lisa and Michael at Dar Charkia, Lynn Perez at Riad Farnatchi, Ursula and Björn at Riad Enija, Sofia and André at Dar Sholmes and the fantastic teams at La Maison Arabe, Riyad El Cadi, Riad Mabrouka, Riad Davia and Caravan Serai. Thanks also to Tom Herzog-Singer and Helmut Fink for their expert advice.

An Additional Note

Please be advised that travel information is subject to change at any time—and this is especially true of prices. We therefore suggest that you write or call ahead for confirmation when making your travel plans. The authors, editors, and publisher cannot be held responsible for the experiences of readers while traveling. Your safety is important to us, however, so we encourage you to stay alert and be aware of your surroundings.

Star Ratings, Icons & Abbreviations

Every hotel, restaurant, and attraction listing in this guide has been ranked for quality, value, service, amenities, and special features using a **star-rating** system. Hotels, restaurants, attractions, shopping, and nightlife are rated on a scale of zero stars (recommended) to three stars (exceptional). In addition to the star-rating system, we also use a **kids** icon to point out the best bets for families. Within each tour, we recommend cafes, bars, or restaurants where you can take a break. Each of these stops appears in a shaded box marked with a coffee-cup-shaped bullet 🍵.

The following **abbreviations** are used for credit cards:

AE	American Express	**DISC**	Discover	**V**	Visa
DC	Diners Club	**MC**	MasterCard		

Frommers.com

Now that you have this guidebook to help you plan a great trip, visit our website at **www.frommers.com** for additional travel information on more than 4,000 destinations. We update features regularly to give you instant access to the most current trip-planning information available. At Frommers.com, you'll find scoops on the best airfares, lodging rates, and car rental bargains. You can even book your travel online through our reliable travel booking partners. Other popular features include:

A Note on Prices

In the "Take a Break" and "Best Bets" sections of this book, we have used a system of dollar signs to show a range of costs for 1 night in a hotel (the price of a double-occupancy room) or the cost of an entree (main course) at a restaurant. Use the following table to decipher the dollar signs:

Cost	Hotels	Restaurants
$	under $60	under $10
$$	$60–$125	$10–$15
$$$	$125–$250	$15–$20
$$$$	$250–$350	$20–$25
$$$$$	over $350	over $25

An Invitation to the Reader

In researching this book, we discovered many wonderful places—hotels, restaurants, shops, and more. We're sure you'll find others. Please tell us about them, so we can share the information with your fellow travelers in upcoming editions. If you were disappointed with a recommendation, we'd love to know that, too. Please write to:

Frommer's Marrakech Day by Day, 1st Edition
Wiley Publishing, Inc. • 111 River St. • Hoboken, NJ 07030-5774

15 Favorite Moments

15 Favorite **Moments**

1 Jemaa el Fna
2 Koutoubia Minaret
3 Souks
4 La Sultana Spa
5 Kosybar
6 Ali Ben Youssef Medersa
7 Pacha
8 Palmeraie
9 Jemaa el Fna food stalls
10 Jardin Majorelle
11 Bahia Palace
12 Riads
13 Mouassine
14 Nikki Beach
15 Essaouira

Legend

- P Police Station
- ✉ Post Office
- ✚ Hospital

0 _____ 1/4 mi
0 _____ 0.25 km

Marrakech is a genie of a city. Name your wish—a romantic riad or haggling in the souks, the show-stopping theatrics of Jemaa el Fna or a top-to-toe scrub in a hammam—and it shall be granted. From the medina's medieval jigsaw to Hivernage's hedonistic clubs, the slinky restaurants of Guéliz to the über-cool beaches of the Palmeraie, Marrakech has a spirit that's impossible to bottle.

① **Being spellbound by magic and madness on Jemaa el Fna.** Snake charmers coaxing cobras, Gnaoua musicians whirling into trances, cartwheeling acrobats, storytellers recounting tales, and clairvoyants reading fortunes—even UNESCO applauded Jemaa el Fna for being the life and soul of Marrakech's 365-day party. *See p 60.*

② **Standing in awe of the Koutoubia Minaret.** Saunter the palm-dotted gardens of this marvel of medieval symmetry, and find different angles of Marrakech's most iconic landmark. Five times a day the muezzin's melodic *adhan* calls the faithful here to pray. *See p 43.*

③ **Getting lost in the souks.** The maze-like souks set your senses on high alert. Pass by carpenters shaving cedarwood and ironworkers hand-crafting lanterns. You will, *insha'allah* (God willing), learn to dodge donkeys, barter Marrakchi-style, and guzzle mint tea for Morocco. *See p 48.*

Be hypnotized by snake charmers on Jemaa el Fna.

The striking minaret of Koutoubia.

④ **Having a vigorous rubdown at La Sultana Spa.** The medina din and dust evaporate like water on a camel's back as you enter the steamy vaulted chamber. Merciless or mild, your *tayeba* (hammam attendant) will scrub you, crack your joints, and pummel you into soapy relaxation. *See p 33.*

⑤ **Coming eye to eye with the storks at Kosybar.** As the setting sun makes Marrakech blush, sip sundowners on the roof terrace of this bar and watch in wonder as the storks swoop down to their nests atop the Badi Palace walls. Their amorous bill-clattering mingles with lounge beats. *See p 124.*

⑥ **Praising Moroccan craftsmanship at Ali Ben Youssef Medersa.** Stand in the divine courtyard of this 14th-century Koranic school and study walls that dance with lace-fine

stucco, polychrome *zellij* (mosaic tilework), and intricately wrought cedarwood. *See p 8.*

7 **Clubbing at Ville Nouvelle's hottest party spot.** Nocturnal hedonists gravitate toward Hivernage and Guéliz in Ville Nouvelle. Party past your bedtime at **Pacha**, where superstar DJs pump out electro, or **Théâtro** for red-hot house anthems. Alternatively, decadent supper club **Le Comptoir Darna** dishes up belly dancing, exotic cocktails, and shisha. *See p 124.*

8 **Hitching a bumpy ride through the Palmeraie.** Make a date with a dromedary camel to ride through the palm oasis on the northern fringes of Marrakech, and enjoy great views of the snow-capped Atlas Mountains. *See p 97.*

9 **Savoring a feast fit for a sultan.** Gluttony is no sin in this appetizing city, where an alfresco feed on Jemaa el Fna is a gastronomic event. Indulge on *harira* (garbanzo bean or chickpea soup), melt-in-your mouth lamb tagines, crispy *pastillas* (pigeon pies), and syrupy pastries under the stars or at Marrakech's top tables. *See p 106.*

10 **Strutting the botanical catwalk at Jardin Majorelle.** Luxuriant with rare foliage, this was the

Essaouira's striking ramparts offer mesmerising views of the Atlantic.

fashionable garden of the late Yves Saint Laurent. Be dazzled by the cobalt blue Art Deco villa sitting amid Californian palms, cacti, and rustling bamboo. *See p 15.*

11 **Walking in royal footsteps at the Bahia Palace.** The grand vizier and his countless concubines lived in jaw-dropping splendor at this 19th-century palace. Rich with stucco, extraordinary cedarwood ceilings, and geometric *zellij*, the chambers are an A to Z of Moroccan artistry. *See p 11.*

12 **Lazing on a sunny riad roof terrace.** Down a twisty alley lies an inconspicuous brass-studded door. Push it open and—voila!—enter a courtyard where a fountain gurgles and birds twitter in the orange trees. Riads offer a serene escape from the medina bustle, sweeping views over the rooftops, and a warm Marrakchi welcome. *See p 144.*

13 **Luxuriating in the everyday in Mouassine.** Ditch the map for a languid wander through the backstreets and hidden corners of Mouassine. Buy bread from the *furan* (communal oven), stumble across decorative fountains, and pause to watch artisans at work in the *foundouks* (caravanserais). *See p 66.*

14 **Sunbathing celebrity-style.** Slap on the factor 30 and boost your x-factor at one of Marrakech's über-cool urban beaches such as **La Plage Rouge** or **Nikki Beach**. Join bronzed supermodels and celebrities as you indulge in champagne cocktails under the palms. *See p 128.*

15 **Spending the day in Essaouira.** This chilled seaside hangout, made famous by Bob Marley and Jimi Hendrix, is *the* must-do day trip whether you want to ride Atlantic waves, learn the secrets of argan oil, munch luscious seafood in a harborside shack, or mosey around the whitewashed medina. *See p 148.* ●

1

The Best
Full-Day Tours

The Best **in One Day**

1. Koutoubia
2. Koutoubia Gardens
3. Ice Legend
4. Souks
5. Ali Ben Youssef Medersa
6. Musée de Marrakech
7. Koubba Ba'adyin
8. Jemaa el Fna
9. Al Ahbab

Bab Taghzout

Rue Bin

Hôpital El Antaki

Place El Antaki

ASSOUEL

EL MOUKEF

RIAD EL AROUS

Fontaine Chrob Ou Chouf

HART ES-SOURA

ARSET BEN CHEBLI

Médersa Ben Youssef

Place du Moukef

Mosquée Ben Youssef

Rue de Souk d. Fassi

Mosquée Eloussta

Rue Bab Doukkala

Koubba Ba'adyin

Mosquée Bab Doukkala

Dar El Glaoui

Musée de Marrakech

Mosquée Azabzed

R'MILA

MOUASSINE

Mosquée Mouassine

Mosquée Sidi Ishak

Zaouia Sidi Ben Salah

EL KSOUR

AZBEZT

BEN SALAH

Ensemble Artisanal

Zaouia Sidi Moulay El Ksour

SOUKS

DERB DABACHI

Rue Dabachi

Avenue Mohammed V

Place Bab Fteuh

MÉDINA

Koutoubia

Place Jemaa El Fna

KENNARIA

DOUAR GRAOUA

Rue Douar Graoua

Koubba de Lalla Zohra

Place Foucauld

Palais Moulay Idriss

Mosquée de la Koutoubia

Consulat de France

Musée Dar Si Saïd

Jardins de la Koutoubia

Maison Tiskiouine

Avenue Houmman El Fetouaki

Hôtel La Mamounia

Pl. Youssef Tachfine

Hôpital Arset El Mokha

Palais de la Bahia

SIDI MIMOUN

Synagogue Lazama

ARSET EL MAÄCH

Marché Couvert

Place des Ferblantiers

MELLAH

Hôpital Ibn Zohr

Bab Er Rob

Mosquée de la Kasbah

Palais El Badi

Zaouia Sidi Es Soheïli

Tombeaux Saadiens

Bab Agnaou

KSIBET

Cimetière Sidi Es Souheïli

Centre Artisanal

P	Police Station
✉	Post Office
✚	Hospital

0 ___ 1/4 mi
0 ___ 0.25 km

Prepare for sensory overload and know your bienvenues (welcomes) from your baleks (watch outs). Whether dodging mission-driven donkey carts in spice-scented souks, hearing the muezzin's otherworldly call rise above Koutoubia, or joining snake charmers at the twilight circus on Jemaa el Fna—you'll be spellbound by Marrakech from day one. START: **Koutoubia**.

Escape the crowds with a cool stroll around Koutoubia.

❶ ★★★ **Koutoubia.** Rearing above the hubbub of Jemaa el Fna and visible from riad rooftops throughout the medina, the 69m (210-foot)-tall minaret of Koutoubia instills awe with its scale and peerless symmetry. A sultan with an eye for aesthetics, Yacoub el-Mansour oversaw the completion of this 12th-century Almohad creation, the blueprint for architectural wonders such as Seville's Giralda. On closer inspection the rose-tinted, crenellated minaret reveals Moorish detail in its keyhole arches, green-white *zellij* (mosaic tilework), and fleur de lys-like *darj w ktarf* motifs. Five times a day, the muezzin's ethereal call to prayer rises from Koutoubia. ⏱ *30 min. Avenue Mohammed V. Closed to non-Muslims.*

❷ ★ **kids Koutoubia Gardens.** You can almost picture sultans swanning around these manicured gardens, fringed by roses, swaying palms, and orange trees. Today Marrakchis from all walks of life flock here for cool respite and neighborhood gossip. The traffic and clip-clop of *calèches* (horse-drawn carriages) on Avenue Mohammed V fade as you enter these birdsong-filled gardens. Keep an eye out for the resident storks. ⏱ *20 min. Avenue Mohammed V. Admission free. Daily 8am–8pm.*

❸ **Ice Legend.** Clued-in locals gravitate toward here, a hole-in-the-wall ice-cream parlor off Jemaa el Fna. Bitter orange with a halo of whipped cream comes a close second to my personal favorite—zingy blackcurrant sorbet. *52 Rue Bab Agnaou.* ☎ *0524-44-42-00. $.*

❹ ★★★ **Souks.** *Bienvenue mon ami!* Come drink mint tea! A chorus of cries greets you in the souks and the warren of covered alleys twisting north of Jemaa el Fna to Ali Ben Youssef Medersa. Bustling **Souk Semmarine** (p 49) is the main artery, where sunrays stream through the slatted roof to spotlight sequined *babouches* (slippers), embroidered *jellabahs* (hooded robes), and twinkling lanterns. Take a serendipitous wander or make for must-see souks such as **Criée Berbere** (p 20) with its Aladdin-worthy carpets, hand-woven with Berber motifs, or the photogenic **Souk Sebbaghine** (Dyer's Souk, p 52),

Haggle hard and dodge the donkeys in bustling Souk Semmarine.

where skeins of vibrant indigo, saffron, and poppy-red wool dry between the sun-baked walls. Filled with color, spices, and banter, the souks are about haggling hard, dodging muleteers, and luxuriating in the everyday. ⏱ *1½ hrs. North of Jemaa el Fna. Most shops daily 10am–9pm; some close Friday.*

5 ★★★ **Ali Ben Youssef Medersa.** Blissfully calm in the late afternoon, this former *medersa* (Koranic school) enlightens with 16th-century Saâdian craftsmanship. Like the pages in the textbooks of the most diligent theology student, no space is left blank on these walls, which dance with geometric detail, swirly calligraphy, and lustrous *zellij*. Head upstairs for a snapshot of scholarly life in two recreated dorms complete with quills, bookstands, and obligatory tagines and tea sets. With mosque doors closed to them, this is as close to divine inspiration as non-Muslims can get in Marrakech. ⏱ *1 hr. Off Place de la Kissaria. Admission 40dh adults, 20dh children under 12, 60dh combined ticket with Musée de Marrakech and Koubba Ba'adyin. Daily 9am–6:30pm.*

6 ★ **Musée de Marrakech.** This late 19th-century palace was the not-so-humble abode of defense minister Mehdi Mnebhi. First up are the former kitchens, today a mosaic-tiled gallery showcasing modern art.

Rest a while in one of the nooks to marvel at the floral stucco and *zellij*, or take in exhibitions of traditional Moroccan arts from Berber carpets to glittering daggers. The womblike darkness of the hammam is both atmospheric and eerie. In the courtyard, many visitors gasp as they catch their first glimpse of the majestic lamp suspended above the marble fountains. ⏱ *1 hr. Place de la Kissaria. Admission 40dh adults, 20dh children under 12, 60dh combined ticket with Ali Ben Youssef Medersa and Koubba Ba'adyin. Daily 9am–6:30pm.*

7 ★ **Koubba Ba'adyin.** The Almohads grumbled that the mosque of their predecessors wasn't properly aligned with Mecca, and so they promptly tore it down and built the Koutoubia in its place. Thankfully this 11th-century *koubba* (cupola) with its graceful ribbed dome was spared a similar fate and stands proud as Marrakech's only **Almoravid** monument. ⏱ *30 min. Place de la Kissaria. Admission 10dh, 40dh combined with Musée de Marrakech, 60dh with Musée de Marrakech and Ali Ben Youssef Medersa. Daily 9am–6:30pm.*

8 ★★★ **Jemaa el Fna.** Storytellers hold audiences captive with tales

Through the doorway to the Musée de Marrakech.

The smoke from the food stalls drifts above Jemaa el Fna every evening.

delivered in rapid-fire lingo, frenzied Gnaoua beats, cobras hypnotized by magic flutes, and wizened fortune-tellers—Jemaa el Fna, translating as 'assembly of the dead', is very much alive. This vast open-air circus demands audience participation, so do your bit by posing for a DIY dentistry ad or embracing a monkey. Bolder than any circus, crazier than any carnival, this UNESCO-listed square is Marrakech through and through. Arrive as the sun drops behind the Atlas Mountains, when mopeds dart like fireflies through the crowds, and smoke rises from grills where chefs are quick with their frying pans and witticisms. If you don't want a henna tattoo or shoeshine, keep walking. ⏱ *1 hr.* See p 60.

9 **Al Ahbab.** For falafel with fries and the juiciest shawarma (spit-grilled meat) in the medina, follow your nose to this easygoing outpost just off Jemaa el Fna. Try to bag a table out front to people-watch as you chomp. *Rue Bab Agnaou.* ☎ *0671-37-71-46. $.*

Tipping: Practical Matters

Morocco is a tipping culture and Marrakchis are the sharpest daggers when it comes to extracting the tourist dirham. When you point your camera at a flamboyant water carrier or snake charmer, remember that this is how they make a living; no photo on Jemaa el Fna is for free. Although performers will persuasively ask for more, 10dh to 20dh is the going rate for a snap of a viper or macaque around your neck. Fix the price ahead and you won't be taken for a magic carpet ride. Keep a few 10dh coins in your pocket and your wallet well hidden.

The Best **in Two Days**

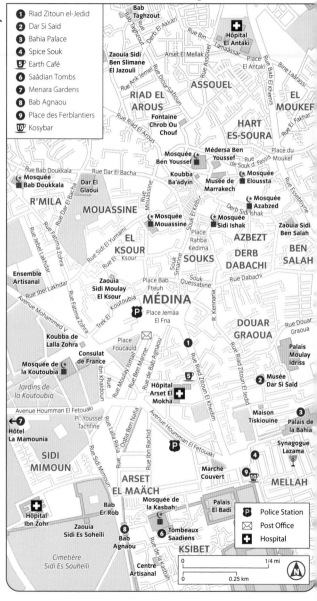

1. Riad Zitoun el-Jedid
2. Dar Si Said
3. Bahia Palace
4. Spice Souk
5. Earth Café
6. Saâdian Tombs
7. Menara Gardens
8. Bab Agnaou
9. Place des Ferblantiers
10. Kosybar

Bab Taghzout

Derb El Akkari

Rue Bin

Hôpital El Antaki

Rue Bab Taghzout

Derb Dour Saboun

Arset El Mellak

Rue Ank Jemel

Place El Antaki

Rue Bab El Khemis

Bine Laârassi

Zaouia Sidi Ben Slimane El Jazouli

ASSOUEL

EL MOUKEF

RIAD EL AROUS

HART ES-SOURA

Rue El Fakhar

Fontaine Chrob Ou Chouf

Rue Riad El Arous

Mosquée Ben Youssef

Médersa Ben Youssef

Place du Moukef

Rue de Souk d. Tassis

Rue Bab Doukkala

Rue Dar El Bacha

Koubba Ba'adyin

Mosquée Eloussta

Rue Essebtiyine

Mosquée Bab Doukkala

Dar El Glaoui

Musée de Marrakech

R'MILA

MOUASSINE

Rue Mouassine

Souk El Kebir

Mosquée Azabzed

Mosquée Mouassine

Mosquée Sidi Ishak

Derb Sidi Ishak

Zaouia Sidi Ben Salah

Rue Dar El Bacha

Rue Jebel Lakhdar

Rue Fatima Zohra

Rue Sidi El Yumami

Rue El

EL KSOUR

Place Rahba Kedima

AZBEZT

Ensemble Artisanal

Rue Ibel Lakhdar

Zaouia Sidi Moulay El Ksour

Place Bab Fteuh

Souk Smarine

SOUKS

DERB DABACHI

BEN SALAH

Souk Quessabine

R. Kennaria

Rue Dabachi

Avenue Mohammed V

Rue Fatima Zohra

Trek El Koutoubia

MÉDINA

Place Jemaa El Fna

DOUAR GRAOUA

Rue Douar Graoua

Koubba de Lalla Zohra

Place Foucauld

Rue Riad Zitoun El Kedim

Rue Riad Zitoun El Jedid

Palais Moulay Idriss

Mosquée de la Koutoubia

Consulat de France

Ibn Khaldoun

Rue Moulay Ismail

Rue de Bab Agnaou

1

2 Musée Dar Si Said

Jardins de la Koutoubia

Avenue Houmman El Fetouaki

5

Hôpital Arset El Mokha

Maison Tiskiouine

3 Palais de la Bahia

←7 Hôtel La Mamounia

Pl. Youssef Tachfine

Rue Lalla Rita

Rue Orba Ben Nafia

Rue Ibn Rachid

Avenue Houmman El Fetouaki

Synagogue Lazama

SIDI MIMOUN

Rue Sidi Mimoun

Marché Couvert

4

9 10 **MELLAH**

ARSET EL MAÂCH

Bab Er Rob

Mosquée de la Kasbah

Palais El Badi

Hôpital Ibn Zohr

Zaouia Sidi Es Soheili

8 Bab Agnaou

6 Tombeaux Saadiens

Rue de la Kasbah

KSIBET

Cimetière Sidi Es Souheili

Centre Artisanal

P	Police Station
✉	Post Office
✚	Hospital

0 — 1/4 mi
0 — 0.25 km

N

On your second day in Marrakech, you'll find Berber cures and banter on **Riad Zitoun el-Jedid,** traditional crafts at Dar Si Said, and a lavish harem fit for a sultan at the Bahia Palace. Glimpse the Atlas Mountains from the olive-lined Menara Gardens and see storks rock the Kasbah from Kosybar's rooftop terrace at sundown. START: **Riad Zitoun el-Jedid.**

❶ ★ Riad Zitoun el-Jedid.
Stroll by offices with scribes busily penning letters and apothecaries boasting miracle cures on this thoroughfare that links the souks to the Kasbah. Carpenters shaving cedarwood in thimble-sized workshops, tailors knocking up tunics on century-old Singer sewing machines, and grocers selling freshly baked flat bread provide a fascinating insight into Marrakchi daily life.
⏲ *30 min. See p 55.*

❷ ★★★ Dar Si Said. Before heading to the souks, stop at this 19th-century mansion for creative inspiration. Showcasing the works of Morocco's *maâlems* (master craftsmen), Dar Si Said presents intricate Berber jewelry, High Atlas carpets, and a pristine collection of hand-carved doors. After an art overload, unwind in the courtyard of pomegranate and citrus trees. ⏲ *1 hr. Rue Kennaria. Admission 10dh. Sat–Thurs 9–11:45am and 2:30–5:45pm, Fri 9–11:30am and 3–5:45pm.*

❸ ★★★ Bahia Palace. Bahia, meaning beautiful, is a fitting name for this sumptuous 150-room palace, bankrolled by grand vizier Si Moussa in the 1860s and extended by his successor Bou Ahmed. You'll be whisked back to an age of tittering courtesans gazing at diamond *zellij* floors, fancy stucco, and kaleidoscopic *zouak* (finely-painted) cedar ceilings; see p 55 for more. The reception room, with separate waiting rooms for Arabs, Berbers, and Jews, leads through to the grand vizier's quarters where the recurring inscription 'health forever' reveals his chief concern. Four wives and 24 concubines inhabited the harem, a lavish tribute to polygamy set around an arcaded courtyard. A fountain gurgles in the fragrant **Andalusian gardens** shaded by orange, pomegranate, and fig trees. Bahia saves the best for last: the chamber of the favorite wife is a fantasy of stained glass and *mashrabiyya* lattice screens to stop

Admire the painted cedarwood and stucco of the Bahia Palace.

The Spice Souk offers plenty of variety.

envious concubines from prying. ⏱ 1½hrs. Riad Zitoun el-Jedid. ☎ 0524-38-95-64. Admission 10dh adults, 3dh children. Daily 8:45–11:45am and 2:45–5:50pm.

4 ★ Spice Souk. Ask Marrakchis to divulge their shopping tips and this spice souk usually makes the grade. Follow your nose to this colorful covered market, brimming with conical towers of Moroccan curry, the 35-spice mix to pep up your tagines, and saffron (the thick Moroccan kind is higher quality than the thin Spanish variety), alongside sacks of ginger roots, lentils, and beans. Indulge in neighborhood chit-chat and obligatory haggling. ⏱ 30 min. Riad Zitoun el-Jedid.

5 ★ Earth Café. Bright sofas and Med-style soul food define Marrakech's first vegetarian and vegan café, which has a chilled vibe and impeccable eco-credentials. Wholesome daytime specials might include warm seasonal salads or vegetable-stuffed spring rolls. Barakat Naim's home-pressed olive oil, organic argan oil, and biscotti make ideal gifts. 2 Derb Zouak, Riad Zitoun el-Kedim. ☎ 0661-28-94-02. $.

6 ★★ Saâdian Tombs. Hailed 'the Victorious' for defeating the Portuguese, Sultan Ahmed el-Mansour (1587–1603) also had a bittersweet taste for trading sugar and slaves—activities that bankrolled these ornate Kasbah burial chambers (rediscovered in 1917). First you'll see the mausoleum where children were buried (those topped with marble slabs denote the sultan's offspring). The chamber of the sultan and his sons is a gilded frenzy of polychrome *zellij*, stucco as fine as piped icing, and calligraphy that curls around the walls. Citrus trees and 200-year-old date palms frame the courtyard where some 100 slaves and servants are interred. ⏱ 1 hr. Rue de la Kasbah. Sat–Thurs 9–11:45am and 2:30–5:45pm, Fri 9–11:30am and 3–5:45pm.

7 ★ Menara Gardens. Take a horse-drawn *calèche* or petit taxi to these gardens for an afternoon amble amid the olive trees and palms. The centerpiece is a shimmering pool with a platform (the best vantage point for photos) and a grand 19th-century pavilion. In the afternoon, when the pool holds up a mirror to the snowy Atlas peaks, the gardens draw families and loved-up couples. ⏱ 1 hr. Avenue de la Menara. Admission free to gardens, 10dh pavilion. Daily 8am–6pm.

Savor healthy, vegetarian fare at the Earth Café.

Marrakech Express

Petit taxis, aka clapped-out Peugeots, are ideal for zipping about town. Either convince the driver to switch on the meter or negotiate a price ahead; pay maximum 20dh by day and 40dh by night (short journeys should cost half that). If you're staying in the medina, you'll have to walk the last stretch anyway, as most *derbs* (alleys) are inaccessible to cars. Before you arrive, ask your riad to arrange a porter to collect your luggage from the nearest taxi stand, and then tip him about 20dh. *Qu'est-ce que vous cherchez?* (what are you looking for?) is the beloved catchphrase of unofficial guides. If you're truly lost, expect to pay around 20dh to be shown the way. Alternatively, find a quiet corner or café to browse your map in peace.

8 Bab Agnaou. Almohads, Saâdian sultans, and many a stubborn donkey—this 12th-century gateway to the Kasbah has seen it all. With its decorative, horseshoe-shaped arches sculpted from ochre-blue Guéliz sandstone (the precise color depends on the time of day), Bab Agnaou is the most striking of Marrakech's 20 city gates. The monumental entrance takes its name from the Berber for 'hornless black ram'. ⏱ *15 min. Medina ramparts.*

9 ★ Place des Ferblantiers. When you see sparks fly, hear the rhythmic tapping of hammers, and smell the varnish, you know you've reached the Place des Ferblantiers (Tinsmith's Square). Using medieval-style tools, the tinsmiths here craft filigree, star-shaped, and bejeweled lanterns that cast extraordinary patterns. Even if there's no space left in my suitcase, I enjoy just poking around the workshops lining the palm-dotted square; some are veritable Ali Baba caves of home lighting. ⏱ *45 min. Place des Ferblantiers. Workshops daily 9am–9pm.*

10 ★★ Kosybar. The rooftop terrace here is the finest place for sundowners, as storks swoop down gracefully to their nests on the neighboring Badi Palace walls and a magenta sky silhouettes the contours of Koutoubia. Bring your camera, sip a glass of Moroccan wine, and catch some of the most bewitching views over Marrakech. *Place des Ferblantiers 47.* ☎ *0524-38-03-42. $$$*

Kasbah mosque rises above the Saâdian Tombs.

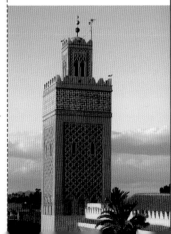

14

The Best **in Three Days**

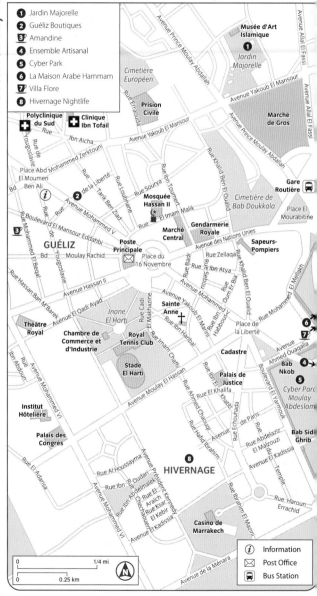

1 Jardin Majorelle
2 Guéliz Boutiques
3 Amandine
4 Ensemble Artisanal
5 Cyber Park
6 La Maison Arabe Hammam
7 Villa Flore
8 Hivernage Nightlife

i Information

✉ Post Office

🚌 Bus Station

0 — 1/4 mi
0 — 0.25 km

My third full-day tour reveals a strikingly different side to Marrakech. Go west to admire Yves Saint Laurent's botanical collection in Jardin Majorelle, and then nibble French pastries and shop for couture kaftans in Guéliz. After an invigorating scrub in La Maison Arabe's candlelit hammam, it's time to party celebrity-style in Hivernage. START: **Jardin Majorelle.**

For quality carpets at fixed prices, head for Ben Rahal.

1 ★★ **Jardin Majorelle.** If gardens were people, this one would be a supermodel, not least because it was part of the stylish collection of late French designer **Yves Saint Laurent** (p 101). French landscape artist Jacques Majorelle (1886–1962) created the botanical haven in 1924, interspersing rare foliage with pots in mouthwatering orange and lemon hues, saving a final splash of color for an Art Deco villa in his trademark cobalt blue. The latter now harbors an intriguing Islamic Art Museum (p 26). A footpath weaves past cacti, rustling bamboo, lofty palms, and pools. Arrive early to beat the crowds and savor the calm. *1½ hrs.*

Off Avenue Yacoub el Mansour. ☎ 0524-30-18-52. www.jardin majorelle.com. Admission 30dh gardens, 15dh Islamic Art Museum. Oct–May daily 8am–5pm; Jun–Sep daily 8am–6pm.

2 ★ **Guéliz Boutiques.** Hop into a horse-drawn *calèche* at Jardin Majorelle for a relaxed trot into Guéliz, where glass-fronted malls and marble-lined boutiques lit by Murano chandeliers are light years away from the medina's din and delirious colors. Refined and modern, Guéliz has style (and prices) to rival Paris. High-end **Rue de la Liberté** is where you'll find insiders' favorite fixed-price carpet shop, Ben Rahal (p 87), and Frédérique Birkemeyer's floaty couture kaftans at Intensité Nomade (p 91). Bear in mind that most shops close on Sunday. ⏱ *1 hr. Guéliz.*

3 ★ **Amandine.** The mention of this patisserie, tucked down a Guéliz backstreet, is enough to make sweet-toothed Marrakchis gush about chocolate-drenched bombes d'amour (love bombs), angelically light meringues, and crisp almond tarts. Drop by for strong espresso, people-watching, and the ultimate sugar rush. *177 Rue Mohammed el-Beqal.* ☎ *0524-44-96-12. $.*

4 ★★★ **Ensemble Artisanal.** Tired of haggling over every last dirham in the souks? This state-run craft complex is every polite Westerner's dream: full of quality handicrafts at fixed prices. No bartering, no hassle. Each of the shops and workshops in the courtyard focuses on a different craft—from pointy *babouches* to hand-woven baskets, ceramics to carpets. It's interesting to see the artisans at work even if you have no intention of buying. 🕐 *30 min. Avenue Mohammed V.* ☎ *0524-38-66-74. Admission free. Mon–Sat 9:30am–7pm.*

5 ★ **Cyber Park.** Royals once went a-strolling in these 18th-century gardens, now a magnet to teenagers who come for upbeat after-school jam sessions by the fountains, flirting under the orange trees, and free WiFi. Should you have no interest in checking your email, the manicured lawns and orange groves are a pleasure to stroll and an escape from the hubbub on Avenue Mohammed V. 🕐 *30 min. Avenue Mohammed V. Admission free. Daily 9:30am–6:30pm.*

6 ★★★ **La Maison Arabe Hammam.** After three days in Marrakech, my dust-filled pores are crying out for La Maison Arabe's hammam. The steam clean takes place beside a rose petal-filled pool in a candlelit *tadelakt* (polished plaster) chamber. *Savon noir* (black soap) with eucalyptus is applied before an invigorating *gommage* (exfoliation) with a rough mitt to remove dead skin. *Rhassoul* clay with orange water leaves skin glowing and ready for a soothing 30-minute massage. You'll leave silky smooth, sleepy, and walking on air.

🕐 *1½ hrs. 1 Derb Assehbe.* ☎ *0524-38-70-10. www.lamaisonarabe.com. Royal Session 800dh. See p 115.*

7 ★★★ **Villa Flore.** Other top tables receive more hype, but this sleek riad achieves perfection in service, cuisine, and atmosphere at comparatively small prices. French architect, Jacques Gering, put his stamp on the light-filled interior, where oriental antiques, ruby-red chairs, and strategically placed roses catch the eye. Much-lauded chef Mustapha Benacher rises early to buy market-fresh ingredients for fluffy couscous infused with saffron and the most tender lamb I've ever eaten. *4 Derb Azzouz.* ☎ *0524-39-17-00. $$–$$$. See p 118.*

8 **Hivernage Nightlife.** The über-cool lounge bars, velvet ropes, and glitzy shows in well-heeled Hivernage are not to everyone's taste, but it's worth spending a night here to see a startlingly different side to Marrakech. Gyrating belly dancers and DJs spinning lounge grooves entertain champagne-sipping socialites at hotspots such as Le Comptoir (p 128), while local tycoons fritter away their fortunes in the swanky casinos. Dress to impress fussy doormen, or head across to Café Extrablatt (p 124) for German aesthetics and relaxed beats. 🕐 *2 hrs. Hivernage.* ●

Marrakshi teenagers surf the web at Cyber Park.

Magical **Marrakech**

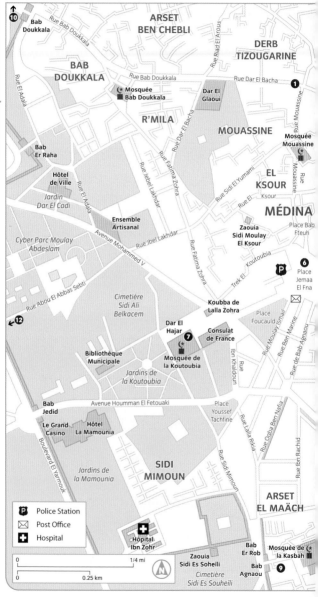

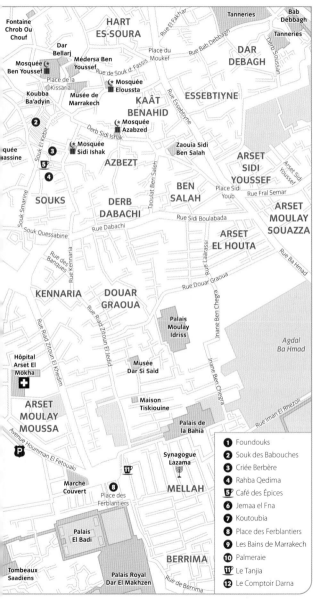

Fontaine Chrob Ou Chouf

HART ES-SOURA

Rue El Fakhar

Tanneries

Bab Debbagh

Dar Bellarj

Place du Moukef

Rue Bab Debbagh

Tanneries

Mosquée Ben Youssef

Médersa Ben Youssef

DAR DEBAGH

Derb Soussan

Rue de Souk d. Fassis

Place de la Kissaria

Mosquée Eloussta

Koubba Ba'adyin

Musée de Marrakech

KAÂT BENAHID

Rue Essebtiyne

ESSEBTIYNE

❷

Derb Sidi Ishak

Mosquée Azabzed

quée assine

❸

Mosquée Sidi Ishak

Souk El Kebir

❺

Zaouia Sidi Ben Salah

ARSET SIDI YOUSSEF

Arset Sidi Youssef

AZBEZT

❹

BEN SALAH

Place Sidi Youb

Rue Fral Semar

ARSET MOULAY SOUAZZA

Souk Smarine

SOUKS

DERB DABACHI

Taoulat Ben Saleh

Rue Sidi Boulabada

Souk Quessabine

Rue Dabachi

ARSET EL HOUTA

Rue Ba Hmad

Rue des Banques

Rue Kennaria

Rue Laarassi

Rue Douar Graoua

KENNARIA

DOUAR GRAOUA

Rue Riad Zitoun El Jedid

Jnane Ben Chegra

Palais Moulay Idriss

Agdal Ba Hmad

Hôpital Arset El Mokha

Rue Riad Zitoun El Khedim

Musée Dar Si Saïd

Jnane Ben Chegra

ARSET MOULAY MOUSSA

Maison Tiskiouine

Rue Iman El Rhezoli

❿

Avenue Houmman El Fetouaki

Palais de la Bahia

Marché Couvert

Synagogue Lazama

⓫

Place des Ferblantiers

MELLAH

Palais El Badi

Tombeaux Saadiens

Palais Royal Dar El Makhzen

BERRIMA

Rue de Berrima

❶ Foundouks
❷ Souk des Babouches
❸ Criée Berbère
❹ Rahba Qedima
❺ Café des Épices
❻ Jemaa el Fna
❼ Koutoubia
❽ Place des Ferblantiers
❾ Les Bains de Marrakech
❿ Palmeraie
⓫ Le Tanjia
⓬ Le Comptoir Darna

Marrakech possesses a magical quality: a place of circus antics, potions, and 1,001 things that go bump in the night. Fall under the spell of this rose-tinted city by deciphering the urban labyrinth of the medina, being hypnotized by cobra charmers on Jemaa el Fna, and bartering like a wizened Berber for your own magic carpet in Criée Berbère. START: **The foundouks are slightly north of Rue Mouassine, as marked on the map. They can only be reached on foot.**

① ★ Foundouks. Nowhere is the mystery of Marrakech, once an important outpost on the trans-Saharan caravan route, more tangible than in the *foundouks* (caravanserais) just north of Rue Mouassine. Behind studded wooden doors lie courtyards where caravans arrived, heavily laden with exotic spices, silks, precious gems, and slaves. Today the first floors, where pack animals once slept, now function as small-scale artisanal workshops. ⏱ *30 min. See p 29.*

② kids Souk des Babouches (Slipper Souk). Delve into the heart of the souks to find the utterly enchanting Souk des Babouches. Never-ending rows of spangled slippers vie for your attention in this

A lantern maker taps out his latest creation, Fondouk al Mizane.

leather-scented souk: from sequined slip-ons, traditional pointed *babouches*, and the ubiquitous Moroccan Adidas (soft leather sneakers). It's a super place to track down fairytale footwear crafted from goat and camel leather. As always, put your haggling hat on. ⏱ *20 min. Souk des Babouches. Daily 9am–7:30pm.*

③ ★★ Criée Berbère (Carpet Souk). Discover your inner Aladdin in the Criée Berbère or Carpet Souk. Just steps from the mayhem on Jemaa el Fna, this shady souk is crammed with hand-woven kélims and vibrant *tapis* (carpets). Merchants with broad grins beckon you to their deep-pile High Atlas creations and scarlet Berber rugs emblazoned with geometric motifs. My favorite time to visit is 4pm when the hardcore hagglers descend for the carpet auction (p 50). ⏱ *30 min. Criée Berbère. Daily 10am–8pm.*

④ ★★ Rahba Qedima. For full-on Marrakchi magic, you can't beat this square framed by herbalist stores. Here potion purveyors rattle off medicinal herbs with encyclopedic prowess. Alongside miracle cures for obesity, rheumatism, and acne, you can pick up *rhassoul* clay for Rapunzel-like glossy locks, Berber whisky (mint tea), and black-seed oil to prevent snoring. The further you venture towards the former slave market, where women sell fabrics under the arches, the more bizarre

Bag miracle lotions and potions on Rahba Qedima.

the offerings. Birds of prey squawk outside compact stores where live chameleons, turtles, and hedgehogs can be found next to alligator and snake skins. *Rahba Qedima.* ⏱ *20 min. Daily 9am–8pm.*

5 ★ **Café des Épices.** When your head starts to spin with the buzz of souk activity, this art-slung café, affording super views over Rahba Qedima, is the perfect antidote. Kick back on the low seats upstairs for a cup of thé épicé (spiced tea), and enticing salads and sandwiches. *75 Rahba Qedima.* ☎ *0524-39-17-70. www.cafedes epices.net. $*

6 ★★★ **Jemaa el Fna.** A picture of well-choreographed chaos, Jemaa el Fna is street theater at its finest. This open-air circus has entertained since the Middle Ages. Dusk is the witching hour when Gnaoua musicians work the crowds into a frenzy with infectious drum beats and upbeat dance moves. Healers extend gnarled fingers to curious passersby and theatrical storytellers

grip audiences with tales in Arabic. Fortune tellers add a spiritual twist with palm and tarot readings under umbrellas, although ironically they often can't predict how much you will have to pay them. Acrobats turning back flips, water sellers in technicolor dreamcoats, men charming snakes, and balancing macaques—Jemaa el Fna is an invigorating assault on the senses. Best after 4pm. ⏱ *1 hr. See p 60.*

7 ★ **kids Koutoubia.** Five times a day, the medina's din is drowned out by voices rising pure and clear from Koutoubia. The *adhan* or call to prayer is eerily beautiful (and an extremely effective alarm clock at 5am). The singular voice that resonates from Koutoubia is particularly enigmatic in the evening as the setting sun paints the sky magenta-indigo. ⏱ *20 min. See p 61.*

8 ★ **Place des Ferblantiers.** Tides of tourists and locals drift past Kasbah's crumbling red walls to this square, where tinsmiths tap out intricate patterns on the floors of rudimentary workshops, as they have done for centuries. Express

Café des Épices for spiced tea and good vibes.

more than a passing interest and you'll be dragged to the back of the shop to view the full collection. ⏱ 30 min. See p 13.

⑨ ★★ Les Bains de Marrakech. Set in a sublime riad snug against the Kasbah's walls, this is one of Marrakech's most enchanting bathhouses. Smooth *tadelakt* (polished plaster) chambers, rose petal-filled fountains, and a palm-fringed pool await you. Sweat it out in a candlelit chamber *à deux* before enjoying a stimulating grapefruit-infused gommage (exfoliation) or mint-clay wrap, followed by an intuitive four-hand massage. All products are 100% natural. The day spa package is a real treat. Reservations essential. ⏱ 1½ hrs. 2 Derb Sedra, Bab Agnaou. ☎ 0524-38-14-28. www.lesbainsdemarrakech.com. 150dh for a 45-min hammam and gommage. 800dh daily spa package. Daily 9am–8pm.

⑩ ★★ kids Dromedary rides in Palmeraie. If you're keen to act out Lawrence of Arabia fantasies, hop in a petit taxi for a quick ride to

A camel offers its hump for rides through the Palmeraie.

the date palm-studded Palmeraie (p 97) just north of the medina. Here dromedary camels take you through the desert-like scrub, with fleeting glimpses of the Atlas Mountains. I get the taxi to drop me off at one of the 'camel car parks', where one-humped beauties with eyelashes to die for take tourists on bumpy rides.

Hot Hammams

Lore has it that a weekly hammam is the Berber secret for a youthful, dewy complexion. The medina din magically slips away when you step inside one of these steamy public bathhouses, found in every neighborhood. For centuries, locals have visited hammams for ablution (cleansing before prayers), relaxation, and soapy socializing. The traditional Moroccan hammam consists of a *guelsa* (changing room), plus cold, warm, and hot chambers. Today hammams vary greatly: from DIY gommage (exfoliation with black soap) in simple wood-heated public bathhouses that cost just a few dirham to palatial riad spas with all the ceremonial mint tea and fluffy bathrobe trappings. Whichever you choose, visiting a hammam is a must-have Marrakech experience, sure to induce Sleeping Beauty-like slumber.

It's a Kinda Magic

If Marrakchi magic has sparked your imagination, time your trip to catch the **Marrakech International Magic Festival** (☎ 0524-43-69-15; www.magiemarrakech.com). Every year on a weekend in March, the city becomes twice as charming, as it welcomes internationally renowned conjurers, magicians, and street entertainers from across the globe. The roll-call in recent years has starred acts such as the musicians Black Fingers and famous illusionists, Bertran Lotth and Jean Louis Galidie. Performances take place across Marrakech, from Jemaa el Fna to the Théâtre Royal. See the website for line-up details.

🕐 *1 hr. Circuit de la Palmeraie. Around 150dh for a 1-hour dromedary ride. Daily 9am–6pm.*

11 ★ **Le Tanjia.** Walking in here is like stepping onto the film set for One Thousand and One Nights, with enormous filigree lanterns casting patterns across the walls. Grab a seat before the svelte belly dancers arrive and feast on the flavorsome house specialty, tanjia (slow-cooked meat with herbs and preserved lemons in a clay pot). The views of Kasbah that unfold from the roof terrace are mesmerizing. *$$$ See p 128.*

12 ★★★ **Le Comptoir Darna.** Take an Art Deco villa, add a young, glamorous crowd, and mix with a troupe of gyrating belly dancers, candle-balancing dervishes, and superstar DJs—et voilà!—I give you Le Comptoir Darna. A near-hallucinatory experience, this decadent lounge club teems with celebrities, playboys, and wannabees, who come more for the hip-wiggling,

Filigree lanterns cast an enticing glow over Le Tanjia.

hookah pipes, and deep house than the food. It's a hedonistic, 21st-century Moroccan fairytale. 🕐 *2hrs. See p 128.*

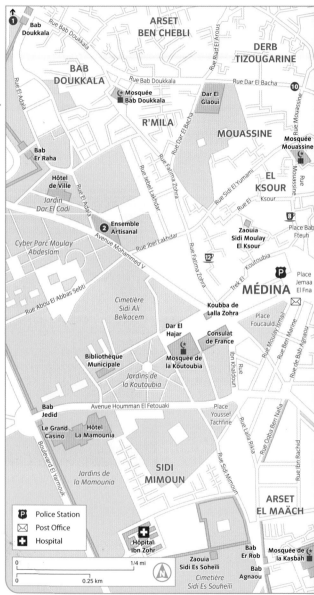

Arts & Crafts

1 Bab Doukkala

Rue Bab Doukkala

ARSET BEN CHEBLI

Rue Riad El Arous

DERB TIZOUGARINE

10

Rue El Adala

BAB DOUKKALA

Rue Bab Doukkala

Rue Dar El Bacha

Rue Mouassine

★ Mosquée Bab Doukkala

Dar El Glaoui

MOUASSINE

Mosquée Mouassine

R'MILA

Rue Dar El Bacha

Bab Er Raha

Rue El Adala

Rue Jebel Lakhdar

Rue Fatima Zohra

Rue Sidi El Yamami

EL KSOUR

Rue Mouassine

Rue El Ksour

Hôtel de Ville

Rue El Adala

Jardin Dar El Cadi

2 Ensemble Artisanal

Avenue Mohammed V

Rue Jbel Lakhdar

Zaouia Sidi Moulay El Ksour

8

Place Bab Fteuh

Cyber Parc Moulay Abdeslam

Rue Abou El Abbas Sebti

12

Rue Fatima Zohra

Trek El Koutoubia

MÉDINA

P

Place Jemaa El Fna

Cimetière Sidi Ali Belkacem

Koubba de Lalla Zohra

Place Foucauld

Rue Moulay Ismail

Rue Ben Marine

Rue de Bab Agnaou

Bibliothèque Municipale

Dar El Hajar

★ Mosquée de la Koutoubia

Consulat de France

Rue Ibn Khaldoun

Jardins de la Koutoubia

Bab Jedid

Avenue Houmman El Fetouaki

Place Youssef Tachfine

Rue Lalla Rkia

Rue Oqba Ben Nafia

Le Grand Casino

Hôtel La Mamounia

Boulevard El Yarmouk

Rue Sidi Mimoun

Rue Ibn Rachid

Jardins de la Mamounia

SIDI MIMOUN

ARSET EL MAÄCH

P Police Station
✉ Post Office
✚ Hospital

✚ Hôpital Ibn Zohr

Zaouia Sidi Es Soheïli

Bab Er Rob

Bab Agnaou

Mosquée de la Kasbah ★

0   1/4 mi

0   0.25 km

Cimetière Sidi Es Souheïli

Fontaine Chrob Ou Chouf

HART ES-SOURA

Rue El Fakhar

Tanneries

Bab Debbagh

Dar Bellarj

Mosquée Ben Youssef

Médersa Ben Youssef

Place du Moukef

Rue Bab Debbagh

Tanneries

Derb Sloussan

DAR DEBAGH

Rue de Souk d. Fassis

Place de la Kissaria

Mosquée Eloussta

Koubba Ba'adyin

Musée de Marrakech

KAÂT BENAHID

ESSEBTIYNE

Souk El Kebir

Derb Sidi Ishak

Mosquée Azabzed

Rue Essebtiyne

Mosquée Sidi Ishak

AZBEZT

Zaouia Sidi Ben Salah

ARSET SIDI YOUSSEF

Arset Sidi Youssef

SOUKS

Taoulat Ben Salah

BEN SALAH

Place Sidi Youb

Rue Fral Semar

Souk Smarine

DERB DABACHI

Rue Sidi Boulabada

ARSET MOULAY SOUAZZA

Souk Quessabine

Rue Dabachi

ARSET EL HOUTA

Rue Ladrassi

Rue Ba Hmad

Rue des Banques

Rue Kennaria

Rue Douar Graoua

KENNARIA

DOUAR GRAOUA

Rue Riad Zitoun ElJedid

Jnane Ben Chegra

Agdal Ba Hmad

Hôpital Arset El Mokha

Palais Moulay Idriss

Jnane Ben Chegra

ARSET MOULAY MOUSSA

Musée Dar Si Saïd

Rue Iman El Rhezoli

Maison Tiskiouine

Avenue Houmman El Fetouaki

Palais de la Bahia

Marché Couvert

Place des Ferblantiers

Synagogue Lazama

MELLAH

Palais El Badi

BERRIMA

Tombeaux Saadiens

Palais Royal Dar El Makhzen

Rue de Berrima

1 Islamic Art Museum
2 Ensemble Artisanal
3 Place des Ferblantiers
4 Aya's
5 Maison Tiskiwin
6 Dar Si Saïd
7 Riads Zitoun
8 Café des Arts
9 Souks
10 Foundouks
11 Musée de Marrakech
12 Le Tobsil

Forget shopping malls: in the souks and Kasbah you can meet the *maâlem* (master craftsman) behind those twinkling lanterns, compliment the handiwork of a carpenter over a mint tea, and get design inspiration exploring fabulous craft museums. Whether you're seeking recycled satchels or handmade *babouches*, this tour reveals Marrakech's crafty side. START: **Islamic Art Museum.**

❶ ★ Islamic Art Museum.

When Yves Saint Laurent and Pierre Bergé were not nurturing exotic blooms, they were avidly hoarding Islamic treasures. This charming museum at the heart of **Jardin Majorelle** (p 15) highlights ethnic jewelry, weapons, traditional dress, and woodwork. Standouts include 19th-century gold-and-horn Tétouan breastplates, peacock-tail-style Koumiya daggers with striking floral patterns, Anti Atlas silk stoles, and intricate *mashrabiyya* screens. ⏱ *30 min. Admission 15dh. Oct–May daily 8am–5pm; Jun–Sep daily 8am–6pm.*

❷ Ensemble Artisanal.

If your haggling spiel is unconvincing, make for this hassle-free crafts cooperative opposite Cyber Park (p 16). Here you can admire artisans diligently fashioning their next masterpiece, be it a hand-knotted rug or a woven basket. Set around a courtyard, these fixed-price shops display original creations from silk throws to lanterns, *babouches* to wood carvings, and calligraphy to bellows. Suitcase space permitting, you can even purchase a striking *zellij* (mosaic tile) tabletop. Many of the shops ship worldwide. ⏱ *30 min. Mon–Sat 9.30am–7pm. Avenue Mohammed V. ☎ 0524-38-66-74. MC, V.*

❸ ★ Place des Ferblantiers.

Take a poke around the workshops where tinsmiths make sparks fly as they swiftly tap out patterns from metal, often using nothing more than a rusty nail, hammer, and an oily rag. Lanterns shaped like stars or inlaid with stained-glass panels, picture frames, and mirrors glint in the sunlight, enticing you over for a closer look. If you speak a smattering of French or Arabic, the *maâlems* (master craftsmen) will delight in telling you the story of each individual piece—some tiny enough for the garden patio, others

Tired of haggling? Go to Ensemble Artisanal for fixed-priced crafts.

Listen out for the tinsmiths on Place des Ferblantiers.

big enough to light a palace. The lanterns take anything from a day to two weeks to make. Although the vendors in these cubby-hole studios are less pushy than those in the souks, there's less margin for bartering—expect a maximum 10% discount. 🕐 *30 min. See p 13.*

④ ★ Aya's. Stop by Aya's for quality hand-crafted gifts from striking tassel-topped flacons to ethnic-chic silver jewelry and soft *babouches*. Sure, these stunning hand-embroidered tunics and elaborate shawls aren't cheap, but everything here is unique. 🕐 *15 min. See p 90.*

⑤ ★★ Maison Tiskiwin. Rarely crowded, this beautiful riad is a fine example of Moroccan craftsmanship with its painted cedarwood doors and carved stucco. Step inside to view the well-traveled collection of Dutch anthropologist **Bert Flint**, who made Morocco his adoptive home more than 50 years ago. The rambling house whisks you on a far-flung journey across Africa, from the pre-Sahara to Southern Mauritania, with crafts including textiles, jewelry, tools, carpets, tribal costumes,

musical instruments, and furniture. Keep an eye out for curiosities such as Neolithic stone carvings, Middle Atlas carpets, Tuareg charm holders, and tasseled leather bags made for young brides. Star exhibits include a full-scale model of a woven Berber tent, mystical fortune-telling boxes, and rain-making masks. Pick up a pamphlet with English descriptions by the entrance. 🕐 *45 min. 8 Rue de la Bahia.* ☎ *0524-38-91-92. Admission 20dh adults, 10dh children under 16. Daily 9am–12:30pm and 3–6pm.*

⑥ ★★★ Dar Si Said. Browse the map by the entrance, and set off on your adventure into Moroccan crafts. This glorious 19th-century *dar* (house) pays homage to almost every epoch and region of Moroccan artistry. Walk and wonder at Safi ceramics emblazoned with floral motifs, well-worn Saharan traveling bags, and time-faded High Atlas carpets. Must-see gems consist of Tuareg jewelry displayed in the one-time chamber of the sultan's favorite wife (the first wife to bear a son) and upstairs, the throne-like marital chairs and magnificently embroidered kaftans. You can take photos of the courtyard but not the collection. 🕐 *45 min. See p 11.*

Colourful tagines for sale in Riads Zitoun.

Best Craft Buys

It's little wonder that Marrakech is carving out its name as one of the world's must-shop cities. The kind of craftsmanship lost in medieval times in the west is still alive here. And in the era of made-in-China products, these skilled artisans rely on tourist sales to support such traditions. Beautifully buffed *tadelakt* vases, filigree lanterns, basketwork, and chunky Berber-style silver jewelry make excellent buys and are easier to slip into your luggage than a carpet. If you've come to Christmas shop, the hand-stitched *babouches* and light *jellabahs*, beat socks as stocking fillers any day.

7 ★ **Riads Zitoun.** A refreshing change from the souks, these parallel streets are brilliant for authentic crafts. **Riad Zitoun el-Jedid** (p 11) is punctuated by cupboard-sized shops selling everything from hand-carved trinkets to kaftans stitched on arthritic Singer sewing machines. For contemporary ceramics in zingy citrus shades and tagine sets, try **Jamade** (p 93). Nearby **Riad Zitoun el-Kedim** is the best street for ethical and eco-friendly gifts, with workshops knocking up photo frames, retro pumps, and even furniture from recycled tires and tarpaulins (see p 144 for more). 🕐 *45 min. Most shops open daily 10am–7:30pm.*

8 ★ **Café des Arts.** Slip into the souks from Jemaa el Fna to find this high-ceilinged café, often the venue for workshops and exhibitions. Admire the surrounding oil paintings while dining on simple dishes such as spaghetti or omelet. *41 bis Souikat Lksour, Bab Fteuh.* ☎ *0661-30-33-75.* $.

9 ★★★ **Souks.** Wear a don't-mess-with-me expression, stick to your first price (even if it means walking out), and compare different shops for quality if you want to buy crafts in the souks. Whether you're

Café des Arts.

looking for leatherwear, textiles, ceramics, or cedarwood, this head-spinning maze is the place to shop. Make for **Souk Smata** (p 51) for *babouches* in myriad colors, **Criée Berbère** (p 20) for hand-woven High Atlas carpets, and **Souk Haddadine** (p 52) for ironwork. If time is an issue, stick to the main artery **Souk Sem-marine** (p 49) for a mix of every-thing. 🕐 *45 min. Most shops daily 10am–9pm; some close Friday.*

🔟 ★★★ **Foundouks.** Gravitate northwest through the souks to Rue Mouassine, home to Marrakech's *foundouks*. Behind creaking wooden doors, you'll find artisans plying their trade, as locals have done for centuries. You might even get to try your own hand at a traditional craft, which is certainly not as simple as it looks. For atmosphere and authen-ticity, you can't beat **Foundouk Tiwtiw** and their beautiful Tuareg jewelry. Nearby is **Foundouk al Mizane**, (p 92) named after the 200-year-old weighing scales at the center of its courtyard. To the right as you enter, you can see the work-shop of award-winning *maâlem* Mr Kharbibi Moulay Mafid. The wood

chips fly as he expertly turns cedar-wood by foot. Opposite, Rasheed sells stylishly contemporary goat-skin lamps colored with natural henna poppy and saffron. 🕐 *30 min: Rue Mouassine and surrounds. Daily 8am–dusk.*

⓫ ★ **Musée de Marrakech.** The marvelously restored 19th-cen-tury **Dar M'Nebhi Palace** shelters a well-curated collection of tradi-tional Moroccan arts in an arcaded courtyard. On show are gem-encrusted daggers, elaborate Ber-ber saddles, and High Atlas carpets. 🕐 *45 min. See p 8.*

⓬ ★★ **Le Tobsil.** Turn up the romance by reserving a table at this intimate riad, buried deep in the medina. The Moroccan diffa (feast) here is legendary: delicious meze, weightless pastillas (pigeon pies), tagines, and fluffy couscous are pol-ished off with mint tea and sticky pastries. *22 Derb Abdellah Ben Hes-saïen, Bab Ksour.* 📞 *0524-44-40-52. $$$$$.*

Essaouira Crafts

The relaxed coastal town of Essaouira is well worth the day trip for its famous thuya woodcarvings and marquetry. Indigenous to Morocco, thuya is a scrub-like conifer that grows widely in the Essaouira area. Tea-light holders and trinket boxes inlaid with mother-of-pearl, lemon-wood, and acacia make unusual gifts. Knotty thuya wood is highly polished with natural oils to reveal its beautiful grain. Essaouira is situated 170km west of Marrakech. For transport details, see p 153.

Coopérative Artisanal des Marqueteurs, Essaouira.

Urban **Escape Acts**

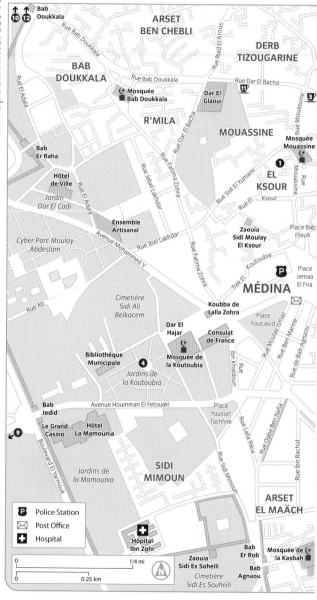

⑩ ⑫ **Bab Doukkala**

ARSET BEN CHEBLI

DERB TIZOUGARINE

Rue Bab Doukkala

Rue Riad El Arous

BAB DOUKKALA

Rue Bab Doukkala

Rue Dar El Bacha

❸

Rue El Adala

🕌 **Mosquée Bab Doukkala**

Dar El Glaoui

⑪

MOUASSINE

Rue Mouassine

R'MILA

Rue Dar El Bacha

🕌 **Mosquée Mouassine**

Bab Er Raha

Rue Jbel Lakhdar

Rue Fatima Zohra

❶

EL KSOUR

Rue Mouassine

Hôtel de Ville

Rue El Adala

Rue Sidi El Yumami

Rue El Ksour

Jardin Dar El Cadi

Ensemble Artisanal

Avenue Mohammed V

Rue Jbel Lakhdar

Zaouia Sidi Moulay El Ksour

Place Bab Fteuh

Cyber Parc Moulay Abdeslam

Rue Fatima Zohra

Trek El Koutoubia

🅿 **MÉDINA**

Place Jemaa El Fna

Rue Ab.

Cimetière Sidi Ali Belkacem

Koubba de Lalla Zohra

✉

Place Foucauld

Dar El Hajar

Consulat de France

Rue Moulay Ismail

Rue Ben Marine

Bibliothèque Municipale

❹

🕌 **Mosquée de la Koutoubia**

Ibn Khaldoun

Rue de Bab Agnaou

Jardins de la Koutoubia

Bab Jedid

Avenue Houmman El Fetouaki

Place Youssef Tachfine

Rue Laila Rikia

Rue Oqba Ben Nafia

Rue Ibn Rachid

←❾

Le Grand Casino

Hôtel La Mamounia

Boulevard El Yarmouk

Rue Sidi Mimoun

SIDI MIMOUN

Jardins de la Mamounia

ARSET EL MAÄCH

🅿 **Police Station**

✉ **Post Office**

➕ **Hospital**

➕ **Hôpital Ibn Zohr**

Zaouia Sidi Es Soheïli

Bab Er Rob

🕌 **Mosquée de la Kasbah**

Bab Agnaou

Cimetière Sidi Es Souheïli

0 _____ 1/4 mi

0 _____ 0.25 km

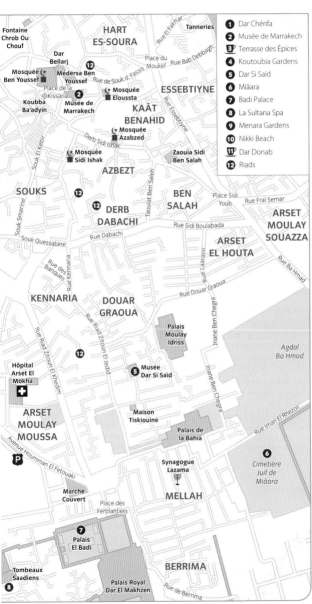

1. Dar Chérifa
2. Musée de Marrakech
3. Terrasse des Épices
4. Koutoubia Gardens
5. Dar Si Said
6. Miâara
7. Badi Palace
8. La Sultana Spa
9. Menara Gardens
10. Nikki Beach
11. Dar Donab
12. Riads

Marrakech revels in contrasts; one minute you're swept up in a wave of medina activity, the next you're on a serene riad rooftop watching the sun burnish the Atlas Mountains, or reflecting over mint tea in a quiet riad courtyard. This tour is about losing the masses in the city's maze-like *derbs* or alleys. START: **Dar Chérifa.**

1 ★★ **Dar Chérifa.** It's certainly a challenge to find this cultural café, tucked down a serpentine alley off Rue Mouassine, but it's worth the effort. Meticulously restored to its original splendor in 2001, this 16th-century Saâdian riad is the medina's oldest, and a veritable oasis of calm. Here the soaring columns and intricately carved stucco and cedar force you to look up in wonder. If the sun's out, head up to the roof for a tea or freshly pressed date juice. Dar Chérifa regularly hosts exhibitions and readings, plus ceramic and cookery workshops. ⏱ *45 min. 8 Derb Chorfa el-Kebir, off Rue Mouassine.* ☎ *0524-42-64-63. Daily 9am–7pm.*

2 ★ **Musée de Marrakech.** No matter when you visit the Musée de Marrakech, the vast inner patio, with its extraordinary lantern and gurgling marble fountains, has an

Dar Chérifa's secret courtyard is a challenge to find, but well worth the effort.

overwhelming sense of tranquility. Enjoy the silence relaxing in an alcove bedecked with spectacular *zellij* tiles and stucco, or wandering the honeycomb of rooms in the former hammam at the back. Listen hard and you may just distinguish the patter of footsteps or the muezzin's call. ⏱ *45 min. See p 8.*

3 **Terrasse des Épices.** Suddenly the clamor of the medina seems distant on this sun-baked roof terrace, where the whole of Marrakech unfurls like a Berber carpet before you. When the souks become stifling, the feeling of space here is refreshing. Savor Atlas Mountain vistas over a lunch of tagliatelle and aubergine mille-feuille. *15 Souk Cherifia.* ☎ *0524-37-59-04. $–$$.*

4 ★ kids **Koutoubia Gardens.** Leave behind the traffic on busy Avenue Mohammed V for a wander through this pocket of greenery tucked behind the Koutoubia. Enjoy shady gardens speckled with palms, fragrant orange trees, and storks' nests. Have your camera handy for close-up snapshots of the minaret. ⏱ *20 min. See p 61.*

5 ★★★ **Dar Si Said.** Vivaldi may well have swapped composing for botany had he seen the lush courtyard garden, inspired by the four seasons, at the heart of this 19th-century mansion. Come in the late afternoon when most of the crowds

Escape the heat and hubbub of Marrakech in the Koutoubia Gardens.

have left, and a blissful sense of calm falls over the garden shaded by pomegranate and cypress trees. 🕐 *30 min. See p 11.*

6 ★ **Miâara.** A million miles away from the bustle of the Kasbah, and yet just 5 minutes' walk, lies the Miâara, a little-known 16th-century cemetery in the Mellah (Jewish Quarter). Only stray dogs and crowing cockerels interrupt the peace in the overgrown graveyard, strewn with shrines and higgledy-piggledy headstones. 🕐 *30 min. Mellah. Sun–Thurs 7am–6pm, Fri 7am–3pm. Donations appreciated.*

7 ★ **Badi Palace.** Abandoned to the elements, Sultan Ahmed el-Mansour's 16th-century palace appears lost in time. Once sublime, today the courtyard and crumbling red brick walls are an overgrown wilderness and a quiet escape from the hubbub of Kasbah. Shafts of daylight pierce the web of vine-strewn underground passageways, recalling something out of an Indiana Jones movie, where your echoing footsteps are likely to be

the only ones. See also p 57. 🕐 *45 min. Near Place des Ferblantiers. No phone. Admission 10dh. Daily 8:30am–11:45am and 2:30–5:45pm.*

8 ★★★ **La Sultana Spa.** La Sultana is the ultimate Kasbah escape. Stress evaporates as you sip mint tea beside the pink marble pool, where only a crackling fire interrupts the silence, or unwind in the domed jacuzzi. Expert *tayebas* (attendants) will show you through to the hammam, where you'll be slathered in pore-awakening eucalyptus *savon noir* (black soap) and given a first-class rubdown. Be prepared for a snooze-inducing massage with warm verbena, rose, or orange-flower oil. Towels, bathrobes. and disposable briefs are provided. Reservations essential. 🕐 *1½ hrs. 403 Rue de la Kasbah.* ☎ *0524-38-80-08. www. lasultanamarrakech.com. 350dh hammam and body wrap. Daily 10am–8pm.*

Peace reigns over the Jewish Cemetery.

Valley Retreat

When Marrakech swelters in summer, cool off on a day trip to the Ourika Valley (p 156) in the High Atlas, where the clean air is refreshing and the mountain views invigorating. Within an hour, you've left the city bustle behind and are passing through mud-brick Berber villages that are home to fragrant herb gardens and rural souks selling fresh produce, second-hand clothing, and alfresco haircuts. Be sure to stop in Setti Fatma (p 156) for a brisk uphill stride to the waterfalls, where you may spot locals taking an impromptu dip. See p 158 for transport options.

9 ★ kids Menara Gardens.
Hop aboard a horse-drawn *calèche* or walk the olive tree-lined Avenue de la Menara to these gardens, which seem to reach beyond Marrakech to touch the foot of the snow-dusted Atlas Mountains. I often come here in the late afternoon to stroll through orchards and olive groves to the 19th-century pavilion. Sit beside the reflecting pools as the last sun tinges the peaks gold. ⏱ *45 min. See p 12.*

10 ★ Nikki Beach. Young and outrageously flirty, this über-chic Palmeraie beach draws jetsetters cooler than its champagne cocktails, as well as mere mortals simply wishing to escape the Marrakech heat. There are bed-style loungers where you can top up the tan or dance to DJs pumping out lounge tunes. The gorgeous outdoor pool is the place for refreshing dips and, naturally, posing in your designer beachwear. The ambiance heats up as the day

Take a tranquil walk through the olive groves and admire Atlas Mountain views in the Menara Gardens.

Unwind with Marrakech's hip set at Nikki Beach.

wears on. See also p 128. ⏱ *2 hrs. Circuit de la Palmeraie.* ☎ *0524-36-87-27. www.nikkibeach.com. Daily noon–7pm.*

🍵 ★★ **Dar Donab.** Insiders (including George Clooney and Uma Thurman) whisper quietly about this exquisite little palace, but frankly the secret is too good to keep. The Eden-like courtyard leads to the restaurant, a feast of Moroccan arts with its striking zellij tilework, cedar cupola, and grand marble fireplace. Dine like the royals on well-prepared classics such as tender chicken tagines with preserved lemons and olives. *53 Rue Dar el-Bacha, Bab Doukkala.* ☎ *0524-44-18-97. $$$.*

⓬ ★★★ **Riads.** Marrakech's beauty makes that of other cities seem superficial, because much of it lies behind closed wooden doors. Ring the bell and you'll be miraculously transported to another world, where thick walls absorb the street din, fountains trickle, and nightingales sing in the orange trees. When the souks get claustrophobic, escape to the roof terrace of

luxurious **Riad Farnatchi** (p 144), discover the secret garden of **Riad Enija** (p 144), or find intimacy and Berber-style romance in **Riyad El Cadi** (p 146). Other ultimate escape acts include **Casa Lalla** (p 111) and **Caravanserai** (p 140).

Riyad El Cadi is an oasis of tranquility.

Celebrity Marrakech

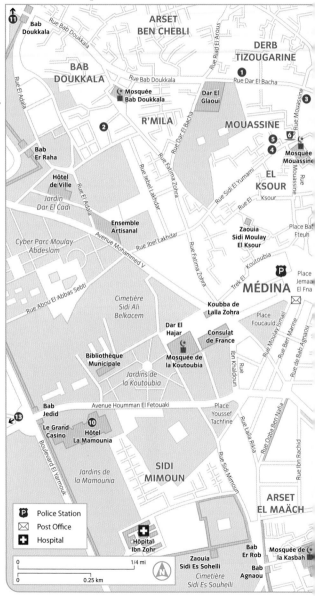

Police Station
Post Office
Hospital

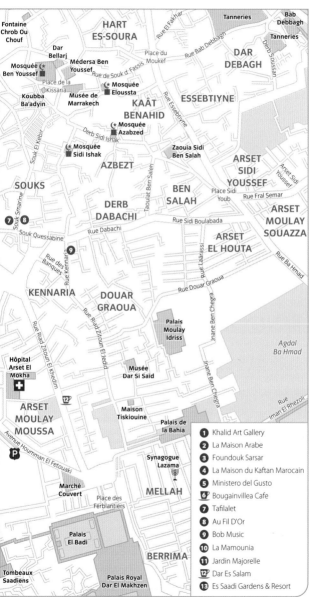

1 Khalid Art Gallery
2 La Maison Arabe
3 Foundouk Sarsar
4 La Maison du Kaftan Marocain
5 Ministero del Gusto
6 Bougainvillea Cafe
7 Tafilalet
8 Au Fil D'Or
9 Bob Music
10 La Mamounia
11 Jardin Majorelle
12 Dar Es Salam
13 Es Saadi Gardens & Resort

Hippie mecca, supermodel magnet, and rock-star refuge; Marrakech has serious celebrity appeal. Since the trippy 1960s when the Stones came rolling in, the red city has turned the heads of artists, musicians, film directors, and fashion divas. From Kate Moss' favorite kaftans to Kate Winslet on camera, this tour follows in the footsteps of the stars. START: **Khalid Art Gallery.**

❶ ★★ Khalid Art Gallery. Film directors, actors, models, and rock stars go gaga for the precious antiques lining this riad gallery, a rabbit's warren of chandelier-lit rooms. Though the age-old Berber rugs, magnificent paintings and rare Jewish jewelry are second mortgage material, it makes for enjoyable window shopping. Don't miss the hall of fame by the entrance, smothered in snapshots of customers Bill Clinton, Silvio Berlusconi, Naomi Campbell, Kate Moss, Brad Pitt, David Bowie, Noel Gallagher, and more. Ridley Scott, director of the visually striking movie *Kingdom of Heaven* (2005), used artifacts from here to dress the set. ⏲ *20 min. See p 86.*

❷ ★★ La Maison Arabe. To relax in true celebrity style, splurge on the 75-minute Royal Session at

Celebrity antique hunters favorite, the Khalid Art Gallery.

La Maison Arabe, which takes place in a candlelit vaulted chamber. The hammam includes a wonderful gommage with eucalyptus-scented *savon noir*, a spice-infused *rhassoul* mask, and a gentle 30-minute massage. Reservations essential. ⏲ *1½ hrs. Derb Assehbe, Bab Doukkala.* ☎ *0524-38-70-10. www.lamaisonarabe.com. 350dh hammam, gommage, and rhassoul wrap, 800dh royal session. Daily 10am–8pm.*

❸ ★★ Foundouk Sarsar. If this centuries-old *foundouk* seems familiar, that's because many of the scenes in the movie *Hideous Kinky* (1998), starring Kate Winslet, were filmed here. Although the film evokes the free spirit of Marrakech in the 1960s and 1970s, the *foundouk* is a far cry from the age of peace and love. Today artisans ply their trade, men wash utensils in the fountain, and kittens dodge the tagines and teapots. ⏲ *20 min. 192 Rue Mouassine.*

❹ ★ La Maison du Kaftan Marocain. Unassuming on the outside, this glitzy store is the beloved haunt of kaftan-crazy celebrities. Jean-Paul Gaultier and Valentino dig the catwalk-worthy collection, while photos of past customers from stage and screen grace the walls. Strike a pose in one of the spangled kaftans, flamboyant tunics, or flouncy *jellabahs* (robes). ⏲ *30 min. See p 91.*

❺ ★★ Ministero del Gusto. Behind a nameless door lies the creative playground of former Italian

In the Spotlight

Serious film buffs will not want to miss the Marrakech **International Film Festival** (☎ 0524-43-24-93; www.festivalmarrakech.info), a nine-day movie fest in November. Held for the first time in 2000, the festival has taken the big screens by storm and looks set to rival the likes of Cannes, London, and Berlin with its first-class program and jury. Guests of honor in recent years include Sigourney Weaver, Martin Scorsese, and Leonardo di Caprio. Screenings take place at numerous venues across the city, including the Palais des Congrès, Cinéma Le Colisée (p 133), and open-air on Jemaa el Fna.

Vogue editor Alessandra Lippini. This eccentric riad gallery is filled with objets d'art, designer clothing, and space-age furniture. Explore the lattice of rooms and you may well spot David Bowie lounging on a leopard-print sofa or Kate Moss trying on a vintage Valentino shift dress for size. You need only look at the limited public open hours to know that this place is exclusive. ⏱ *30 min. See p 86.*

6 Bougainvillea Café. Birdsong fills the pink-walled courtyard of this café, draped with namesake bougainvillea. Rest your feet and refresh over a tea or non-alcoholic cocktail. If you're feeling peckish, try the salads, sandwiches, or sweet crepes. *33 Rue Mouassine.* ☎ *0524-44-11-11. $*

7 ★★ Tafilalet. Celebrities in search of gem-encrusted sparkle for the red carpet flock to this shoebox-sized jewelry store in the souks. Moroccan royals, the president of Qatar, Bill Clinton, Leonardo di Caprio, and *Casino Royale* Bond girl Caterina Murino have all shopped here. Prices are (just about) within the reach of mere mortals. ⏱ *15 min. See p 94.*

8 Au Fil D'Or. Opposite Tafilalet, this boutique is equally prized by the jet-set for its chic prêt-à-porter kaftans in high-quality fabrics, cool linen shirts, and handmade babouches in butter-soft leather. Ask to see the special collection downstairs. ⏱ *10 min. 10 Souk Semmarine.* ☎ *0524-44-59-19. Daily 9am–1pm and 3–7:30pm. See p 90.*

Bougainvillea Café.

Making a Celebrity Splash

Who needs the sea when you have a dreamy white-sand beach just outside the city? The brainchild of the Michelin-starred Pourcel brothers, **La Plage Rouge** (p 128) is one of the city's hippest party spots. It's Hollywood film-set stuff with its Balinese beds, azure pool, eye-candy staff, and an Atlas Mountain backdrop. Join the sunbathing socialites for cocktails, French fusion cuisine, and late-night clubbing by taking a taxi to La Plage Rouge, 10km from central Marrakech.

9 ★★ **Bob Music.** Bob's groovy souk store harbors a terrific collection of traditional Moroccan instruments for budding musicians—from hand-carved lutes to Berber saxophones. As the fading photos on the wall testify, Rachid (the owner) has jammed with Robert Plant of Led Zeppelin. Learn to play like a Gnaoua pro with one-to-one tuition. ⏱ *20 min. See p 94.*

10 ★★★ **La Mamounia.** Sir Winston Churchill once described this grand Art Deco hotel to Roosevelt as being the most lovely spot in the world'; praise that led to a suite being named in his honor. When Charles de Gaulle stayed here after the 1943 Casablanca Conference, a custom-made bed was brought in to accommodate all 6ft 5 inches of the general. Since opening in the 1920s, opulent La Mamounia has provided a backdrop for films such as Hitchcock's *The Man Who Knew Too Much* (1956) and *Morocco* (1930) starring Marlene Dietrich. A peek inside the Livre d'Or reveals other famous past guests including Tom Cruise, Sylvester Stallone, and Nicole Kidman. ⏱ *15 min. Avenue Bab Jdid.* ☎ *0524-38-86-00. www. mamounia.com.*

11 ★★ **Jardin Majorelle.** It's just a short petit taxi ride north to Jardin Majorelle. Late fashion icon Yves Saint Laurent, and his partner Pierre Bergé, restored French painter Jacques Majorelle's avant-garde oasis in 1980. The exotic cacti and slender palms seem to strut like models on a botanical catwalk, set against a backdrop of acid yellow and the artist's trademark cobalt blue. At the heart of the foliage lies a memorial to Yves Saint Laurent (1936–2008). ⏱ *1 hr. See p 15.*

Browse jewelry fit for royalty at the gem of the souks, Tafilalet.

See the botanical vision of Yves Saint Laurent at Jardin Majorelle.

12 ★★ **Dar Es Salam.** Just like Alfred Hitchcock's Oscar-winning The Man Who Knew too Much, shot here in 1956, this lavish 17th-century palace is a timeless classic. Both Sean Connery and Winston Churchill have eaten in the chandelier-lit opulence. Book a table to dine on Moroccan flavors such as fragrant couscous followed by lamb tagine with prune and almonds and sticky Moroccan sweets (menus 250–400dh). *170 Riad Zitoun el-Kedim.* ☎ *0524-44-35-20. $$$.*

13 ★ **Es Saadi Gardens & Resort.** For true rock-star chic, it has to be this glamorous Hivernage retreat, where Mick Jagger and Keith Richards escaped the paparazzi in 1967. The hotel is the epitome of luxury with its 8-hectare palm-dotted gardens, casino and lavish rooms—some with four-poster beds and private pools. For the celebrity treatment without staying here, book a traditional hammam, sesame oil gommage, or a calming cabana-bed massage at the Oriental Spa. *Es Saadi Gardens & Resort, Avenue El Quadissia.* ⏱ *1½ hrs.* ☎ *0524-44-88-11. www.essaadi.com. 290dh for 45-min hammam and gommage. Daily 9am–9pm. See p 141.*

All Aboard The Train

Close your eyes, think of a Marrakech tune, and nine times out of ten it will be '**Marrakech Express**' by Crosby, Stills, and Nash. From the 1950s to the 1970s, free-spirited hedonists in search of exotica and themselves boarded the train to Marrakech, a milestone on the hippie trail from Europe to Asia. The red-ochre city rocked The Beatles and Stones, and Beat Generation writers such as Jack Kerouac and Paul Bowles. Although the backpacker digs, purple haze, and bellbottoms have since been replaced by boutique riads, spas, and fashionable kaftans, the boho vibe, creativity, and yes, that catchy jingle live on.

Architectural Elements

1. Koutoubia Minaret
2. Ramparts
3. Bab Agnaou
4. Saâdian Tombs
5. Earth Café
6. Bahia Palace
7. Dar Si Said
8. Musée de Marrakech
9. Koubba Ba'adyin
10. Ali Ben Youssef Medersa
11. Chouf Fountain
12. Maison Arabe

P Police Station
⊠ Post Office
➕ Hospital

0   1/4 mi
0   0.25 km

Delve into Moroccan decorative arts and architecture on this close-up tour. Kaleidoscopic mosaics and lacey stucco, Kufic calligraphy and painted cedarwood—no surface is left untouched in Marrakech. At the end of this tour you'll appreciate that even the everyday can be extraordinary in this geometrically minded, aesthetically pleasing city. **START Koutoubia.**

1 ★★★ Koutoubia Minaret. Standing sentinel above Marrakech is the 70m-high minaret (by law no building can be taller) of Koutoubia (p 61). With its admirable symmetry, fleur-de-lys-like *darj w ktarf* (cheek-and-shoulder) motifs, and crenellations, it's the city's most powerful image. Yet the width to height ratio of 1:5 affords the slender tower an incredible lightness. Look up to the top to spy the three gilded copper balls; lore has it they were originally made from pure gold and donated by Sultan Yacoub el Mansour's wife as repentance for daylight snacking during Ramadan. ⏲ *25 min. See p 3.*

A feat of symmetry and ornament - the minaret of Koutoubia.

bluish pink Guéliz stone. Approach it from Rue Sidi Mimoun and you'll be struck by its scalloped arches, profusion of floral ornament, graceful Kufic script, and the *trompe l'oeil* effect of the bas relief. ⏲ *10 min. See p 13.*

4 ★★ Saâdian Tombs. Enter Sultan Ahmed el-Mansour's extravagant tombs and on the left lies the Chamber of the Twelve Pillars. Here geometric *zellij* (mosaic tiles) and swirling calligraphy guide the eye to Carrara marble

2 ★ Ramparts. Built by the Almoravids to fortify Marrakech in the 12th century, the soaring ramparts encircling the medina are among Morocco's finest. Towering up to 6m (19 feet) high and stretching for 19km around the medina, the *pisé* (clay and chalk) walls are flanked by 20 gates and 200 towers. To find out why Marrakech is nicknamed 'the red city', return at dusk when the ramparts blush. ⏲ *15 min. See p 62.*

3 Bab Agnaou. There is magnetism about Bab Agnaou, Marrakech's most striking city gate, shaped like a horseshoe and carved from

Watch the ramparts 'blush' at dusk.

columns and *muqarnas*, vaulted sta-lactite-like niches carved from stucco. Another typical feature of Islamic architecture is the *mihrab* niche in the wall, showing the direction of Mecca. Across the way is the mausoleum of the sultan's mother, boasting a colorfully painted cedar ceiling. ⏱ *45 min. See p 12*.

5 ★ **Earth Café.** Revive over a Yogi tea, freshly squeezed juice, or a healthy vegetarian special at the bohemian-style café. It's also a fine spot to pick up first-rate argan and olive oil. *2 Derb Zouak, Riad Zitoun el-Kedim.* ☎ *060-54-38-99-15. $.*

6 ★★★ **Bahia Palace.** Bahia translates as 'beautiful' or 'brilliant' and it's no overstatement; the grand vizier's lavish late 19th-century palace is like a textbook on Moroccan craftsmanship. Wander courtyards and chambers where vivid *zellij* perform cartwheels across the walls and rise to delicate calligraphy and stucco. Concubines saw little outside life but could day-dream gazing up to their chamber's carved, painted cedarwood ceilings, graced with flowers, birds, stars, and other naturalistic motifs. *Zouak* is the term to describe such wood-work, finely hand painted with pigments such as poppy (red), saffron

Mashrabiyya screens in the Bahia Palace.

(yellow), and mint (green). Another characteristic element of Moroccan architecture is the fountain in the great courtyard, which allowed the grand vizier to whisper sweet noth-ings to his concubines without his wives eavesdropping. Before you exit the palace, take in the chamber of the 'favorite wife' to see *mashrabiyya*, lattice-like turned-wood screens. ⏱ *1 hr. See p 11*.

7 ★★★ **Dar Si Said.** This sub-lime 19th-century palace is famed for its ingeniously hand-painted cedar ceilings. Allow time to

Knocking on Heavenly Doors

Generally overlooked in the west, doors have a decorative purpose in this secretive city. Wandering the medina you'll find doors that are carved, painted, or framed by stonework, providing a beautiful transition between public and private life, commotion and calm. Confusingly many have no name or number. The next time you arrive at a riad door, pause to contemplate details such as doorknockers shaped like the good-luck Fatima hand or, in the Jewish district of Mellah (p 56), the Star of David.

Moroccan Artistry Lexicon

Get more out of your visit to Marrakech by identifying some of the city's key decorative arts and architectural elements:

Calligraphy: One of the highest art forms in the Muslim world. It is a visual expression of the word of the Koran, which forbids the depiction of animate objects.

Mashrabiyya: Lattice-like turned-wood screens that take their name from the Arabic word sharaba (to drink or absorb), denoting their original purpose as water storage shelves.

Mihrab: The niche in the wall of a mosque that indicates the direction of Mecca.

Muqarnas: Stucco niches carved like stalactites.

Tadelakt: Polished lime-based plaster first used by Berbers to make their earthen cisterns waterproof. Tadelakt is applied wet-on-wet, dried naturally, and hand buffed with a stone.

Zellij: Mosaic tilework, assembled from thousands of precisely cut puzzle-like pieces. Zellij can take a lifetime to master and has bamboozled mathematicians with its infinite variations and repeated, interwoven patterns.

Zouak: A painting technique using a fine brush and often natural pigments, which is used to elaborately decorate cedarwood doors and ceilings.

appreciate the upstairs wedding chamber, where lustrous *zellij* tilework ascends to stalactite like *muqarna* niches and coffered ceilings that are a kaleidoscope of geometric patterns, colors, and inlaid eight-point stars. Each panel is a mini work of art that dazzles with its complexity. ⏱ *45 min. See p 11.*

8 ★ Musée de Marrakech. I find it hard to tear myself away from this museum's vast central courtyard, where fountains gurgle and daylight filters through a glass roof supported by a filigree brass lantern. Take a seat in a *bhou* (alcove) to marvel at the polychrome *zellij* tilework, keyhole arches, and honeycomb-like stucco. The labyrinth of chambers beyond reveal finely painted coffered cedar ceilings. ⏱ *45 min. See p 8.*

9 ★ Koubba Ba'adyin. Marrakech's best-preserved example of Almoravid architecture is this 11th-century *koubba* (cupola). Once an

Koubba Ba'adyin.

Symbols & Meanings

The further you explore Marrakech, the more you find recurring patterns and numbers. Keep an eye out for the **Khamsa** (literally meaning 'five'), or **Fatima hand**, used in amulets and jewelry to ward off the 'evil eye'. Five is a symbolic number, representing the five sacred pillars of Islam. Eight, revealed in patterns of octagons and eight-pointed stars, also has special importance because it's considered the number of Paradise in Islam.

ablutions annex for Ben Youssef mosque, the *koubba* is the blueprint for many of the designs you see elsewhere in Marrakech, with its pyramid-like *merlons* (battlements), graceful keyhole arches, and interior adorned with intertwined floral and foliate patterns, and calligraphy. 🕐 *30 min. See p 8*.

⑩ ★★★ Ali Ben Youssef Medersa. Often as fine as piped icing on a cake, stucco (decorative plaster) is another time-honored decorative art in Marrakech, given the abundance of lime in the surrounding hills. Ali Ben Youssef Medersa's arcaded courtyard is a mind-blowing masterpiece of floor-to-ceiling *zellij* mosaics, Kufic inscriptions, carved cedar, and stucco entwined with naturalistic motifs (flowers, leaves, pinecones, and birds), which is as delicate as Chantilly lace. 🕐 *1 hr. See p 8*.

⑪ Chouf Fountain. Every Marrakech neighborhood once had a communal fountain but few could match this 16th-century Saâdian masterpiece, a UNESCO World Heritage site. Linger to notice the calligraphy and wooden lintel carved like honeycomb and sheltered by a green-tiled roof. 🕐 *10 min. See p 69*.

⑫ ★ Maison Arabe. Appreciate the majestic zouak painted ceilings and arched mirrors as Andalusian musicians strum in the restaurant of this venerable 1940s riad. Dinner here is a feast of traditional Moroccan arts and cuisine. *1 Derb Assehbe, Bab Doukkala.* ☎ *0524-38-70-10. $$$.* ●

Admire the zouak painted cedar ceiling of Maison Arabe's restaurant.

Central Souks **& Around**

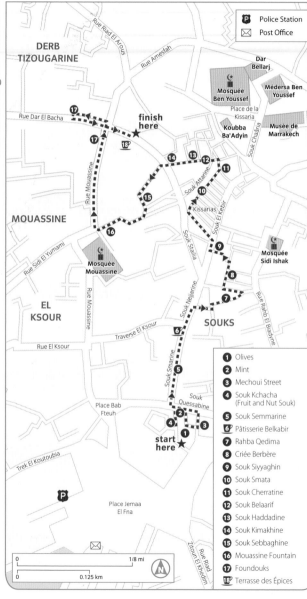

| | Police Station |
| | Post Office |

DERB TIZOUGARINE

Rue Riad El Arous

Rue Amesfah

Dar Bellarj

Mosquée Ben Youssef

Médersa Ben Youssef

Place de la Kissaria

Rue Dar El Bacha

finish here

Koubba Ba'Adyin

Musée de Marrakech

Souk Chaaria

MOUASSINE

Rue Sidi El Yumami

Souk 'Attarine

Kissarias

Souk El Kebir

Mosquée Mouassine

Souk Stailia

Mosquée Sidi Ishak

EL KSOUR

Rue Mouassine

Rue El Ksour

Souk Nejjarine

Traverse El Ksour

SOUKS

Rue Rahb El Biadyne

Souk Smarine

Souk Quessabine

Place Bab Fteuh

Trek El Koutoubia

start here ★

Place Jemaa El Fna

Rue Riad Zitoun El Khedim

0 — 1/8 mi
0 — 0.125 km

1	Olives
2	Mint
3	Mechoui Street
4	Souk Kchacha (Fruit and Nut Souk)
5	Souk Semmarine
6'	Pâtisserie Belkabir
7	Rahba Qedima
8	Criée Berbère
9	Souk Siyyaghin
10	Souk Smata
11	Souk Cherratine
12	Souk Belaarif
13	Souk Haddadine
14	Souk Kimakhine
15	Souk Sebbaghine
16	Mouassine Fountain
17	Foundouks
18'	Terrasse des Épices

Throw away your pocket-watch and marvel as things get curiouser and curiouser on this spin of the labyrinthine souks. Whether you're dodging donkey carts to warning cries of *balek!* or haggling like a Berber for *babouches* (slippers), this hallucinogenic wonderland will enchant you. The souks open daily from around 9am to 8pm, with some closing Friday for the Jumu'ah prayer and COUSCOUS. START: **Northeast corner of Jemaa el Fna.**

1 ★ Olives. Enter the souks from Jemaa el Fna and you'll be struck by the tangy aroma of lemons and herbs wafting from the olive souk. Pairing well with any tagine, olives are a staple part of the Marrakchi diet and quality is second-to-none. Only the heads of vendors are visible amid the mountains of glossy green, red, and black olives (the color depends on when they were harvested), alongside jars of preserved lemons, chilis, capers, and pickles. Sample and buy some olives for around 18dh per kilo. ⏲ *10 min. Souk Ableuh.*

2 Mint. Immediately opposite the olives you'll find fresh and dried mint in bunches, another favorite ingredient in Marrakchi cuisine. Target these makeshift wooden stands if you're planning to recreate Moroccan tea ceremonies back home. ⏲ *5 min. Souk Ableuh.*

3 ★ Mechoui Street. The aroma of *mechoui* lamb (see p 113), slow roasted in the embers of a wood fire to achieve its rich flavor and fall-off-the-bone tenderness, will lure you over to these hole-in-the-wall joints. Chefs puff up with pride when you give an admiring nod to the quality of their cuts, telling you that their humble TV-and-plastic-chair eateries were the first restaurants in Marrakech. Apart from the delicious lamb, there are also sheep heads for the brave. Around 70dh will buy you a small feast. ⏲ *10 min. Souk Ableuh. Daily 10am–9pm.*

Follow your nose to the olive souk.

4 Souk Kchacha (Fruit and Nut Souk). Amble back towards the mint stalls, bear left (east), and you'll shortly reach Souk Kchacha, where the stalls are heaped with dried fruit and nuts. The plump apricots, sticky dates and figs, walnuts, and cashews are great for grazing between purchases. Expect to pay between 40dh and 120dh per kilo. A friendly *assalam aleikum* (hello) and a winning smile will boost your chances of being allowed to take photos. ⏲ *30 min. Souk Kchacha.*

5 ★★★ Souk Semmarine. Every visitor will walk through this bustling souk at least once. As you pass through the stucco arch at the entrance, you encounter gossiping

The bustling Souk Semmarine.

women, grubby kids with quick smiles (and quicker fingers, so watch your wallet), stubborn mules, and men lugging carpets among the dazed tourists. Light filters through the slatted roof to reveal bejeweled slippers, leather pouffes, and brilliant throws, and unlike many other souks this main artery sells a hotchpotch of everything. Gems include Omar's jewelry at Tafilalet (p 94), sleek kaftans at Au Fil d'Or (p 90), and Adil's quality throws at Sabra Mode (p 93). Remember the golden rule: if you can find your way back to Souk Semmarine, you can find your way out of the souks. ⏲ *30 min. Souk Semmarine.*

6 **Pâtisserie Belkabir.** Pause for syrupy Moroccan treats at this cupboard-sized patisserie. Oozing honey and nuts, these traditional sweetmeats make great gifts too. A kilo costs around 100dh. *63–65 Souk Semmarine. No phone. $.*

7 ★★ **Rahba Qedima.** Look for the 'château des souks' sign on Souk Semmarine, and then turn right at the next gate to reach this mystical square flanked by herbalist's stores and centered on a market selling hand-woven baskets and beanies. Simply name your ailment and the men in white will produce a miracle cure—be it Berber viagra (ginseng), anti-snoring nigella, or Ramadan tea to fight the flab. This is also the place for hammam gear, natural perfumes, and clay pots of crimson 'Berber lipstick' made from crushed insects. Gawp at iguanas, alligator skins, and other peculiarities before delving back into the souks. ⏲ *20 min. See p 20.*

8 ★★ **Criée Berbère.** Weave northeast from Rahba Qedima to the cool, dark carpet souk, also dubbed the Criée Berbère or Souk des Tapis. Even if a $1,000 rug isn't on your wish list, this souk should be for its colorful Berber designs and grinning vendors spinning yarns. My Aladdin vote goes to Bazar Ben Allal (p 87). Size, quality, and detail determine the price, but brace yourself for a haggling marathon. For bids and banter, arrive at 4pm for the daily carpet auction. ⏲ *20 min. See p 20.*

A carpet from Bazar Ben Allal.

How Low Can You Go?

You want how much? The ability to haggle like a pro is a rite of passage in Marrakech's souks. Waver in your bartering spiel and the grinning sharks will have you (and your holiday bucks) for breakfast. But how to begin? Well, a good benchmark is to knock 70% off the first price. Be direct and tough, even when the vendor unleashes sob stories about his starving kids and crumbling business. Gradually work your way up to a more reasonable 50% of the original amount and always be prepared to walk away—chances are the no-can-do salesman will call you back. Ultimately, though, there is no one 'right price'; a bargain is what you're happy and willing to pay. Think of haggling like a game of karate: a verbal combat of blows and kicks, with handshakes and smiles all round at the end.

9 Souk Siyyaghin. Exit the carpet souk and walk a few paces north on Souk Semmarine to enter the glittering jewelry souk on the right, crammed with treasures from filigree bangles to silver chains. If you're intent on buying, find out the going rate for gold back home before shopping here, because overcharging is de rigueur.
🕐 *10 min. Souk Siyyaghin.*

10 ★ Souk Smata. Diagonally opposite the jewelry souk is an archway that leads to the enticing slipper souk. This bazaar of vibrant *babouches* and belts is full of decisions. Pointy or round? Spangled or sleek? Plain or embroidered? Or perhaps you'll go for a smart pair of beach-ready *babouches climatisées* (air-conditioned slippers), aka sandals. Pause to admire new creations in the making. 🕐 *20 min. Souk Smata.*

11 Souk Cherratine. Passing through a white gate, you'll be struck by the pungent smell of pelts in the leather souk, dotted with thimble-sized workshops where leatherworkers sharpen tools and deftly cut and stitch leather goods by hand. Top buys include *babouches*, satchels, handbags, wallets, and multi-colored pouffes.
🕐 *15 min. Souk Cherratine.*

12 Souk Belaarif. Donkeys bray, stereos pump out electro beats, and TVs bleep at the medieval-meets-modern high-tech souk, where young Marrakchi shout into

Pointed or round? Find a pair that fit in the slipper souk.

The dazzling colours of Marrakech's dyers' souk.

their mobiles above the noise. Jam-packed with electrical goods, these hole-in-the-wall stores are interesting just to look around. ⏲ *10 min. Souk Belaarif.*

⑬ ★★ Souk Haddadine. Once the digital din has faded, you'll hear (probably before you see) the iron-workers' souk. Out of the shadows, grease-smeared men emerge from cupboard-sized workshops; some frantically hammer away at wrought-iron chairs, others expertly weld filigree lanterns. You can barely hear yourself think above the clang of metal, the whirr of drills, and the tapping of hammers. It's an immensely atmospheric place to shop for lamps, bellows, candelabras, and lucky *Fatima* hand door knockers. ⏲ *15 min. Souk Haddadine.*

⑭ Souk Kimakhine. So you've heard the catchy Gnaoua beats on Jemaa el Fna, now here's your

chance to take some home. Sidling up to Souk Haddadine, the stringed instrument souk is a one-stop shop for music lovers, with everything you need to stage your own Berber jam session. I come to watch *maâlems* (master craftspeople) beautifully carving *rababas* (single-stringed fiddles), banjos, mandolins, and lutes. ⏲ *10 min. Souk Kimakhine.*

⑮ ★★★ Souk Sebbaghine. Walk south of the Souk Kimakhine and have your digicam poised to snap the photogenic dyers' souk (*souk des teinturiers* in French). Shrinking violets beware, because Sebbaghine is somewhere over the rainbow: flames of henna orange, flashes of mint green and indigo, bursts of saffron yellow, and splashes of poppy red and fuchsia suffuse the narrow alleyways. Skeins are hung out to dry between mud-brick walls, while workers stoke the fires of their steaming vats of dye. Tip one

The great scales of Foundouk al Mizane.

of the shop owners a few dirham to visit a roof terrace with a bird's-eye view over this technicolor souk. ⏱ *20 min.*

16 Mouassine Fountain. Close to the dyers' souk lies the Mouassine mosque, directly adjacent to the city's largest and most important public fountain. Embellished with geometric patterns, carved wood, and calligraphy, this triple-arched Saâdian fountain is a splendid example of the fountains that were once fundamental to daily life in Marrakech. ⏱ *5 min. Rue Sidi Yamani.*

17 ★★★ Foundouks. Head north along Rue Mouassine from the mosque and let curiosity drag you through the heavy wood doors of the *foundouks* (caravanserais). Framing an inner courtyard, small-scale workshops make use of the former stables and provide an insight into different crafts and a flavor of bygone Marrakech. My favorites include Foundouk Sarsar (p 38), where scenes in *Hideous Kinky* were filmed and Foundouk al Mizane (p 92) with its woodworkers, lantern makers, and centuries-old weighing scales. ⏱ *30 min. See p 70.*

18 Terrasse des Épices. The clamor of the medina seems distant on the high-slung roof terrace of this restaurant, where Marrakech unfurls like a Berber carpet before you. Pick an alcove to sip a mint tea and drink in views as the city starts to twinkle. It's a great spot for light meals such as tagliatelle and aubergine millefeuille. *184 Rue Mouassine.* ☎ *0524-42-97-28. $$.*

Mint Tea & Retail Sympathy

You might get a motherly slap on the wrist for slurping your tea elsewhere, but it's the done thing in Morocco. From grand palaces to grimy workshops, mint tea—jokingly referred to as 'Berber whisky'—is the drink of choice. This sweet, refreshing blend of gunpowder green tea, fresh mint, and sugar symbolizes hospitality and is used to welcome (and sweeten up) shoppers in the souks. Tradition says that tea was first introduced in the 17th century during the reign of Moulay Ismail as a British gift to the Moroccan court, but it didn't become widespread until the mid-19th century. Traditionally, mint tea is poured from a great height into tinkling glasses. It's polite to accept the offer, even if you take just a sip.

Mint tea provides refreshment from haggling in the souks.

Kasbah, Mellah & Around

1 Riad Zitoun el Jedid
2 Dar Si Said
3 Maison Tiskiwin
4 Bahia Palace
5 Spice Souk
6 Mellah
7 Lazama Synagogue
8 Furan
9 Miâara
10 Place des Ferblantiers
11 Badi Palace
12 Herboristerie Palais El Badia
13 Bab Agnaou
14 Kasbah Mosque
15 Saâdian Tombs
16 Royal Palace
17 Agdal Gardens
18 Tatchibana

P Police Station
✉ Post Office
✚ Hospital

Rue Diour-Sabourir

0   1/4 mi
0   0.25 km

Fontaine
Chrob Ou
Chouf

HART
ES-SOURA

Médersa Ben
Youssef

Mosquée
Ben Youssef

Rue de Souk d. Fassis

Koubba
Ba'adyin

Musée de
Marrakech

Mosquée
Eloussta

Rue Essebtiyne

Mosquée
Mouassine

Derb Sidi Ishak

Mosquée
Azabzed

Mosquée
Sidi Ishak

Zaouia Sidi
Ben Salah

Souk El Kebir

Place
Rahba
Kedima

AZBEZT

BEN
SALAH

DERB
DABACHI

SOUKS

Souk
Smarine

Souk
Quessabine

Rue Dabachi

MÉDINA

Rue Kennaria

Place Jemâa
El Fna

start
here

DOUAR
GRAOUA

Rue Douar
Graoua

P

Koubba de
Lalla Zohra

Place
Foucauld

Palais
Moulay
Idriss

Consulat
de France

Musée
Dar Si Said

Mosquée de
la Koutoubia

Ibn Khaldoun

Rue Moulay Ismail

Rue Ben Marine

Rue de Bab Agnaou

Hôpital
Arset El
Mokha

Rue Riad Zitoun El Jedid

Rue Riad Zitoun El Khedim

Maison
Tiskiouine

Palais de
la Bahia

Avenue
Houmman El Fetouaki

Pl. Youssef
Tachfine

Rue Laila Rikia

Oqba Ben Nafia

Rue Ibn Rachid

Avenue Houmman El Fetouaki

Marché
Couvert

P

MELLAH

SIDI
MIMOUN

Rue Sidi Mimoun

ARSET
EL MAÄCH

Mosquée de
la Kasbah

Palais
El Badi

Hôpital
Ibn Zohr

Bab
Er Rob

Tombeaux
Saadiens

BERRIMA

Zaouia
Sidi Es Soheïli

Bab
Agnaou

KSIBET
NHAS

Mosquée
Berrima

Cimetière
Sidi Es Souheili

Centre
Artisanal

Rue de la Kasbah

Arset El
Bab Er Rob

KASBAH

Palais Royal
Dar El Makhzen

Méchouar
Extérieur

finish
here

Rue de Méchouar

Méchouar
Intérieur

Bab
Er Rih

18

Kasbah is the romantic Marrakech of trans-Saharan tales. The adobe walls of the fortified citadel seem to reach towards the snow-capped Atlas Mountains and tangled alleys wind to concealed riads and spice-filled souks. From majestic 19th-century palaces to the backstreets of the Jewish quarter, this full-day tour takes you through a corner of Marrakech that has resisted the tides of time. START: **Riad Zitoun el-Jedid.**

1 ★ Riad Zitoun el Jedid. Linking Jemaa el Fna to Kasbah, this street is terrific for a leisurely saunter and shop, dotted with cubbyhole tailors, apothecaries, grocers, and colorful *babouche* stores. It's slightly more relaxed than the souks. Be sure to nip into Jamade (p 93) for hip Moroccan ceramics. ⏱ *30 min. See p 11.*

2 ★★★ Dar Si Said. Swing left onto a narrow alley to this elegant 19th-century mansion. The edifice alone is worth a visit for its polychrome *zellij* tilework, gracefully painted cedar ceilings, and central courtyard full of fruit trees and birdsong. Downstairs, seek out tasseled Saharan traveling bags, faded High Atlas carpets, Berber jewelry, and Safi ceramics. Upstairs, throne-like palanquins used to carry newly-wed brides and the star-shaped octagonal ceiling will grab your attention. ⏱ *1 hr. See p 11.*

3 ★★ Maison Tiskiwin. One block south, Dutch anthropologist Bert Flint's small but perfectly formed collection whisks you on a dusty journey along the trans-Saharan caravan route from Morocco to Timbuktu. Each room showcases new treasures such as Tuareg saddles, gazelle-shaped sugar hammers, ceremonial rain-making masks, and even a reconstructed nomadic tent. At the entrance, pick up a booklet with English descriptions. ⏱ *45 min. See p 27.*

4 ★★★ Bahia Palace. Grand vizier Si Moussa's 19th-century

Wander the courtyards to appreciate the beauty of the Bahia Palace.

palace is indeed *bahia* (beautiful) and so too, rumor has it, were his concubines. Explore the one-time harem, the sweet-scented gardens, and the chamber where the grand vizier romanced his favorite wife beneath *mashrabiyya* (lattice wood) screens, as a band of blind musicians played. Rap star, P Diddy's hedonistic birthday bash here in 2002 is proof of the palace's timeless appeal. ⏱ *1 hr. See p 11.*

5 ★ Spice Souk. This tiny souk, across the way from Bahia Palace, is a real treat for the nostrils. This is where the locals go to buy their spices in cupboard-sized stores, each eager to outdo its neighbor with perfect cones of paprika, curry, and Moroccan 35-spice mix. ⏱ *15 min. See p 12.*

6 Mellah. Just east of Place des Ferblantiers, a lattice of tight *derbs* (alleys) unfolds in Mellah, Marrakech's little-visited Jewish quarter. Low on sights, high on atmosphere, the streets here are full of neighborly chit-chat, stray cats, men playing backgammon, and women scrubbing vegetables. It hasn't received the tourist clean up, and so is dirtier and slightly dodgier than other areas—don't walk here alone or after dark—but it's certainly still worth exploring. Look out for the idiosyncratic two-storey houses with wrought-iron balconies. ⏱ *15 min. East of Place des Ferblantiers.*

7 Lazama Synagogue. Wander south down a couple of ramshackle Mellah backstreets and you will, *insha'allah* (God willing), find this inconspicuous synagogue on the left. There's no sign, but would-be

Sample bread fresh from the furan (communal oven).

guides can show you the way for a few dirham. Look for the Star of David in the blue-white *zellij* tiling in the inner courtyard before tipping the man at the entrance. Built in 1492 when Spain expelled the Jews, the synagogue has been restored and modernized over the years, with an upstairs gallery for women. Despite the air of calm, there's a kind of downtrodden feel about the place—perhaps because of the disused school or the fact that this is the last of 35 such synagogues in Marrakech. ⏱ *20 min. 36 Derb Ragrada. Small contribution (10–20dh) appreciated. Sun–Thurs 9am–6pm, Fri 9am–1pm.*

8 Furan. Mosey southeast towards the Jewish cemetery and the smell of freshly baked bread may entice you into the local *furan* (communal oven), where the baker is more than happy to give you a peek inside the fiery furnace. Be prepared to tip if you take photos. ⏱ *10 min. Mellah. Daily 9am–5pm.*

9 ★ Miâara. A visit to this vast Jewish cemetery, overgrown with black pepper trees and overrun with stray dogs, is a strangely emotional experience. There's an air of abandon about the 17th-century graveyard with its higgledy-piggledy slab headstones. The brothers that tend the cemetery will show you around for a nominal contribution and provide invaluable background information. Among the humped graves are 11 ornate shrines to Jewish saints, embellished with stucco and cedar. ⏱ *20 min. See p 33.*

10 Place des Ferblantiers. For a cheap, tasty feed with views across the palm-dotted square and the occasional stork wheeling above, you can't beat the row of open-fronted eateries. Around 50dh buys you a flavorsome tagine and mint

Find herbs, spices and remedies at Herboristerie Palais El Badia.

tea. Many of these cafés have pavement terraces for chilling and catching a few rays. *Place des Ferblantiers. $.*

⑪ ★ Badi Palace. No place in Marrakech kindles the imagination quite like Sultan Ahmed el-Mansour's 16th-century palace. Within these crumbling red walls you can imagine the original splendor—the sumptuous marble, gold, and onyx chambers, and the lavish parties held in the 135m-long central courtyard with its sunken gardens. Nowadays the ruins are movie-set stuff, with tumbledown pavilions, eerie underground passageways (the former dungeons), and a roof terrace guarded by storks. It's worth the extra 10dh to see the Koutoubia minbar pulpit, a masterpiece of 12th-century marquetry. ⏱ *45 min. See p 33.*

⑫ Herboristerie Palais El Badia. The friendly pharmacists at this Berber herbalist store near the palace have natural remedies for everything from baldness to clumsiness. Step past baskets overflowing with spices, ginseng, and rose buds into the store lined with natural pigments, scents, and mysterious roots. Relax your shoulders with a speedy 20dh argan-oil massage in the shop opposite. ⏱ *15 min. See p 88.*

⑬ Bab Agnaou. Head back the same way or save your legs with a petit taxi ride to 12th-century Bab Agnaou, the main gateway to Kasbah and the most spectacular of Marrakech's city gates. The name 'Agnaou' refers both to the Berber for 'hornless black ram' and the swarthy commoners who once entered Kasbah via this gate. ⏱ *10 min. See p 13.*

⑭ Kasbah Mosque. A short amble west of Badi Palace next to

Kasbah mosque rises above the Saâdian Tombs.

the Saâdian Tombs stands this eye-catching Almohad mosque, a focal point of Kasbah. Its terracotta mina-ret bears many of the same features as Koutoubia, with green-and-white *zellij*, merlon crenellations, and fleur-de-lys-like *darj w ktarf* (cheek

Marrakech's imposing Royal Palace.

and shoulder) patterns. 🕐 *10 min. Rue de la Kasbah.*

⑮ ★★ Saâdian Tombs. The sul-tan with a Midas touch, Ahmed el-Mansour (1578–1603) chose to die as he lived—in extravagant finery. Thus he poured the wealth he acquired from trading Portuguese slaves and sugar into this trio of opulent mausoleums. Easily the most striking is the **Chamber of the Twelve Pillars**, dripping with Carrera marble and gilt stucco sta-lactites, where the sultan is buried alongside his favorite sons. Fragrant with citrus trees and rosemary, the garden is where loyal servants, offi-cials, and wives were buried facing Mecca. At the back, the tomb of the sultan's mother boasts a beautiful cedar ceiling. Sultan Moulay Ismail (The Bloodthirsty) walled up the tombs in the early 18th century in an attempt to erase past glories, but they were unearthed in 1917. 🕐 *45 min. See p 12.*

⑯ Royal Palace. Veer south past the stores on bustling Rue de la Kas-bah, turning left onto Rue Bab

Jewish Marrakech

The Star of David in mosaic tiles and door knockers, the Seal of Solomon on cedar ceilings, narrow alleyways, and tall houses are all hallmarks of **Mellah**, Marrakech's Jewish quarter. The area was conceived as a Jewish ghetto in 1558 by Saâdian sultan, Moulay Abdallah, who decided it would be easier to control and tax the city's Jews (many of them successful bakers, tailors, jewelers, and sugar traders) by confining them to one area within earshot of the palace. The name *mellah* meaning 'salt' in Arabic refers to the gruesome practice of forcing Jewish residents to rub salts into the heads of decapitated felons before they were displayed in public. Horror stories aside, Mellah was once a flourishing community home to rabbis, synagogues, and markets. Today, residents are overwhelmingly Muslim, as most Jews left long ago for Casablanca, Israel, or France; only an estimated 250 still reside in Marrakech.

Méchouar to reach the plaza in front of the grand rose-tinted Royal Palace (*Palais Royal* in French). High crenellated walls allow King Mohammed VI privacy when he's in residence, but you can still admire the regal abode from afar. ⏱ *15 min.*

⑰ ★ **Agdal Gardens.** The entrance to these royal gardens from the palace isn't evident, but a guard will point you in the right direction down a path that cuts south between the lofty walls. Planted with orange, pomegranate, olive, and fig trees, and centered on carp-filled pools, these gardens have a wilder feel than most. Ignore the roguish types by the pavilion who demand an entrance fee—it's free. ⏱ *45 min. See p 101.*

⑱ **Tatchibana.** Amble south to round out your Kasbah tour at this sleek Japanese restaurant. Choose between the courtyard lit by paper lanterns or the salon where alcoves add a cozy touch to the streamlined decor. The Japanese chef cooks

authentic sushi, sashimi, and tempura. Save room for refreshing desserts such as green tea cake with lemon cream. *38 Route de Bab Ksiba.* ☎ *0524-38-71-71. $$$.*

Glimpse the Atlas Mountains from the Agdal Gardens.

Jemaa el Fna **& Around**

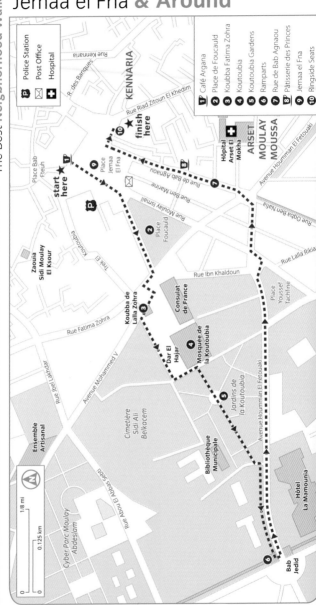

Police Station
Post Office
Hospital

1 Café Argana
2 Place de Foucauld
3 Koubba Fatima Zohra
4 Koutoubia
5 Koutoubia Gardens
6 Ramparts
7 Rue de Bab Agnaou
8 Pâtisserie des Princes
9 Jemaa el Fna
10 Ringside Seats

Jemaa el Fna was once an execution ground; it still makes your head spin today. Part zoo, part pantomime, this medina square seems unfathomable—thudding to Gnaoua drums, whirling with agile acrobats and fire-eaters, shimmying transvestites, and snake charmers. This half-day walk around Jemaa el Fna finds method in the round-the-clock madness. START: **Terrasses de l'Alhambra.**

1 Café Argana. Get your caffeine fix on the terrace of this café overlooking the action on Jemaa el Fna. Although service can be slow, it's an inviting spot for coffee and pastries, ice-cream, or a quick tagine. *Place Jemaa el Fna.* 📞 *0524-44-53-50. $.*

2 Place de Foucauld. Cross Jemaa el Fna and head towards the Koutoubia Minaret (p 43) to reach this palm-strewn square, where the city's *calèches* (horse-drawn carriages) line up for business. If you fancy a trot around town, expect to pay between 100dh and 150dh per hour. This spectacular approach to the mosque will have you reaching for your camera. 🕐 *15 min. Place de Foucauld.*

3 ★ Koubba Fatima Zohra. Cross Avenue Mohammed V and you'll spy the pearl-white domed tomb of Fatima Zohra, often eclipsed by the monumental scale of Koutoubia that rises up behind. Topped by a meringue-like cupola, this 17th-century mausoleum commemorates Fatima Zohra: the daughter of a religious leader who reputedly had the ability to transform into a white dove by night and was a gifted fortune teller. 🕐 *10 min. Avenue Mohammed V.*

4 ★★★ kids Koutoubia. Directly behind the tomb is the all-seeing Koutoubia (p 7), the highest building in Marrakech with a 69-m (210-foot) tall minaret. Although access to the 12th-century mosque is for muslims only, non-Muslims can still walk

Learn the legend behind Koubba Fatima Zohra.

around it to appreciate details such as the crenellations and *darj w ktarf* patterns. Listen out for the muezzin's *adhan* (call to prayer). In the past, the muezzin was a blind man to prevent him from peeking at women in the palaces and riads. The name Koutoubia loosely translates as 'booksellers' mosque', referring to the book market that once stood here. 🕐 *20 min. Avenue Mohammed V.*

5 ★ Koutoubia Gardens. Escape the heat and the noise with a quiet saunter through these tranquil gardens, dotted with palms, orange trees, and storks' nests. Bring your camera to capture different views of Koutoubia. Note the Muslim graveyard to the right as you enter but whatever you do, don't point—it's considered disrespectful. Children who point at graves are told they will have to eat mud as punishment. 🕐 *15 min.*

The ochre-red walls of medieval Kasbah.

6 ★ **Ramparts.** Saunter west along Avenue Bab Jdid, where opulent La Mamounia (p 133) stands proud, to pass through one of the medina's gates and reach the ochrered ramparts. In the 12th century, the Almoravids built these walls 19km long and up to 6m (19 feet) tall in a fruitless attempt to protect Marrakech from would-be invaders. Today the ramparts, honeycombed by pigeon holes, frame the old city and draw sporty locals for languid strolls and impromptu soccer matches. Come in the late afternoon to see the fortifications glow in the sunlight. ⏲ *20 min. Boulevard el Yarmouk.*

7 **Rue de Bab Agnaou.** Retrace your steps back to Avenue Mohammed V and cross over to Rue Bab Agnaou. This bustling pedestrian thoroughfare, feeding back to the square, is lined with ice-cream parlors, cafés, hotels, fast-food joints, and souvenir shops. Nip into **Grand Hotel Tazi** (p 124) for a cheap beer within easy walking distance of the (almost) teetotal Jemaa el Fna. ⏲ *15 min. Rue de Bab Agnaou.*

8 **Pâtisserie des Princes.** For raspberry torte, crumbly apple tart, and pain au chocolat that would make a Parisian proud, pop into this patisserie, which also tempts with Moroccan sweets such as cornes de gazelle (almond paste-filled cookies). *32 Rue de Bab Agnaou.* ☎ *0524-44-23-19. $.*

9 ★★★ **Jemaa el Fna.** Jemaa el Fna is sensory overload, bombarding you with feats of strangeness, circus tricks, and a tornado of colors, sounds, and sights. Its moniker, loosely translating as 'assembly of the dead', alludes to the square as a former site of execution (severed heads were displayed here in medieval times). In the morning, there are little more than a handful of herbalists, juice carts, and persistent henna tattooists. Come dusk, however, Jemaa pulsates with life: acrobats and Gnaoua musicians, storytellers and snake charmers, would-be dentists and chefs all fire your imagination and appetite. You'll be happy to know that there is (at least some) method in this madness.

Street musicians and water carriers on Jemaa el Fna.

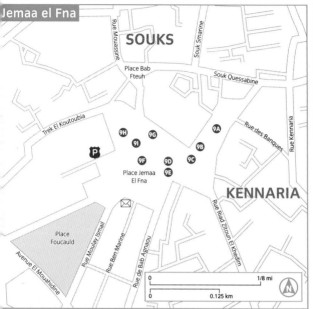

In the northeast corner, close to the entrance to the souks, **story-tellers** captivate their audience with tales told theatrically in Arabic. Nearby you'll find the gaily painted **juice carts**, where freshly squeezed orange juice (make sure it isn't diluted) costs 3dh, and **dried-fruit carts** that are heaped with apricots, dates, and figs. Vying for attention in the same area are **healers**, performing miracles with walnut roots and ostrich eggs, and **dentists** whose rusty pliers and mounds of rotten molars make you thank your lucky stars you don't have a toothache. Head to the center for **snake-charmers and monkey men** for that must-have snapshot with a cobra or an impish macaque. Just north, the smoke-enshrouded **food stalls** do a roaring trade after dark. Edging further west, **acrobats** perform gravity-defying acts and **Gnaoua musicians** wow the crowds with their infectious rhythms. 🕐 1½ hrs. Jemaa el Fna. Tip around 10–20dh for photos. Daily 9am–midnight.

10 Ringside Seats. When you tire of dodging donkeys and mopeds, bag a ringside seat to enjoy the show. **Terrasses de L'Alhambra** (p 117) affords prime Jemaa el Fna views in a relaxed setting. The rooftop **Grand Balcon du Café Glacier** (p 124) has arguably the best panorama, as clicking cameras confirm, but I was overcharged for drinks on my last visit. For dinner with a view, try cheap and friendly **Chez Chegrouni** (p 112) or Berber chic **Le Marrakchi** (p 117).

North of **Souks & Mouassine**

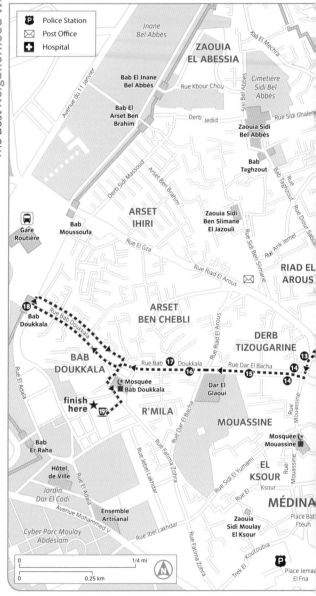

Legend:
- 🅿 Police Station
- ✉ Post Office
- ✚ Hospital

Jnane Bel Abbès

ZAOUIA EL ABESSIA

Bab El Jnane Bel Abbès

Rue Kbour Chou

Cimetière Sidi Bel Abbès

Avenue du 11 Janvier

Bab El Arset Ben Brahim

Derb Jedid

Rue Sidi Ghalen

Zaouia Sidi Bel Abbès

Bab Taghzout

Derb Sidi Massoud

Arset Ben Brahim

Zaouia Sidi Ben Slimane El Jazouli

Rue Bab Taghzout

Rue Djour Sabor

Gare Routière

Bab Moussoufa

ARSET IHIRI

Rue El Gza

Rue Sidi Ben Slimane

Rue Ank Jemel

RIAD EL AROUS

Rue Riad El Arous

Rue Bab Doukkala

ARSET BEN CHEBLI

Rue Riad El Arous

DERB TIZOUGARINE

18 Bab Doukkala

BAB DOUKKALA

Rue Bab 17 Doukkala

16

Rue Dar El Bacha

13

14

15

14

Rue El Adala

Mosquée Bab Doukkala

Dar El Glaoui

Rue Mouassine

finish here ★ 19

R'MILA

MOUASSINE

Rue Dar El Bacha

Mosquée Mouassine

Bab Er Raha

Rue Fatima Zohra

Rue El Adala

EL KSOUR

Rue Mouassine

Hôtel de Ville

Jardin Dar El Cadi

Rue El Adala

Avenue Mohammed V

Ensemble Artisanal

Rue Jebel Lakhdar

Rue Sidi El Yamami

Rue El Ksour

MÉDINA

Place Bab Fteuh

Cyber Parc Moulay Abdeslam

Rue Jbel Lakhdar

Rue Fatima Zohra

Zaouia Sidi Moulay El Ksour

Trek El Koutoubia

🅿

Place Jemaa El Fna

0 _____ 1/4 mi
0 _____ 0.25 km

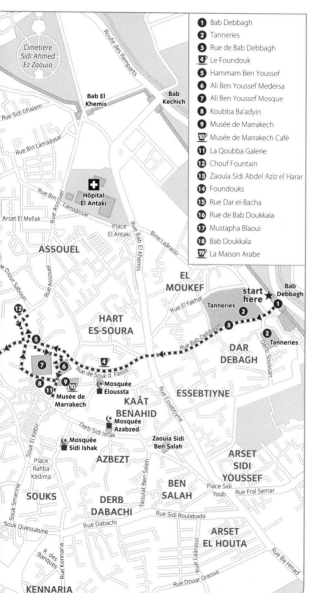

1. Bab Debbagh
2. Tanneries
3. Rue de Bab Debbagh
4. Le Foundouk
5. Hammam Ben Youssef
6. Ali Ben Youssef Medersa
7. Ali Ben Youssef Mosque
8. Koubba Ba'adyin
9. Musée de Marrakech
10. Musée de Marrakech Café
11. La Qoubba Galerie
12. Chouf Fountain
13. Zaouia Sidi Abdel Aziz el Harar
14. Foundouks
15. Rue Dar el-Bacha
16. Rue de Bab Doukkala
17. Mustapha Blaoui
18. Bab Doukkala
19. La Maison Arabe

The everyday is fascinating in Marrakech. Skirting north of the souks and Mouassine, this full-day tour rambles through untouristy neighborhoods: from the swirling colors of the Bab Debbagh tanneries to vibrant Rue de Bab Doukkala. Each corner reveals a new perspective; be it a communal *furan* (bread oven), a saintly *zaouia* (shrine), or a UNESCO-listed Saâdian drinking fountain. START: **Bab Debbagh.**

❶ Bab Debbagh. On the western edge of the medina in an untouristy corner of town, the keyhole arch in this red-brick Almoravid gate marks the entrance to the malodorous tanners' quarter. It's also a fascinating transition between Marrakech new (modern brick buildings and satellite dishes on one side) and old (pre-industrial tanneries on the other). Designed to slow down would-be invaders, the three-turn gate represents a sophisticated 12th-century defense system. Before venturing further—most likely with a horde of school children behind you—make sure that your cash is well hidden. ⏱ *10 min. Bab Debbagh, Rue de Bab Debbagh.*

Sunlight streams through the slatted roof on Rue de Bab Debbagh.

❷ ★★ Tanneries. A far cry from the beauty and banter of the dyers' souk, the tanneries on and around Rue de Bab Debbagh paint a very different picture of Marrakech: one of stench, squalor, and medieval trades. With a little care, it's safe to explore the tanneries alone, although you'll certainly be approached by unofficial tip-hungry guides; some are unsavory characters, and so it's preferable to arrange for an official guide to show you around. As the pungent odor can be overwhelming in the midday heat, I recommend arriving in the morning for an astonishing insight into the tanning process. Behind mud-brick walls lay honeycomb-like stone vats, where hardy laborers dip the hides first into acidic pigeon excrement, and then into natural dyes such as mint green, saffron yellow, and poppy red, diluting them with water from a nearby stream. Be sure to wear old shoes. ⏱ *30 min. Rue de Bab Debbagh. Daylight hours; best in the morning.*

❸ Rue de Bab Debbagh. There are no real 'sights' on this street linking the tanneries to the souks, nevertheless it provides a genuine snapshot of daily life in the medina and a flavor of off-the-beaten track Marrakech. Overladen donkey carts, men lugging heavy loads, and youngsters jostle for space amid the butchers, postage stamp-sized grocery stores, apothecaries, and grimy workshops. Take care in this area after dark. ⏱ *15 min. Rue de Bab Debbagh.*

Fresh from the Furan

When the enticing scent of freshly baked bread curls around your nostrils in Marrakech, you've most probably stumbled across a *furan* (communal oven). These neighborhood bakeries have been around as long as Marrakech itself. The *furan* tucked down Derb Zaouiat Lakhdar, just east of Ali Ben Youssef Medersa, has been turning out crusty loaves since the 14th century. Given the space premium in the tight-knit medina, communal ovens are a necessity, because few homes have their own. Locals flock here in the morning with dough-laden baskets, and the baker produces up to 300 flatbread loaves daily. Visit the *furan* for a peek at this time-honored tradition and a chance to taste the bread (small loaves cost 1.5dh, large loaves 3dh).

4 ★ **Le Foundouk.** Bear left onto Souk Hal Fassi and push the heavy wood door to enter this dimly lit restaurant, a glamorously restored caravanserai. If it's sunny, I head straight up to the flower-draped roof terrace, where the medina unfolds before me and trickling fountains provide a welcome contrast to the hubbub below. Lunch on delicious Moroccan fare such as tagines and seven-vegetable couscous, or refresh over mint tea and pastries. *55 Souk Hal Fassi.* ☎ *0524-37-81-90. $$$–$$$$.*

5 Hammam Ben Youssef. Close to the *furan*, you'll find another neighborhood must-have: the community hammam. The sign is inconspicuous, but bathhouse goers with baskets of *savon noir* (black soap) and *rhassoul* (Atlas clay) give the game away. If you want to join the locals for a steam and scrub, bring a change of underwear, your own towel, and mat. ⏱ *1 hr. Derb Zaouiat Lakhdar.* ☎ *No phone. Admission 10dh. Daily: men 6am–11pm; women 11am–9pm.*

6 ★★★ **Ali Ben Youssef Medersa.** It's little wonder that students of the Koran found inspiration in the 14th-century walls of this *medersa* (Koranic school). The courtyard is a work of genius: a riot of intricately wrought cedarwood, meticulously carved stucco, *mashrabiyya* lattice screens, kaleidoscopic *zellij* stars,

Break your sightseeing with lunch on the roof terrace of Le Foundouk.

The exterior of Ali Ben Youssef Medersa.

and Kufic inscriptions. Peek through keyhole arches and explore the cramped dorms (there are 132 in total) for a true sense of the medersa's history. 🕐 *1 hr. See p 8.*

⑦ Ali Ben Youssef Mosque.
This striking 12th-century Almoravid mosque is the oldest and second largest in Marrakech. Over the years it has been pulled down and rebuilt on several occasions; the last Merenid-style facelift was in the 19th century. Although the inside is out of bounds to them, non-Muslims can still admire its high ochre-red walls, archetypal minaret, and lustrous green tiled roof. 🕐 *10 min. Place de la Kissaria.*

⑧ ★ Koubba Ba'adyin. Opposite the mosque rises this sand-hued *koubba* (cupola), Marrakech's best-preserved example of Almoravid architecture, originally intended for ablutions (ritual cleansing and purification before prayers). Hearing the muezzin's *adhan* (call to prayer) here can be quite an emotional experience. 🕐 *30 min. See p 8.*

⑨ ★ Musée de Marrakech.
Mehdi Mnebhi, the minister of defense to Sultan Moulay Abdelaziz (1894–1908), was a lucky man—blessed with charisma, wealth, wit, and this late 19th-century

Afternoon light illuminates Koubba Ba'adyin.

Browse or buy innovative Moroccan artworks at La Qoubba Galerie.

palace. Although the rotating exhibitions of contemporary Moroccan art and traditional crafts (from Berber daggers to Jewish costumes) are intriguing, it's the remarkable building that will impress. ⏱ *1 hr. See p 8.*

10 Musée de Marrakech Café. If you're suffering from culture overload, take time out with a mint tea or coffee at this inexpensive courtyard café by the museum entrance. There's a decent selection of fresh sandwiches, salads, and sticky Moroccan pastries if you're feeling peckish. *No phone. $.*

11 La Qoubba Galerie. Just a few paces south of the Musée de Marrakech (p 8) in Souk Talaa, this small but exciting gallery is part of Marrakech's flourishing contemporary art scene. Vivid abstract works, emotive scenes of Morocco, and color-charged landscapes capture the attention and imagination. ⏱ *15 min.*

12 Chouf Fountain. Retrace your steps and wander north of Ali Ben Youssef Medersa to this communal fountain, tucked down a narrow *derb*, a flashback to the days when running water was a rarity. *Chouf* loosely translates as 'drink and look' in Arabic, as an inscription denotes. The late 16th-century fountain hails from the reign of the Saâdian sultan Ahmed el-Mansour (1578–1603), nicknamed 'The Golden One'. It was awarded UNESCO World Heritage status in 1985. ⏱ *15 min. Rue Assouel.*

13 Zaouia Sidi Abdel Aziz el Harar. Bear southwest along Rue Amesfah and Derb el Maaden to locate this well-hidden *zaouia* (shrine) to one of Marrakech's seven *marabouts* (saints), who range from lepers to theologians. As with mosques, non-Muslims aren't allowed to enter the *zaouia*, but they can admire the stonework of the tomb from outside. This one is dedicated to 15th-century theologian Sidi Abdel Aziz el Harar. ⏱ *15 min. Derb el Maaden.*

world of *foundouks* (p 20), one-time stopovers on the trans-Saharan trade routes. The spice-bearing camels are long gone but an air of mystery still reigns in these courtyards. Some have been renovated, with the stables converted into craft workshops, while others feature little more than cracked paintwork and a gas burner for tea. 🕐 *30 min. Rue el Mouassine and Bacha el Glaoui.*

🅱 **Rue Dar el-Bacha.** Walk south and turn right onto this smart street on the northern fringes of Mouassine, harboring elegant riads, gourmet restaurants, and antique shops. As you stroll, look out for Khalid Art Gallery (p 86) on the right, a treasure-trove of antiques and a celebrity favorite. Opposite on the left is the sublime palace Dar Donab (p 112), sheltering luxurious rooms and an exquisite Moroccan restaurant. Soon you'll spy the high pink-hued walls of **Dar el Bacha**, the one-time royal residence and

Sure to brighten up any home - stylish lamps in Fondouk al Mizane.

🅳 ★★★ **Foundouks.** Continue straight for a peek behind the wooden doors into the concealed

Khalid Art Gallery is a treasure-trove of precious antiques.

harem of the infamous Pasha of Marrakech Thami el-Glaoui (1879–1956), Berber warlord and friend of the French colonizers. ⏱ *30 min. Rue Dar el Bacha.*

⓰ ★ Rue de Bab Doukkala. Continue onto Rue de Bab Doukkala, a friendly neighborhood punctuated by specialty stores from cobblers to butchers, barbers to bookshops. The street hums with activity from the crack of dawn, with children playing in the alleys and plump ladies emerging with baskets full of fresh bread from the *furans.* Roughly half way down, you'll glimpse the slender minaret of the 16th-century Bab Doukkala mosque. A short ramble west brings you to Bab Doukkala food souk, where the aroma of grilled sardines fills the air, light filters through the slatted wooden roof, and vendors sell fruit, herbs, and earthenware cooking pots from makeshift stalls. It's an untouristy place from which to watch daily life unfold. ⏱ *30 min. Rue de Bab Doukkala.*

⓱ Mustapha Blaoui. Fling open the unmarked wooden doors to enter this cavernous warehouse, brimming with top-quality Moroccan furniture, lamps, twinkling mirrors, ceramics, and antique tapestries. It's a rambling attic of a store well worth exploring at leisure over a mint tea. The helpful staff can arrange overseas shipping. ⏱ *20 min. 142–144 Rue de Bab Doukkala.* ☎ *0524-38-52-40. Daily 9am–8pm.*

⓲ Bab Doukkala. With its double horseshoe arches and distinctive saw-like crenellations, this red-brick gate leads to a roundabout and the main bus station. This bustling transport hub is where the medina

Feast on traditional Moroccan cuisine in refined surrounds at La Maison Arabe's restaurant.

meets 21st-century Guéliz: motorbikes splutter past mule-driven carts and men wearing skullcaps and *jellabahs* (robes) shine the shoes of businessmen. Like magic, the claustrophobic medina unfolds into the broad boulevards of Ville Nouvelle. ⏱ *10 min. Bab Doukkala.*

⓳ ★★★ La Maison Arabe. Trace the ramparts south to this riad, where Andalusian musicians serenade diners in sumptuous surrounds. Tuck into Moroccan classics from fragrant salads to fall-off-the-bone lamb flavored with herbs and preserved lemons. *1 Derb Assehbe, Bab Doukkala.* ☎ *0524-38-70-10. $$$$. See p 115.*

Ville Nouvelle

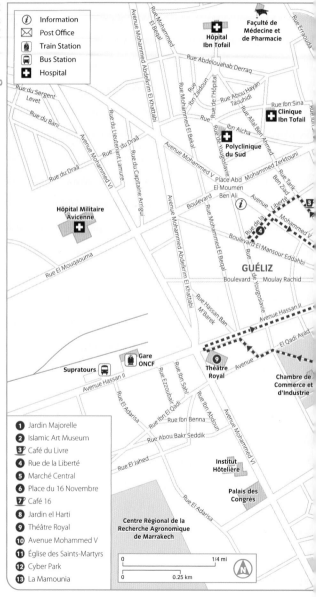

Key (map legend):
- (i) Information
- ✉ Post Office
- 🚆 Train Station
- 🚌 Bus Station
- ✚ Hospital

Map labels:
Rue Mohammed El Beqal
Avenue Mohammed Abdelkrim El Khattabi
Rue Errraoudia
Hôpital Ibn Tofail
Faculté de Médecine et de Pharmacie
Rue Abdelouahab Derraq
Rue du Sergent Levet
Rue du Bani
Rue de l'Hôpital
Rue Ibn Zaidoun
Rue Mohammed El Beqal
Rue Abou Hayan Taouhidi
Rue Ibn Sina
Clinique Ibn Tofail
Rue du Lieutenant Lamure
Rue du Draâ
Rue du Capitaine Arrigui
Avenue Mohammed V
Rue Allal Ben Ahmed
Ibn Aicha
Rue de Yougoslavie
Polyclinique du Sud
Avenue Mohammed V
Place Abd El Moumen Ben Ali
Mohammed Zerktouni
Rue Tarik Ben Ziad
Hôpital Militaire Avicenne
Boulevard Mohammed El Beqal
Boulevard
(i)
Rue de la Liberté
Avenue Mohammed V
Boulevard El Mansour Eddahbi
Rue El Mouqaouma
Avenue Mohammed Abdelkrim El Khattabi
GUÉLIZ
Boulevard de Moulay Rachid
Rue Hassan Ben M'Barek
Avenue Hassan II
El Qadi Ayad
Supratours
Gare ONCF
Rue Ibn Sahl
Rue Ezzoubair
Théâtre Royal
Avenue
Chambre de Commerce et d'Industrie
Avenue Hassan II
Rue El Adarisa
Rue Ibn El Qadi
Rue Ibn Benna
Rue Ibn Abdoun
Rue Abou Bakr Seddik
Rue El Jahed
Avenue Mohammed VI
Institut Hôtelière
Palais des Congrès
Rue El Adarisa
Centre Régional de la Recherche Agronomique de Marrakech

1. Jardin Majorelle
2. Islamic Art Museum
3. Café du Livre
4. Rue de la Liberté
5. Marché Central
6. Place du 16 Novembre
7. Café 16
8. Jardin el Harti
9. Théâtre Royal
10. Avenue Mohammed V
11. Église des Saints-Martyrs
12. Cyber Park
13. La Mamounia

0 ——— 1/4 mi
0 ——— 0.25 km

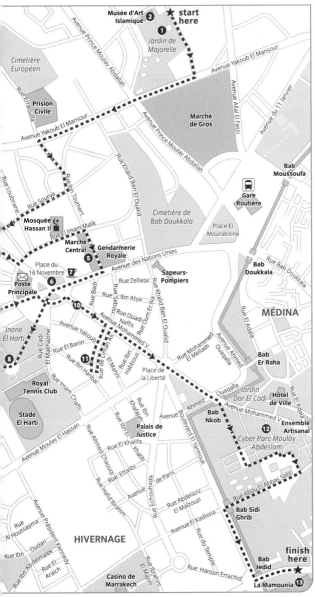

★ start here

❶

❷ Musée d'Art Islamique

Jardin de Majorelle

Cimetière Européen

Avenue Prince Moulay Abdallah

Avenue Yakoub El Mansour

Avenue Allal El Fassi

Avenue du 11 Janvier

Prison Civile

Rue Erraouda

Marché de Gros

Avenue Yakoub El Mansour

Rue Loubnane

Rue Ibn Tournert

Rue Khalid Ben El Oualid

Rue Sourya

Bab Moussoufa

Gare Routière

Place El Mourabitine

Mosquée Hassan II ★

Rue El Imam Malik

Marché Central

❺ Gendarmerie Royale

Cimetière de Bab Doukkala

Avenue des Nations Unies

Rue Bab El Doukkala

Bab Doukkala

Place du 16 Novembre

❼

❻ Poste Principale

Rue Badr

Rue Zellaqa

Sapeurs-Pompiers

Rue El Adala

MÉDINA

Rue Ibn Atya

Rue Ouadi Naffis

Rue Seboù

❿

Rue Khalid Ben El Oualid

Rue Oum El Banine

Avenue Yakoub

Avenue Mohammed V

Rue Mohammed El Meilakh

Avenue Ahmed Ouaqalla

Bab Er Raha

Jnane El Harti

Rue Cadi El Makhzine

Rue El Banin

Rue Ibn El Marrin

Rue Ibn Habbous

❽

Rue de Oran

❶❶

Rue Ibn Hanbal

Place de la Liberté

Ouaqalla

Jardin Dar El Cadi

Hôtel de Ville

Rue El Adala

Royal Tennis Club

Rue Imam Chafiti

Rue Ibn Khalifa

Ahmed

Avenue Mohammed V

Bab Nkob

❶❷ Ensemble Artisanal

Stade El Harti

Avenue Moulay El Hassan

Rue Ahmed Chaouqi

Rue Ibn El Khatib

Palais de Justice

Avenue

Boulevard El Yarmouk

Cyber Parc Moulay Abdeslam

Rue El Khatib

Rue Ettalibi

Avenue de Paris

Rue Echouhada

Rue Abdelaziz El Malzouzi

Rue Abou El Abbas Sebti

Rue Hafid Ibrahim

Bab Sidi Ghrib

HIVERNAGE

Rue Al Houssayma

Avenue Président Kennedy

Rue Ibn Oudari

Rue Ibn Abdelmalek

Rue El Araich

Avenue El Kadissia

Rue Ibrahim El Mazni

Rue du Temple

Rue Haroun Errachid

Bab Jedid

finish here ★

Casino de Marrakech

La Mamounia ❶❸

Marrakech is a tale of two cities. Beyond the ochre-red walls of the medina lies Ville Nouvelle, the new city built under French colonial rule, comprising Guéliz and Hivernage. The neighborhood reveals a totally different side to Marrakech with its wide tree-fringed boulevards, bistros, and über-chic lounge bars. Come for the gardens, boutique shopping, and pavement cafés. START: **Jardin Majorelle.**

① ★★ Jardin Majorelle. Every season's color is green at the late Yves Saint Laurent's haute-couture garden. Get here early before the crowds descend for a dewy morning stroll past slender Brazilian cacti, bamboo, and lofty California palm, leading to a cobalt blue villa housing the designer's art collection. Revive over a cup of fragrant jasmine blossom tea in the orange tree-shaded courtyard café before stepping inside. ⏱ 1 hr. See p 15.

② ★ Islamic Art Museum. Housed in a startling blue Art Deco villa at the heart of the garden, this museum shelters Yves Saint Laurent's precious stash of decorative arts. First up, is a room displaying the lithographs of Jacques Majorelle (1886–1962). The French painter revealed his love of his adopted home of Morocco in imaginative scenes of High Atlas Kasbahs and souks. Delve further to find curiosities from interlaced *mashrabiyya* screens, vivid yellow-blue faience, and a16th-century Anti Atlas *minbar* (mosque pulpit). Past the Middle Atlas carpets and carved cedar doors, you reach a room dedicated to all the nomadic essentials, including the daggers and tasseled storage bags, required to survive in the Sahara. ⏱ 30 min. See p 26.

③ ★ Café du Livre. If books are food for the soul, the literati won't go hungry at this boho café serving up tasty snacks, free WiFi, and good vibes. Browse the shelves for second-hand novels for riad reading, and then bag a sofa to enjoy brunch (Sandra's pancakes come

The botanical lushness of Jardin Majorelle is refreshing on a hot day.

Read and refuel over coffee and snacks at laid-back Café du Livre.

recommended) or homemade soups and hamburgers. *44 Rue Tarik Ben Ziad.* ☎ *0524-43-21-49. $.*

④ ★★ Rue de la Liberté. You won't bag souk-like bargains, but you will find posh boutiques and one-off creations on Rue de la Liberté, the main shopping drag in Guéliz. For snazzy leather footwear, slip into Atika (p 89), where stylish Marrakchi buy their loafers. Where the road bisects Avenue Mohammed V, chandelier-lit Intensité Nomade lures couture lovers in search of flamboyant kaftans and imaginative garb by young Moroccan designers. Ben Rahal (p 87), meanwhile, is a must if you crave a quality Berber carpet; the charming staff will patiently explain the origins and meaning of anything that catches your eye. Next, head across to home design favorite L'Orientaliste (p 93), stocking

everything from Tuareg camel leather lamps to floral fragrances. Right next door Al Jawda (p 94) is sugar-coated heaven—pick up a box of sticky pastries or almond-filled *cornes de gazelle*. Côté Sud (p 91) and nearby sister boutique Maison Rouge (p 93) offer an inspiring range of Moroccan crafts from hand-embroidered linens to adorable children's bathrobes. ⏱ *1½ hrs. Most shops Mon–Sat 9:30am–12:30pm and 3:30–7:30pm.*

⑤ Marché Central. Head south from Jardin Majorelle along Rue ibn Toumert to reach this local market. I recommend vegetarians and animal lovers keep a wide berth from the southern flank with its filthy chicken cages and butchers selling horse meat. The rest is a more appealing mix of fresh fruit and vegetables, spices, basketwork, *babouches*, clothing, and bric-a-brac. ⏱ *20 min. Rue ibn Toumert. Daily 8am–7pm.*

⑥ Place du 16 Novembre. Were it not for the distinctive red hue of the buildings, the nearby mosque, and the odd palm tree, you'd be forgiven for thinking you

Frédérique Birkemeyer's couture kaftans grace Intensité Nomade.

Cutting-Edge Creativity

Guéliz has recently given rise to a flourishing crop of new galleries. Once a contemporary art wasteland, talented creatives are now being given the attention they deserve in Marrakech. Daring **Galerie 127** (p 86) exhibits a mix of home-grown and international photography in an edgy industrial-style space, while **Galerie Noir Sur Blanc** (p 86) turns the spotlight on innovative works such Larbi Cherkaoui's vivacious calligraphy-inspired pieces. For a comprehensive rundown of cutting-edge art, visit the slick **Matisse Art Gallery** (p 86), showcasing big Moroccan names such as Hassan El Glaoui and Nourredine Chater.

were in an entirely different country (let alone city) on this bustling plaza. Here well-off Marrakchi ladies eschew traditional headscarves for designer labels and do lunch on the terrace of Café 16. Shiny marble floors, glass-fronted shops, and even a Moroccan-styled McDonald's complete the picture of 21st-century Marrakech. ⏱ *15 min. Place du 16 Novembre.*

Café 16 on Place du 16 Novembre.

7 Café 16. Über-cool decor—blonde wood with lime and orange highlights and cubic flower lanterns—gives street cred to this café on the square. Skip mediocre lunches and go straight for desserts such as sharp lemon tart and raspberry mousse. *Place du 16 Novembre.* ☎ *0524-33-96-70. $$.*

8 kids Jardin el Harti. Take a breather from the Guéliz traffic with a leisurely saunter through this attractive garden of palms, cacti, and pools. If you have youngsters in tow, the playground is a great place for tots to let off excess energy. There are also tennis courts and a soccer pitch. ⏱ *20 min. Rue Ouadi el-Makhazine. Admission free. Daily 8am–7pm.*

9 ★ Théâtre Royal. Acclaimed Tunisian-born architect **Charles Boccara** left his indelible imprint on Marrakech's voluminous **theatre**, which forces you to gaze up to its soaring sand-hued dome and Egyptian-style columns. Though something of a white elephant, there's no denying that the theatre has given the city a much-needed cultural injection and Guéliz an eye-catching landmark. ⏱ *15 min. See p 134.*

Théâtre Royal illuminated after dark.

⑩ ★ Avenue Mohammed V.
All roads eventually lead to this buzzy avenue, which proves handy for getting your bearings. Stretching several kilometers, Marrakech's main artery links Guéliz to the medina and is lined with shops, banks, and travel agencies. Walking south from Place du 16 Novembre you'll glimpse the ochre-red **Hôtel de Ville** (City Hall) on the left, an imposing oblong-shaped edifice set amid palms and orange trees. On the same side of the street is **Ensemble Artisanal** (p 15), a temple of fixed-price crafts, while right opposite is the high-tech greenery of **Cyber Park** (p 16). Continue farther south and you get the full-on effect of **Koutoubia** (p 61) just before crossing to enter the gates to the medina. The traffic on Avenue Mohammed V can be a nightmare, and so try to tag onto a group of locals to make it safely across the street. ⏱ *20 min.*

Architectural Trailblazer

Marrakech's most dazzling new landmark is the ONCF train station opposite the Théâtre Royal. Inaugurated in late 2008, the **Gare de Marrakech** (www.oncf.ma) took 29 months of labor and a cool 120 million dirham to build. With its striking mélange of classic and avant-garde styles, it looks set to become an icon. The architect Youssef Méléhi seized inspiration from the gates of the medina for the monumental arched entrance, while the interior is an ultramodern take on Moroccan decorative art forms, featuring mosaic marble floors, palm-like columns, and pyramidal lanterns.

A wrought-iron sign on Marrakech's main artery, Avenue Mohammed V.

⓫ Église des Saints-Martyrs. Just off Avenue Mohammed V, on Rue el Imam Ali, there's a fascinating juxtaposition between this peach-hued Catholic church and the beautiful mosque opposite with its stucco arches and keyhole-shaped doors. Dating from 1930, the church was one of the first landmarks in Guéliz. Ring the bell in the garden to see the high-ceilinged interior, flooded by daylight and striking in its simplicity. *Rue el Imam Ali.* ☎ *0524-43-05-85. Admission free. Daily 10:30am–7:30pm summer, 10:30am–6:30pm winter.*

⓬ ★ kids Cyber Park. This central park attracts all sorts, from mums with their youngsters to couples, and from Marrakchi teenagers who come to flirt, jam, and surf the web in the cyber café to tourists seeking a green escape from the traffic-clogged Avenue Mohammed V. It's one of my favorite spots for a wander, with gravel paths interlacing orange and olive trees, banana palms, and fountains. Pick a bench to regain your cool before heading back out into the heat of the city. ⏱ *30 min. See p 16.*

⓭ ★★★ La Mamounia. Set in exotic gardens perfumed by orange trees, which afford far-reaching views to snowy Atlas peaks, it's easy to see why the British Prime Minister, Winston Churchill, found this luxurious 1920s hotel a source of inspiration for his paintbrush. ⏱ *10 min. See p 133.* ●

Hivernage Nightlife

Party in style till the sun rises over the Atlas is Hivernage's philosophy. Here evenings of blackjack at the swanky Casino de Marrakech (p 133) and belly dancing and hubbly-bubblies at sexy Art Deco villa Comptoir Darna (p 128) spill into late nights of champagne-fuelled debauchery at Marrakech's clubs. Dress to impress the fussy doormen at hedonistic hotspots such as Le Théâtro (p 127), where glammed-up Marrakchis groove to techno and R&B. Otherwise jump in a taxi and head out to Pacha (p 126), the biggest club in Africa. It's heaving come midnight, but arrive any earlier and the vibe is more school disco than dirty dancing.

Shopping Best Bets

Best **Couture Kaftans**
★ Intensité Nomade, *139 Avenue Mohammed V (p 91);* and ★ La Maison du Kaftan Marocain, *65 Rue Sidi el-Yamani (p 91)*

Best **Instruments for Berber Jamming**
★★ Bob Music, *21 Rue Kennaria Dabachi (p 94)*

Best **Magic Carpets**
★★ Ben Rahal, *28 Rue de la Liberté (p 87)*

Best **Costumes for Children**
Alrazal, *55 Rue Sourya (p 89)*

Best **Argan Oil**
★ Assouss Argane, *94 Rue Mouassine (p 87)*

Best **Antique Treasure-Trove**
★★ Khalid Art Gallery, *14 Rue Dar el-Bacha (p 86)*

Best **Unique Beach Tunics**
★ Warda la Mouche, *127 Rue Kennaria (p 91)*

Find herbs, spices and remedies at Herboristerie Palais El Badia.

Best **Herbal Miracle Cures**
★ Herboristerie Palais El Badia, *22 bis Arset Lamaach Touareg Jdad (p 88)*

Best **Marrakchi Clubwear**
★ Kulchi, *1 bis Rue el-Ksour (p 91)*

Best **Funky Loafers**
★ Atika, *34 Rue de la Liberté (p 89)*

Best **Fixed-Price Crafts**
★★★ Ensemble Artisanal, *Avenue Mohammed V (p 91)*

Best **Hammam Bubbles**
★ L'Art du Bain, *13 Souk el-Lbadine (p 88)*

Best **Authentic Jewelry**
★★ Tafilalet, *5 Souk Semmarine (p 94)*

Best **Baby Jellabahs**
★★ Kifkif, *8 Rue Laksour (p 93)*

Best **Born-Again Gifts**
Recycle Alley, *Riad Zitoun el-Kedim (p 92)*

Best **Home-Grown Art**
★ La Quobba Galerie, *91 Souk Talaa (p 86)*

Best **Babouches**
★ Au Fil d'Or, *10 Souk Semmarine (p 90)*

Best **Sticky Moroccan Sweets**
Al Jawda, *11 Rue de la Liberté (p 94)*

Best **Foundouk Shop**
★★ Foundouk al Mizane, *Rue Mouassine (p 92)*

Best **Creative Candles**
★ Zen Bougie, *10 Rue Laksour (p 93)*

Kasbah & Around Shopping

Aya's **1**
ETS Bouchaib **2**
Grande Bijouterie **3**
Herboristerie Palais El Badia **4**
Jamade **5**
Warda la Mouche **6**

Bab Taghzout
Bab Taghzout
Derb El Akkari
Rue Bin
Arset El Mellak
Hôpital El Antáki
Rue Assouel
Rue Bab El Khemis
Lamaâssar
Place El Antaki
Bine Laârassi
Rue Ark Jemel
Rue Diour Saboun
ASSOUEL
Bine Laârassi
RIAD EL AROUS
EL MOUKEF
Fontaine Chrob Ou Chouf
Rue El Fakhar
ARSET BEN CHEBLI
Rue Riad El Arous
HART ES-SOURA
Place du Moukef
Rue Riad El Arous
Mosquée Ben Youssef
Médersa Ben Youssef
Rue de Souk d. Fassis
Rue Bab Doukkala
Rue Dar El Bacha
Koubba Ba'adyin
Mosquée Eloussta
Mosquée Bab Doukkala
Dar El Glaoui
Musée de Marrakech
Rue Essettyine
R'MILA
MOUASSINE
Rue Mouassine
Derb Sidi Ishak
Mosquée Azabzed
Rue Dar El Bacha
Rue Sidi El Yumami
Rue Sidi El Kebir
Mosquée Mouassine
Mosquée Sidi Ishak
Zaouia Sidi Ben Salah
Rue Fatima Zohra
EL KSOUR
Place Rahba Kedima
AZBEZT
BEN SALAH
Rue El Ksour
Souk Smarine
SOUKS
DERB DABACHI
Ensemble Artisanal
Rue Jbel Lakhdar
Souk Quessabine
Rue Dabachi
Avenue Mohammed V
Rue Fatima Zohra
Zaouia Sidi Moulay El Ksour
Place Bab Fteuh
MÉDINA
R. Kennaria
Trek El Koutoubia
Place Jemâa El Fna
DOUAR GRAOUA
Rue Douar Graoua
Koubba de Lalla Zohra
Place Foucauld
6
Rue Riad Zitoun El Jedid
Palais Moulay Idriss
Mosquée de la Koutoubia
Consulat de France
Rue Bab Marine
5
Musée Dar Si Saïd
Rue Ibn Khaldoun
Rue Moulay Ismail
Rue de Bab Agnaou
Jardins de la Koutoubia
Hôpital Arset El Mokha
Maison Tiskiouine
Avenue Houmman El Fetouaki
Rue Riad Zitoun El Kedim
Palais de la Bahia
Hôtel La Mamounia
Pl. Youssef Tachfine
Rue Laila Rikia
Rue Orba Ben Nafia
Rue Ibn Rachid
Avenue Houmman El Fetouaki
3
Synagogue Lazama
SIDI MIMOUN
P
Marché Couvert
1
4
Place des Ferblantiers
MELLAH
ARSET EL MAÄCH
Rue Sidi Mimoun
Mosquée de la Kasbah
Palais El Badi
P Police Station
Hôpital Ibn Zohr
Bab Er Rob
Tombeaux Saadiens
Post Office
2
Zaouia Sidi Es Soheïli
Bab Agnaou
KSIBET
Hospital
Cimetière Sidi Es Souheïli
Rue de la kasbah
Centre Artisanal
0   1/4 mi
0   0.25 km

Ville Nouvelle Shopping

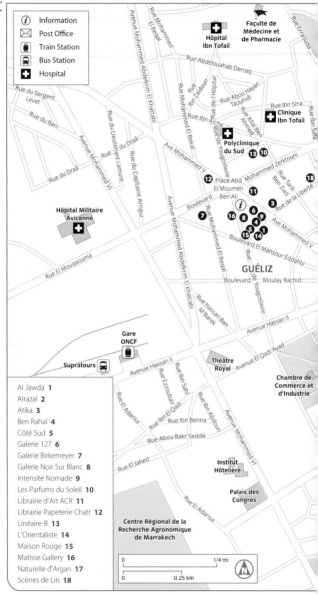

(i) Information

✉ Post Office

🚉 Train Station

🚌 Bus Station

➕ Hospital

Al Jawda **1**
Alrazal **2**
Atika **3**
Ben Rahal **4**
Côté Sud **5**
Galerie 127 **6**
Galerie Birkemeyer **7**
Galerie Noir Sur Blanc **8**
Intensité Nomade **9**
Les Parfums du Soleil **10**
Librairie d'Art ACR **11**
Librairie Papeterie Chatr **12**
Linéaire-B **13**
L'Orientaliste **14**
Maison Rouge **15**
Matisse Gallery **16**
Naturelle d'Argan **17**
Scènes de Lin **18**

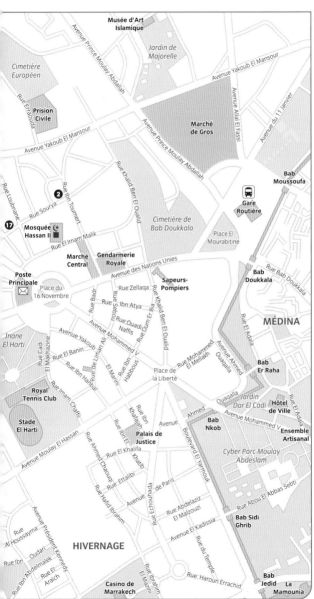

Cimetière
Européen

Musée d'Art
Islamique

Jardin de
Majorelle

Avenue Prince Moulay Abdallah

Avenue Yakoub El Mansour

Rue Erraouda

Prision
Civile

Avenue Yakoub El Mansour

Avenue Prince Moulay Abdallah

Marché
de Gros

Avenue Allal El Fassi

Avenue du 11 Janvier

Bab
Moussoufa

Rue Loubnane

Rue Ibn Tournert

Rue Khalid Ben El Oualid

Rue Sourya

2

17

Mosquée
Hassan II

Rue El Imam Malik

Gare
Routière

Cimetière de
Bab Doukkala

Place El
Mourabitine

Bab
Doukkala

Rue Bab Doukkala

Marché
Central

Gendarmerie
Royale

Avenue des Nations Unies

Sapeurs-
Pompiers

MÉDINA

Poste
Principale

Place du
16 Novembre

Rue Zellaqa

Rue Badr

Rue Seboul

Rue Ibn Atya

Rue Ouadi
Naffis

Rue Oum El Bia

Rue Khalid Ben El Oualid

Rue El Adala

Jnane
El Harti

Avenue Yakoub Mohammed V

Rue Cadi
El Makhzine

Rue El Banin

Rue de Liman Ali

El Marini

Rue Ibn
Habbous

Place de
la Liberté

Rue Mohammed
El Mellakh

Avenue Ahmed
Ouaqaila

Bab
Er Raha

Royal
Tennis Club

Rue Imam Chaffii

Rue Ibn Hanbal

Ouaqaila

Ahmed

Jardin
Dar El Cadi

Hôtel
de Ville

Rue El Adala

Stade
El Harti

Avenue Moulay El Hassan

Rue Ahmed Chaouqi

Rue Ibn
Khatab

Rue Ibn El
Khatib

Rue El Khalifa

Avenue

Bab
Nkob

Avenue Mohammed V

Ensemble
Artisanal

Palais de
Justice

Rue Ettalibi

Rue Hafid Ibrahim

Avenue

Rue Echouhada

de Paris

Boulevard El Yarmouk

Cyber Parc Moulay
Abdeslam

HIVERNAGE

Rue
Al Houssayma

Avenue Président Kennedy

Oudari

Rue El
Araich

Rue Ibn Abdelmalek

Rue Abdelaziz
El Malzouzi

Avenue El Kadissia

Rue du Temple

Rue Ibrahim
El Marini

Rue Abou El Abbas Sebti

Bab Sidi
Ghrib

Casino de
Marrakech

Rue Haroun Errachid

Bab
Jedid

La
Mamounia

Souks & Mouassine Shopping

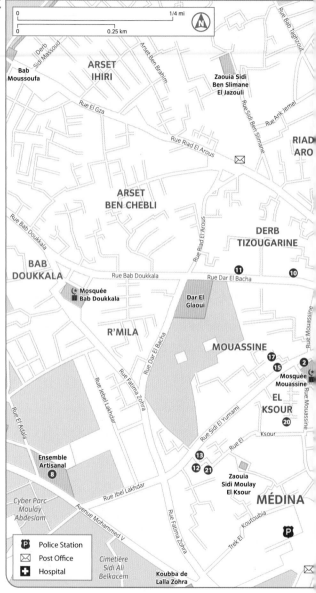

0 _____ 1/4 mi
0 _____ 0.25 km

Bab
Moussoufa

Derb Sidi Massoud

**ARSET
IHIRI**

Arset Ben Brahim

Zaouia Sidi
Ben Slimane
El Jazouli

Rue El Gza

Rue Sidi Ben Slimane

Rue Arik Jemel

Rue Bab Yaghzout

**RIAD
ARO**

Rue Riad El Arous

⊠

**ARSET
BEN CHEBLI**

Rue Bab Doukkala

Rue Riad El Arous

**DERB
TIZOUGARINE**

**BAB
DOUKKALA**

Rue Bab Doukkala

⑪

Rue Dar El Bacha

⑩

Rue Bab Doukkala

Mosquée
Bab Doukkala

Dar El
Glaoui

R'MILA

Rue Dar El Bacha

MOUASSINE

Rue Mouassine

⑰

⑮

❷

Mosquée
Mouassine

Rue Jebel Lakhdar

Rue Fatima Zohra

Rue Sidi El Yamami

**EL
KSOUR**

⑳

Rue Mouassine

Ksour

Rue El

⑬

**Ensemble
Artisanal**

❽

Rue El Adala

⑫ **㉑**

Zaouia
Sidi Moulay
El Ksour

MÉDINA

Cyber Parc
Moulay
Abdeslam

Rue Jbel Lakhdar

Avenue Mohammed V

Rue Fatima Zohra

Koutoubia

Trek El

Ⓟ

Ⓟ	Police Station
⊠	Post Office
✚	Hospital

Cimetière
Sidi Ali
Belkacem

Koubba de
Lalla Zohra

⊠

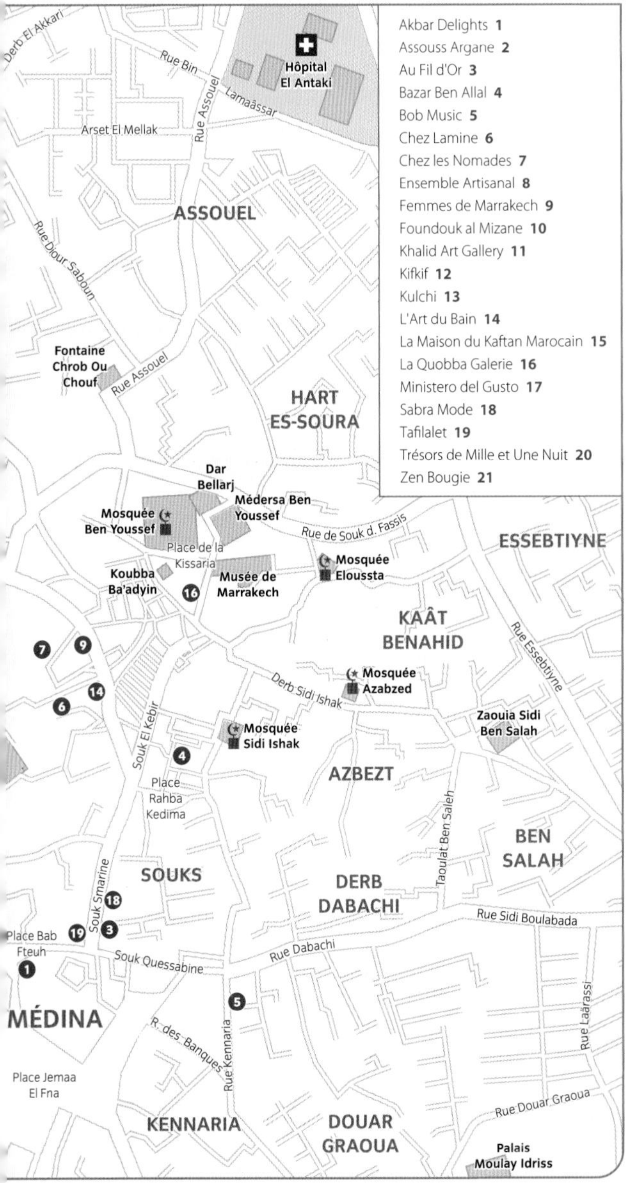
Akbar Delights 1
Assouss Argane 2
Au Fil d'Or 3
Bazar Ben Allal 4
Bob Music 5
Chez Lamine 6
Chez les Nomades 7
Ensemble Artisanal 8
Femmes de Marrakech 9
Foundouk al Mizane 10
Khalid Art Gallery 11
Kifkif 12
Kulchi 13
L'Art du Bain 14
La Maison du Kaftan Marocain 15
La Quobba Galerie 16
Ministero del Gusto 17
Sabra Mode 18
Tafilalet 19
Trésors de Mille et Une Nuit 20
Zen Bougie 21
Derb El Akkari
Rue Bin Lamaâssar
Hôpital El Antaki
Rue Assouel
Arset El Mellak
ASSOUEL
Rue Diour Saboun
Fontaine Chrob Ou Chouf
HART ES-SOURA
Dar Bellarj
Médersa Ben Youssef
Mosquée Ben Youssef
Place de la Kissaria
Rue de Souk d. Fassis
ESSEBTIYNE
Koubba Ba'adyin
Musée de Marrakech
Mosquée Eloussta
KAÂT BENAHID
Rue Essebtiyne
Derb Sidi Ishak
Mosquée Azabzed
Zaouia Sidi Ben Salah
Souk El Kebir
Mosquée Sidi Ishak
AZBEZT
Place Rahba Kedima
Taoulat Ben Saleh
BEN SALAH
SOUKS
Souk Smarine
DERB DABACHI
Rue Sidi Boulabada
Place Bab Fteuh
Souk Quessabine
Rue Dabachi
MÉDINA
R. des Banques
Rue Kennaria
Rue Laârassi
Place Jemaa El Fna
KENNARIA
DOUAR GRAOUA
Rue Douar Graoua
Palais Moulay Idriss

Marrakech **Shopping A to Z**

Antiques & Art

Galerie 127 VILLE NOUVELLE
You ascend a spiral staircase to Marrakech's first contemporary photography gallery. Exposed brick walls create an urban cool backdrop for works by acclaimed photographers such as Bernard Descamps and Jean-Christophe Ballot. *127 Avenue Mohammed V.* ☎ *0524-43-26-67. MC, V. Map p 82.*

Galerie Noir Sur Blanc VILLE NOUVELLE   This dynamic gallery turns the spotlight on emerging and established Moroccan artists, staging contemporary exhibitions as well as workshops and cultural events. The knowledgeable staff are happy to give background on the artworks and their meanings. *48 Rue de Yougoslavie.* ☎ *0524-42-24-16. MC, V. Map p 82.*

★★ **Khalid Art Gallery** SOUKS & MOUASSINE   Antiques expert Khalid has a magpie's eye for spotting valuables to adorn his chandelier-lit riad, much loved by luminaries including Naomi Campbell, Silvio Berlusconi, and Brad Pitt. His gallery is a rambling attic of Islamic art and time-faded Berber carpets, bejeweled chests, and painted cedarwood doors—all with gulp-inducing price tags. *14 Rue Dar el-Bacha* ☎ *0524-44-24-10. AE, MC, V. Map p 84.*

★ **La Quobba Galerie** SOUKS & MOUASSINE   If Guéliz art is too obscure for your tastes, nip into this compact gallery near Place de la Kissaria for a diverse selection of color-charged works, from evocative portraits to Moroccan landscapes. *91 Souk Talaa.* ☎ *0524-38-05-15. www.art-gallery-marrakech.com. MC, V. Map p 84.*

Browse or buy innovative Moroccan artworks at La Qoubba Galerie.

Matisse Gallery VILLE NOUVELLE Homegrown and international art with an oriental twist graces the walls of the Matisse Gallery. Works reach from avant-garde Moroccan paintings to more abstract pieces. *Passage Ghandouri, 61 Rue de Yougoslavie.* ☎ *0524-44-83-26. www.matisse-art-gallery.com. AE, MC, V. Map p 82.*

★★ **Ministero del Gusto** SOUKS & MOUASSINE   Behind an unmarked door lies the dreamlike world of Alessandra Lippini, the former fashion editor of Italian Vogue. Follow in the footsteps of David Bowie and Kate Moss into the light-filled courtyard and theatrical showroom, where the fantastical collection skips from Hassan Hajjaj's Day-Glo Pop Art to 1970s Chanel shift dresses and vintage Murano glass. *22 Derb Azzouz.* ☎ *0524-42-64-55. www.ministerodelgusto.com. AE, MC, V. Map p 84.*

Trésors de Mille et Une Nuit
SOUKS & MOUASSINE Through bustling souks, and down a winding *derb*, you'll find the cavernous Ali Baba's cave of precious antiques. Prices are often sky high, but do still visit this beautifully restored riad to wander the warren of rooms, crammed with centuries-old Tuareg jewelry, twinkling mirrors, and mother-of-pearl-chests. *8 Derb Sania, Rue el-Ksour.* 📞 *0524-44-09-31. AE, MC, V. Map p 84.*

Books

Librairie d'Art ACR VILLE NOUVELLE Whether you're seeking a tagine recipe, an insight into traditional Moroccan arts such as *zellij* (mosaic tilework), or just an arty postcard, this well-stocked bookshop delivers. Specialist titles on everything from calligraphy to basketry share shelf space with an array of English-language phrasebooks and guides. *55 Boulevard Zerktouni.* 📞 *0524-44-67-92. MC, V. Map p 82.*

Librairie Papeterie Chatr VILLE NOUVELLE Pop into one of Marrakech's best and biggest bookstores for reading matter from Moroccan cookery books to phrasebooks in both French and English. The store also stocks a wide range of maps and newspapers. *19 Avenue Mohammed V.* 📞 *0524-44-79-97. MC, V. Map p 82.*

Carpets

Bazar Ben Allal SOUKS & MOUASSINE 'Small shop, small prices, best quality!' informs Ahamed Brahim, as he welcomes you with a broad grin into his tiny store. Although his carpets and kélims are comparable to others in the souks, there's less pressure to buy, always a mint tea on offer, and prime views of the daily carpet auction (see p 50). Prices are negotiable. *Criée Berbère, 27 Rahba Qedima.* 📞 *0524-43-32-73. MC, V. Map p 84.*

★★ Ben Rahal VILLE NOUVELLE Piled high to the ceiling, the richly embroidered Berber carpets and antique kélims won't cost you a sultan's ransom. Even the owners of Marrakech's plushest riads swear by the quality. Browse at your leisure and arrange shipping later. *28 Rue de la Liberté.* 📞 *0524-43-32-73. MC, V. Map p 82.*

Chez les Nomades SOUKS & MOUASSINE Near Souk Sebbaghine (Dyers' Souk), this textile trove harbors hand-knotted Chichaoua carpets, flat-woven Zemmour rugs, and deep-pile Middle Atlas carpets. Friendly staff can explain regional variations and the symbolism in Berber motifs. *32–34 Bradia el-Kedima.* 📞 *0524-44-22-59. www.chezles nomades.com. MC, V. Map p 84.*

Cosmetics, Herbal Remedies & Fragrances

★ Assouss Argane SOUKS & MOUASSINE No time to go to Essaouira? Stock up on first-rate cosmetic and culinary argan oil (around 150dh per bottle), produced by a women's cooperative, at this attractive souk store. The *rhassoul* (clay)

Find your own magic carpet at Bazar Ben Allal in the carpet souk, Criée Berbere

Ten Years Younger

Healers wax lyrical about the wonders of ostrich eggs, but will they really fit in your bathroom cabinet? Throughout the medina, you'll come across *herboristes* (herbalists' stores), where savvy pharmacists whip out hammam must-haves, fennel-flower toothpicks, and a zillion other mystery lotions and potions. Top buys include saffron (Moroccan, not Spanish), star anise, and vanilla pods. Otherwise, bag the following natural remedies:

Argan oil: Hold back the years or treat acne, eczema, and psoriasis with vitamin E-rich argan oil, the Berber elixir of youth.

Ginseng: Banish fatigue and boost you memory with ginseng roots.

Nigella oil: Cleopatra used nigella or black-seed oil for silky locks, but it also alleviates seasickness and nerves.

Orange oil: Ease stress and insomnia with extract of orange.

Rhassoul: Apply this mineral-rich Atlas clay for glossy tresses and to prevent hair loss.

masks, natural soaps, and creams scented with essential oils make great gifts. **94 Rue Mouassine. ☎ 0524-38-01-25. www.assouss-argane.com. MC, V. Map p 84.**

★ **Herboristerie Palais El Badia** KASBAH & AROUND There's frankincense, myrrh, and three wise men rattling off herbal health benefits at this jar-lined store near Badi Palace. Alongside natural pigments, fennel toothpicks, and ginseng roots are home blends such as the ever-popular Ramadan weight loss tea. Nip over to the shop right opposite for a soothing argan-oil shoulder massage for 20dh. **22 bis Arset Lamaach Touareg Jdad. ☎ 0524-38-90-74. Cash only. Map p 81.**

★ **L'Art du Bain** SOUKS & MOUASSINE If you desire a silk-smooth Berber complexion, make for this closet-sized store, overflowing with luscious soaps and suds. Alongside handmade palm-oil soaps, there's *savon noir* (black

soap) and *rhassoul* clay for the hammam. The soaps infused with orange flower, mint, jasmine, and rosemary smell good enough to eat. **13 Souk el-Lbadine ☎ 0668-44-59-42. MC, V. Map p 84.**

Herboristerie Palais El Badia.

Get bathtime inspiration at L'Art du Bain.

Les Parfums du Soleil VILLE NOUVELLE Sniff out the citrus and floral fragrances at this Guéliz perfumery, decorated in traditional *tadelakt* (polished plaster). Choose from soaps and candles with patchouli, orange flower, Atlas cedar, and their classic rose water. Signature perfumes, said to capture Morocco's essence, include Soir de Marrakech and Casablanca. *Rue Tarik Ibn Ziad.* ☎ *0524-42-26-27. www.lesparfumsdusoleil. com. MC, V. Map p 82.*

★ **Linéaire-B** VILLE NOUVELLE Many people stop by Linéaire-B before heading to the hammam and emerge half an hour later with a bag full of organic beauty essentials such as *savon noir* with eucalyptus and rose-scented *rhassoul* clay. The relaxing creams with lavender, hibiscus, and Barbary Fig are attractively presented in calligraphy-labeled bottles. *13 Rue Moulay Ali.* ☎ *0524-43-34-69. www.lineaire-b.com. MC, V. Map p 82.*

Naturelle d'Argan VILLE NOUVELLE Cold-pressed organic argan oil is the big draw in this smart Guéliz boutique. The argan-oil exfoliating soap is a good buy. They also do a range of massage oils and creams enriched with shea butter and beeswax to leave skin soft and supple. *5 Rue Sourya.* ☎ *0524-44-87-61. www.naturelledargan.com. MC, V. Map p 82.*

Fashion & Footwear
★ **Akbar Delights** SOUKS & MOUASSINE Marrakech meets Mumbai in French designer Yann Dobry's slinky couture kaftans, embroidered with floral patterns, colorful beads, and braiding. There's also an Akbar showroom in Guéliz (42 Rue de la Liberté). *45 Place Bab Fteuh.* ☎ *0524-39-19-89. AE, MC, V. Map p 84.*

kids Alrazal VILLE NOUVELLE If you have children in tow, eager to act out fairytale fantasies, hey presto: here's an enchanting boutique full of glittery princess-like kaftans, sultan-worthy hand-embroidered tunics, and mini *jellabahs* (loose, floor-length robes). Sizes range from 3 months to 10 years old. *55 Rue Sourya.* ☎ *0524-43-78-84. MC, V. Map p 82.*

Atika VILLE NOUVELLE Marrakech's funkiest feet race toward this dapper Guéliz store. At around 600dh a pair, the soft suede loafers and gregarious snakeskin shoes cost a fraction of what you would pay for similar quality back home. *34 Rue de la Liberté.* ☎ *0524-43-64-09. MC, V. Map p 82.*

Help! I Need Somebody

It's fun to take part in the ceremonial mint tea slurping and haggling rituals (see p 51 for tips), but for major purchases—think Middle Atlas carpets or made-to-measure silk kaftans—call SOS **personal shopper**. The trick is getting it right, as many commission-hungry guides drag you to seventh-cousin-once-removed Ali's slipper/carpet/jewelry shop, where dear old Al takes you for every last dirham. **Lisa** at **Dar Charkia** (p 140), **Laetitia Trouillet** (www. lalla.fr), and **Kati Lawrence** (☎ 0897-96-69-69) are highly recommended souk mavens, who guide you through the maze *and* save you money in the process.

★ **Au Fil d'Or** SOUKS & MOUASS-INE   Vogue-worthy prêt-a-porter and made-to-measure kaftans lure well-dressed locals, celebrities, and (rumor has it) Spanish royalty here. Whether you're seeking light *jella-bahs*, sumptuous silk tunics, or simply a pair of *babouches* (slippers), Au Fil d'Or obliges. *10 Souk Semmarine.* ☎ *0524-44-59-19. AE, MC, V. Map p 84.*

★ **Aya's** KASBAH & AROUND   Like exotic butterflies, Aya's multi-colored cotton kaftans and vibrant hand-embroidered tunics appear light enough to flutter off the rails. Clothing is complemented by

one-off gifts from Indian pashminas to tassel-topped bottles and Joanna Bristow's ethnic silver jewelry. *11 bis Derb Jdid, Bab Mellah.* ☎ *0524-38-34-28. MC, V. Map p 81.*

★ **Galerie Birkemeyer** VILLE NOUVELLE   Forget fashion statements—Birkemeyer stocks timelessly elegant leather jackets, handbags, and trunks. The atmosphere is pretty stuffy and bargains are nonexistent, but there are no quibbles about the quality. *169–171 Rue Mohammed el-Bequal.* ☎ *0524-44-69-63. www.galerie-birkemeyer. com. AE, MC, V. Map p 82.*

Haute couture with a Marrakshi twist at Intensité Nomade.

★ **Intensité Nomade** VILLE NOUVELLE Frédérique Birkemeyer's couture creations are tailor-made for special occasions—from red-carpet worthy robes to extravagant kaftans à la Elton John. Style-conscious Marrakchi trawl the chandelier-lit boutique for Moroccan design originals such as Noureddine Amir's metrosexual jackets and Julia's funky Berber-inspired T-shirts. *139 Avenue Mohammed V.* ☎ *0524-43-13-33. AE, MC, V. Map p 82.*

★ **Kulchi** SOUKS & MOUASSINE Florence Taranne interweaves classic cuts with a Summer of Love spirit at her petit boutique. Marrakchi clubbers and boho chicks dig the shimmery kaftans, coquettish flower-embroidered dresses, tie-dyed shirts, and Hassan Hajjaj Pop Art tees. *1 bis Rue el-Ksour.* ☎ *0524-42-91-77. MC, V. Map p 84.*

★ **La Maison du Kaftan Marocain** SOUKS & MOUASSINE Jean-Paul Gaultier, Valentino, Gloria Gaynor: the celebrities that shop at this chic store are every bit as rich and flamboyant as its kaftans. Step inside to gawp at the technicolor coats, hand-embroidered *jellabahs*, glittering tunics, and flouncy silk numbers. *65 Rue Sidi el-Yamani.* ☎ *0524-44-10-51. AE, MC, V. Map p 84.*

★ kids **Warda la Mouche** KASBAH & AROUND Sandrine's flowery, Franco-Moroccan threads make great beachwear. Fine-tune your summer look with chiffon tunics and pompom-topped ballet pumps. Tots love the twinkly *babouches* and mini kaftans. *127 Rue Kennaria.* ☎ *0524-38-90-63. MC, V. Map p 81.*

Homeware, Crafts & Gifts
★ **Chez Lamine** SOUKS & MOUASSINE Add a splash of Marrakchi riad glamor to your home with decorative *tadelakt* creations such as candle holders and lamp stands

Warda la Mouche.

from this tiny souk store. *7 Souk Sebbaghine (Dyers' Souk).* ☎ *0524-38-48-45. MC, V. Map p 84.*

Côté Sud VILLE NOUVELLE This sister boutique of Maison Rouge (p 93) presents Moroccan crafts with a novel twist. Browse the shelves for embroidered cushions, sequined wicker bags, ceramic teapots, and stained-glass vases. It also stocks the *Les Sens de Marrakech* range of natural cosmetics. *4 Rue de la Liberté.* ☎ *0524-43-84-48. MC, V. Map p 82.*

★★★ **Ensemble Artisanal** VILLE NOUVELLE Marrakchis beg to differ, but the truth is that haggling doesn't come naturally to everyone. Ensemble Artisanal is the souks in fast-forward mode, minus the madness and mint tea. Shop for fixed-price *babouches*, lanterns, kaftans, and other Moroccan crafts. *Avenue Mohammed V.* ☎ *0524-38-66-74. MC, V. Map p 84.*

ETS Bouchaib KASBAH & AROUND For fixed prices and

Pick up creative, fairtrade crafts at Kifkif.

clued-up staff, visit this Kasbah craft emporium. Downstairs you'll find suitcase-sized gifts from ethnic money brooches to hubbly-bubbly pipes, glazed earthenware, and *jellabahs*. Step upstairs for intricately knotted Tuareg carpets, cactus-silk kélims, and Berber wedding belts. The store ships worldwide. *7 Derb Baïssi.* ☎ *0524-38-18-53. www. bouchaib.net. MC, V. Map p 81.*

★ Femmes de Marrakech
SOUKS & MOUASSINE   Nine women joined creative forces to set up this cooperative, specializing in fair-trade threads in loose cotton and linen. Slip into slinky, sleeveless kaftans with bold prints and tailored tunics in pastel hues. *67 Souk Kchachbia.* ☎ *0524-37-83-08. MC, V. Map p 84.*

★★ Foundouk al Mizane
SOUKS & MOUASSINE   The friendly *maâlems* (master craftsmen) at this age-old caravanserai gladly reveal their artisanal secrets. Mr Kharbibi Moulay Mafid, expertly turns cedarwood with his bare feet to shape lucky charms, and opposite, Rasheed sells natural dyed, handmade goatskin lamps. Pick from one of 145 designs or ask him to create a bespoke piece for you. *Rue Mouassine. No phone. Cash only. Map p 84.*

Recycle Alley

When that fake fez or wooden cobra simply won't do, dig deeper for less-predictable gifts. For eco-friendly and durable creations, look no further than the workshops punctuating **Riad Zitoun el-Kedim**, where local craftsmen diligently transform recycled materials into one-off creations. Watch in amazement as old truck tarpaulins are deftly cut, and then stitched on Singer sewing machines to become retro-style backpacks, bike satchels, and sandals. Other unique crafts to put some va-va-voom into your shopping include Michelin-tire photo frames, pots, and furnishings.

Jamade KASBAH & AROUND Jamade's candy bright ceramics are a break from the Berber norm. Enliven your home with chili-red candlesticks or tagine sets and teapots in citrus shades. The collection also comprises beads, leather bags, purses, and jewelry. *1 Place Douar Graoua, Riad Zitoun el-Jedid.* ☎ *0524-42-90-42. AE, MC, V. Map p 81.*

★★ kids Kifkif SOUKS & MOUASSINE I'm a huge fan of this curiosity shop, filled with ethical, fair-trade gifts; from fabrics embroidered by women with disabilities to crockery hand-painted in rural villages. The children's collection is superb—think cuddly camels, baby argan oil, and cute *jellabah*-inspired bathrobes emblazoned with the Kasbah (6 months to 8 years of age). *8 Rue Laksour.* ☎ *0661-08-20-41. MC, V. Map p 84.*

L'Orientaliste NOUVELLE VILLE For home design inspiration, check out L'Orientaliste's Tuareg camel-leather lamps, ceramics, antique chests, and wooden photo frames. Light and natural, their signature fragrances such as mimosa, rose, amber, and patchouli are beautifully presented in tassel-topped bottles. *11 and 15 Rue de la Liberté.* ☎ *0524-43-40-74. MC, V. Map p 82.*

Maison Rouge NOUVELLE VILLE Bejeweled candle holders, scarlet-and-gold cushion covers, hand-embroidered tablecloths, and silver-topped flacons are among the trinkets at this split-level store. The tasseled children's bathrobes are adorable and the hand-painted plates depicting Moroccan daily life make ideal souvenirs. *6 Rue de la Liberté.* ☎ *0524-44-81-30. MC, V. Map p 82.*

★ Sabra Mode SOUKS & MOUASSINE It's a tough call, but Adil's spangled throws are probably the finest in the souks. Some 10,000 pieces are crammed into his compact store in all sizes and every color of the rainbow. Prices are reasonable given the quality, with a standard size costing around 320dh. *46 Souk Semmarine.* ☎ *0524-44-58-62. Cash only. Map p 84.*

Scènes de Lin VILLE NOUVELLE Slightly snooty service detracts nothing from the quality of linens here, which can be ordered in any color and length. Well-to-do Marrakchi socialites praise the store's luxurious tablecloths, cushion covers, sequined throws, and attention-grabbing lamps. *70 Rue el-Houria.* ☎ *0524-43-61-08. MC, V. Map p 82.*

★ Zen Bougie SOUKS & MOUASSINE This scarlet-walled shop is the best place to buy artisanal candles in myriad shades and styles. Standouts include candles embellished with copper Fatima hands and lit by

Zen Bougie candles.

a tea-light within, and hand-carved thuya wood tea-light holders. *10 Rue Laksour.* ☎ *0524-39-19-89. www.zenbougie.com. AE, MC, V. Map p 84.*

Jewelry & Accessories
Grande Bijouterie KASBAH & AROUND   A carved stucco arch opposite Bahia Palace leads through to this covered souk, where tiny jewelers sparkle with gold bangles, silver chains, gem-encrusted belts, and semi-precious stones. *Rue Bab Mellah. No phone. MC, V. Map p 84.*

★★ **Tafilalet** SOUKS & MOUASS-INE   All that glitters in souk jewelers is not gold, but Tafilalet is the exception. Omar travels the globe in search of semi-precious stones to ensure that the quality is high and prices are comparatively low for Bulgari imitations, ethnic Berber jewelry, rubies, sapphires, and diamonds. *5 Souk Semmarine.* ☎ *0524-44-10-57. MC, V. Map p 84.*

Moroccan Sweets
Al Jawda VILLE NOUVELLE   Listen for the joyous squeals of abandoned diets as you enter this tiny Guéliz patisserie, where shelves brim with honey-drenched pastries infused with orange-flower water, feather-light macaroons, almond paste-filled *cornes de gazelle* (cookies), and petits fours (around 160dh per

Bob Music.

kilo). *11 Rue de la Liberté.* ☎ *0524-43-38-97. www.al-jawda.com. MC, V. Map p 82.*

Musical Instruments
★★ **Bob Music** MITTE   Looking for a mahogany-finished oud, a henna-painted storyteller hand drum, or a cow-horn Berber saxophone? You'll need plenty of willpower and puff to produce a tune on the latter, but help is at hand—owner Rachid offers expert demonstrations and private music lessons. As photos on the wall testify, even Led Zeppelin frontman Robert Plant found musical inspiration here. *21 Rue Kennaria Dabachi.* ☎ *0524-37-72-81. www.musouk.com. MC, V. Map p 84.* ●

Best **Outdoor Pursuits**

Palmerai

Nikki Beach

Superette Jardin de la Palmeraie

Le Palmeraie d'Or

Circuit de la Palmeraie

Route de Fés

Hôpital Ibn Tofail

Cimetière Européen

Prison Civile

Rue Erraouda

Polyclinique du Sud

Clinique Ibn Tofail

Rue de Yougoslavie

Ibn Aicha

Place Abd Mohammed Zerktouni El Moumen Ben Ali

Rue de la Liberté

Rue Tarik Ben Ziad

Rue Loubnane

Rue Souraya

Rue Ibn Tournert

Mosquée Hassan II

El Imam Malik

Avenue Mohammed V

Rue Mohammed V

Bd Boulevard El Mansour Eddahbi

Rue de Yougoslavie

Rue Boulevard El Bekal

Rue Mohammed El Bekal

Rue Hassan Ban M'Barek

GUÉLIZ

Bd Moulay Rachid

Poste Principale

Place du 16 Novembre

Marché Central

Gendarmerie Royale

Avenue des Nations Unies

Rue Zellaqa

Rue Badil

Rue Ibn Atya

Rue Saebou

Rue El Bia

Rue Khalid Ben El Oualid

Sapeurs-Pompiers

Gare Routière

Cimetière de Bab Doukkala

Place El Mourabitin

Rue Mohammed El Meillakh

Avenue Hassan II

Avenue El Qadi Ayad

Avenue Yakoub El Mansour

Avenue Mohammed V

Rue Cadi El Makhazine

Rue Ibn Habbous

Rue Oum Er Bia

Sainte Anne

Place de la Liberté

Théâtre Royal

Rue Ibn Aboun

Avenue Mohammed VI

Institut Hôtelière

Palais des Congrès

Rue El Adarsa

Jnane El Harti

Chambre de Commerce et d'Industrie

Royal Tennis Club

Stade El Harti

Rue Imam Chafii

Rue Ibn Hanbal

Cadastre

Avenue Moulay El Hassan

Palais de Justice

Rue El Khalifa

Rue Ahmed El Khatib

Rue Ahmed Chaoui

Rue Harid Ibrahim

Rue El Khalifa

Avenue de Paris

Rue Echouhada

Rue Abdelaziz El Malzouzi

Avenue El Kadissia

Avenue Ahmed Ouaqalla

Bab Nkob

Boulevard El Yarmouk

Cyber Pa. Moulay Abdesla

Bab Si Ghrib

Temple

Rue Ibrahim El Mazni

Rue Haroun Errachid

HIVERNAGE

Rue Al Houssaymia

Rue Ibn Oudari

Avenue President Kennedy

Rue Abdelmalek Es Araich

Rue Chechaouen El Kebir

Rue Ksar El Kadissia

Avenue El Kadissia

Avenue Mohammed VI

Casino de Marrakech

Avenue de la Ménara

1	Camel Trekking
2	City Strolls
3	Golf
4	Horse Riding
5	Hot-Air Balloon Flights
6	Tennis
7	Water Parks

i	Information
✉	Post Office
🚌	Bus Station

The Atlas Mountain views alone are enough to coax active types out of their riad rooftop lounger for a little outdoor adventure. Just minutes from the medina you can camel trek through a date palm oasis, play golf in La Palmeraie, or join an exhilarating buggy raid to a Berber village; and the ski slopes of Oukaïmeden and Essaouira's crashing Atlantic waves are but a day trip away.

❶ Camel Trekking. When the sun's out, hop in a taxi to the Palmeraie for a bumpy morning ride through the date palms. Simply ask your driver to stop at one of the lay-bys, where camels and their masters vie for custom. Pick your beast of burden and barter for a good price. Frankly the experience is more inspiring than the scrubby landscape, and so an hour-long trek should be long enough for your camera and your bottom. It's the closest you'll get to the Sahara without going the extra hundred miles. *Circuit de la Palmeraie. Around 150dh for one-hour camel rides. Daily during daylight hours.*

❷ City Strolls. Shake the riad sleepy dust from your eyes and work off last night's Moroccan *diffa* (feast) with an early morning walk around the ramparts near **Bab Hmar**. Marrakchis turn up in track

suits for an impromptu workout, as the sun rises above the Atlas Mountains and paints the ramparts pink. Nearby you'll spot youngsters playing soccer. *Bab Hmar, Avenue Tassaltante, near Agdal Gardens. Daily 6:30–8am.*

❸ Golf. Within minutes of Marrakech, avid golfers can take their pick from three world-class golf courses. Reasonable green fees, fine weather, Atlas Mountain vistas, and open tracts of land studded with lakes and palms make the area prime golfing terrain. Among the best is the lush 18-hole, par-72 **Palmeraie Golf Course**, designed by Robert Trent Jones. *Palmeraie Golf Course, Circuit de la Palmeraie.* ☎ *0524-36-87-66. www.palmeraie-golf-club.com. Green fees: 300dh 9 holes, 500dh 18 holes. Daily 7am–7pm.*

Explore the date palm-strewn Palmeraie by camel.

Rise high above hill and dale in a hot-air balloon.

4 Horse Riding. If camels are too humpy for your taste, there are several stables in Marrakech where you can jump into the saddle of a horse. One of the most central and reputable is the Palmeraie Golf Palace, where children enjoy a short pony trot in the paddocks. Alternatively, take your trusty stead on a trek around the Palmeraie. *Palmeraie Golf Palace, Circuit de la Palmeraie.* ☎ *0524-36-87-93. www.pgp.co.ma. Horses 150dh per hour, 800dh per day; ponies 90dh per hour. Daily 8am–12pm and 3–8pm summer, 8am–12pm and 3–6pm winter.*

5 Hot-Air Balloon Flights. Your idea of action, on the other hand, might involve drifting over rippled valleys and Atlas peaks in a hot air balloon. Run by friendly French pilot Maurice, Ciel d'Afrique offers passenger flights year-round, which include a 4x4 pick-up service. Flights aren't cheap but the experience is one of quiet exhilaration, affording tremendous aerial views. Most take off at daybreak (weather permitting) and advance bookings are essential. The office is in Guéliz. *15 Rue Mauritanie.* ☎ *0524-43-28-43. www.cieldafrique.info. 2050dh flight per person.*

Adrenaline Overdrive

One of the latest adrenalin-loaded crazes in Marrakech is buggy raiding, where you can race through challenging terrain at speeds of up to 150kph, pausing to refuel over tea in a Berber village. Half-day treks including transfers and insurance with **Raid Buggy** (☎ 0661-55-23-78; www.raidbuggy.com), with longer excursions to the Agafay Desert available. Or channel your inner speed demon go-karting on the outskirts of Marrakech at the 1.3km circuit at **Atlas Karting** (Route de Safi; ☎ 0661-23-76-87). If getting dirty in the dunes and desert appeals, **Nomade Quad** (Route de Fés. ☎ 0524-43-85-40; www.nomade-quad-maroc.com) offers quad biking in La Palmeraie. Contact companies directly for meeting points, times, and prices.

Out of Town Action

Those craving more outdoor action will find it on a day trip from Marrakech. **Essaouira** (p 148) is a magnet to surfers, windsurfers, and kite surfers from May to September, when huge waves roll in from the cobalt Atlantic to pummel its wide bay. If you're keen to hit the surf, pack your wetsuit and head to the coast. Come winter when the first snow dusts the Atlas Mountains, skiers and snowboarders carve up the slopes of **Oukaïmeden** (p 156), Africa's highest and Morocco's only real ski resort. Situated 70km south of Marrakech (just over an hour by taxi), the high-altitude village sits at 3,273m (10,742 feet) and receives frequent dumps of snow from late December to late March.

⑥ Tennis. Master your backhand with the pros at the **Royal Tennis Club** in the Jardin el Harti (p 76). Dating back to 1926, the club comprises nine clay courts, offering wonderful Atlas views, some of which are floodlit after dark. *Jardin el Harti, Rue Ouadi el-Makhazine.* ☎ *0524-43-19-02. www.frmt.ma. 100 dh court per hour. Daily 7am–12pm and 2:30–10pm.*

⑦ Water Parks. When Marrakech gets too hot for tots, take them to the Oasiria water park 5km out of town. Children love the shallow splash pools, pirate ship, whizzy slides, wave pool, and lazy river. Grown-ups, meanwhile, can relax in the verdant gardens or try activities from volleyball and water polo to aqua aerobics and soccer. Feeling a bit of a daredevil? Prepare to scream on the *steeeep* kamikaze slide. A free shuttle bus runs roughly hourly from the medina (opposite Koutoubia) and Guéliz (Place el Harti) from June to August. *Route du Barrage 4km.* ☎ *0524-38-04-38. www.oasiria marrakech. Admission 100dh adults, 50dh concessions, free for children under 80cm in height. Apr–Aug daily 10am–6pm, Sep–Mar Fri–Sun 10am–6pm.*

Total whiteout - skiing in Oukaïmeden in the Atlas Mountains.

Green Marrakech

1/4 mi
0.25 km

Maison de
la Culture

Avenue du 11 Janvier

**KAA
EL MECHRA**

Souk
El Khemis

Route des Remparts

Musée d'Art
Islamique
5
*Jardin de
Majorelle*

Jnane
Bel Abbès

Cimetière
Sidi Ahmed
Ez Zaouia

Avenue

Allal El Fassi

Avenue Yakoub El Mansour

Bab El Jnane
Bel Abbès

Bab El
Arset Ben
Brahim

*Cimetière
Sidi Bel
Abbès*

Bab El
Khemis

Avenue Prince Moulay Abdallah

Marché
de Gros

Avenue du 11 Janvier

Bab
Moussoufa

Zaouia Sidi
Bel Abbès

Bab
Taghzout

Bab
Kechich

Rue Bab El Khemis

*Cimetière de
Bab Doukkala*

Ave des Nations Unies

Gare
Routière

**ARSET
IHIRI**

Zaouia Sidi
Ben Slimane
El Jazouli

ASSOUEL

**RIAD EL
AROUS**

Bab
Doukkala

Rue Bab Doukkala

**ARSET
BEN CHEBLI**

Mosquée
Ben Youssef

**HART
ES-SOURA**

Médersa Ben
Youssef

Rue Essebtyne

Place de
la Liberté

Bab
Nkob

**BAB
DOUKKALA**

Bab
Er Raha

Mosquée
Bab Doukkala

Dar El
Glaoui

MOUASSINE

Koubba
Ba'adyin

Mosquée
Mouassine

Musée de
Marrakech

**KAÂT
BENAHID**

Rue Echouhada

Hôtel
de Ville

Ensemble
Artisanal

Avenue Mohammed V

SOUKS

MÉDINA

Rue Dabachi

4
*Cyber Parc Moulay
Abdeslam*

Bab Sidi
Ghrib

*Cimetière
Sidi Ali
Belkacem*

Koubba de
Lalla Zohra

Place
Jemaa
El Fna

Place
Foucauld

KENNARIA

Rue Riad Zitoun El Khedim

Musée
Dar Si Saïd

Palais
Moulay
Idriss

Bab
Jedid

3
*Jardins de
la Koutoubia*

Mosquée de
la Koutoubia

Ave Houmman El Fetouaki

Place
Youssef
Tachfine

Palais de
la Bahia

Hôtel
La Mamounia

Ave Houmman El Fetouaki

MELLAH

Avenue de la Ménara

Boulevard El Yarmouk

*Jardins de
la Mamounia*

**SIDI
MIMOUN**

Mosquée de
la Kasbah

Place des
Ferblantiers

Palais
El Badi

Mosquée
Berrima

*Oliveraie de
Bab Jdid*

Bab
Er Rob

Bab
Agnaou

Tombeaux
Saadiens

Bab
El Aghdar

Route Secondaire N501

*Cimetière
Sidi Es Souheili*

Palais Royal
Dar El Makhzen

Arset El
Bab Er Rob

KASBAH

**DERB
CHTOUKA**

Bab
Irhli

Rue de Bab Irhli

1
*Jardins
de l'Agdal*

1 Agdal Gardens
2 Menara Gardens
3 Koutoubia Gardens
4 Cyber Park
5 Jardin Majorelle
6 Palmeraie
7 Jnane Tamsna

🅿 Police Station
✉ Post Office
🚌 Bus Station

6 →
7 →
← 2

Though it appears arid on the surface, Marrakech hides some of Morocco's lushest gardens. Gaze up to snow-dusted Atlas peaks, walking in sultans' footsteps in the orchard-like Adgal Gardens and the olive-strewn Menara Gardens. In summer, Marrakchis seek cool respite in the central the palm-shaded Cyber Park and Koutoubia Gardens, or with languid strolls through Jardin Majorelle.
START: **Agdal Gardens.**

❶ ★ Agdal Gardens. A garden fit for an Almohad sultan, these 12th-century royal orchards south of the medina are only open Fridays and Sundays when the king isn't in residence. Agdal is the Berber name for a walled meadow, referring to the *pisé* (clay and mud) walls that frame the 400-hectare gardens, which nurture citrus, apricot, and pomegranate trees. Follow the avenue punctuated by olive and cypress trees to the grand basin, where royals once frolicked on boats and held lavish picnics. Here you can feed the carp and wonder at views of the Atlas Mountains, which are particularly bewitching after the first snow in winter. Look out for **Dar al Baida pavilion**, where Sultan Moulay Hassan had his harem. The gardens are a short taxi ride from the center, but I prefer to walk along the passageway that shadows the high walls of the Royal Palace. ⏲ *45 min. See p 59.*

❷ ★ kids Menara Gardens. Walk west along Avenue de la Menara, skirting the Bab Jdid olive grove

The fragrant orange groves of the Agdal Gardens.

and the swish hotels of Hivernage, to these romantic gardens. These olive tree-speckled gardens, framing a rectangular pool, are the ideal escape from the heat and hubbub of Marrakech. Visit the green-tiled pavilion to admire painted cedarwood, stucco, and fine vistas. The best views are from the small amphitheater north of the symmetrical pool, where the **Atlas Mountains** reflect in the water in the late afternoon. ⏲ *1 hr. See p 34.*

❸ Koutoubia Gardens. When the souks are sweatier than a hammam, find cool respite in these gardens behind Koutoubia. Aside from perfectly symmetrical snapshots of the minaret, this pocket of verdure offers shade under the orange and palm trees. Keep an eye out for the resident bill-clattering storks. ⏲ *20 min. See p 32.*

❹ ★ kids Cyber Park. You can't literally surf the web, but you can stroll the Cyber. Dotted with Internet kiosks, this one-time royal garden is now the meeting point for Marrakchi teenagers dodging homework to hang out under the fragrant orange trees. Escape the bustle on Avenue Mohammed V with a refreshing amble through palms and citrus trees, interspersed with benches and fountains. ⏲ *30 min. See p 16.*

❺ ★★ Jardin Majorelle. The late fashion icon Yves Saint Laurent's botanical garden wears every season well. Jacques Majorelle was a feted landscape painter, but in 1924 he surpassed himself with this exotic picture, drenched with vivid

Paradise City

From riad courtyards to royal orchards, gardens in Marrakech are often based on the Garden of Paradise mentioned in the Koran. Distinctive features include symmetry, water, and shade. Many gardens are quadripartite, divided into four equal sections by foot-paths or waterways and enclosed by walls (an allusion to the gates of heaven). The focal point is a basin or fountain, symbolic of water as a fundamental source of life, especially in arid climates. Citrus, fig, and pomegranate trees create a vision of lushness and provide shade, fragrant aromas, and fruit. In larger gardens, such as those at Menara and Agdal, you'll notice pavilions which, according to the Koran, are where the righteous reside.

color and light. When temps soar, this is my favorite spot in Marrakech for a ramble. A pathway snakes past lofty Californian palms, bulbous cacti, rustling bamboo, and bougainvillea. At the heart of the foliage, ponds hold up a mirror to the beautiful blues of the Art Deco villa housing the **Islamic Art Museum** (p 74). 🕐 *1 hr. See p 15.*

6 ★ **Palmeraie.** With its tall palms and ostentatious neo-Moorish villas, the Palmeraie is like the Beverly Hills of Marrakech. Nestled at the foot of the mountains, this oasis is known for its namesake 120,000 date palms, though trees

Grand villas stud the Palmeraie, a magnet to the rich and famous

are wilting and numbers dwindling because of property development and disease. The palms are watered by **khettara**, a clever 12th-century network of underground irrigation channels that brings water from the Ourika Valley. Today the Palmeraie is the much-loved refuge of sun-seeking royals, rock stars, and upwardly mobile Marrakchis, home to luxurious retreats and an 18-hole golf course (p 97). Explore the popular **Circuit de la Palmeraie** by horse-drawn *calèche* or on the hump of a camel. 🕐 *1½ hrs. (p 22).*

7 ★ **Jnane Tamsna.** Alfresco fans flock to this serene villa estate set in 6-hectare gardens fragrant with citrus trees and flowers. The chef uses homegrown ingredients from the organic garden to prepare light, aromatic dishes such as Senegalese yassa (chicken slow cooked in lemon and onions) served with garden vegetables, and refreshing grapefruit-ginger sorbet. Come for a three-course lunch (350dh) and you can spend the afternoon by the secluded pool or playing tennis. *Douar Abiad, La Palmeraie.* ☎ *0524-32-84-84. $$$$.* ●

Dining Best Bets

Best **Jemaa el Fna View**
★★ Le Marrakchi $$$ *52 Jemaa el Fna (p 117)*

Best **Literary Brunch**
★ Café du Livre $ *44 Rue Tarik Ben Ziad (p 74)*

Best **Arabian Nights**
★★★ La Sultana $$$$ *403 Rue de la Kasbah (p 115);* and ★★ La Maison Arabe $$$$ *1 Derb Assehbe, Bab Doukkala (p 115)*

Best **Veggie Café**
★★ Earth Cafe $ *2 Derb Zouak, Riad Zitoun el-Kedim (p 12)*

Best **Romantic Riad**
★★ Le Tobsil $$$$$ *22 Derb Abdellah Ben Hessaïen, Bab Ksour (p 117);* and ★★★ Villa Flore $$–$$$ *4 Derb Azzouz (p 118)*

Best **Moroccan Soul Food**
★★ Al Fassia $$–$$$ *55 Boulevard Zerktouni (p 110)*

Best **French Menu**
★★★ Le Bis $$$–$$$$ *6–7 Rue Sakia el Hamra, Semlalia (p 116);* and ★ Chez Pascal $$–$$$ *32 Boulevard Zerktouni (p 112)*

Candles light the way to La Maison Arabe's restaurant.

Best **Stork Snapshots**
★ Nid' Cigogne $ *60 Place des Tombeaux Saâdians (p 117)*

Best **Intimate Courtyard**
★ Casa Lalla $$$$ *Derb Jamaa, Riad Zitoun el-Kedim (p 111)*

Best **Decadent Thai Lounge**
★ Narwama $$$ *30 Rue Koutoubia (p 117)*

Best **Foundouk Flavors**
Le Foundouk $$$–$$$$ *55 Souk Hal Fassi (p 67)*

Best **Palace Dining**
★ Dar Donab $$$ *53 Rue Dar el-Bacha, Bab Doukkala (p 112)*

Best **Cheap Eat**
★ Chez Chegrouni $$ *Place Jemaa el Fna (p 112)*

Best **Theatrical Feast**
★ Dar Yacout $$$$$ *79 Derb Sidi Ahmed Soussi (p 113)*

Best **Colonial Charm**
★ Grand Café de la Poste $$$ *Avenue Imam Malik cnr Boulevard el-Mansour Eddahbi (p 114)*

Best **Creative Moroccan**
★★ Lotus Privilege $$$$$ *9 Derb Sidi Ali ben Hamdouch, Bab Doukkala (p 117)*

Best **Ice-Cream**
★ Ice Legend $ *52 Rue Bab Agnaou (p 7)*

Best **Market-Fresh Fish**
★ La Table du Marché $$$–$$$$ *4 Rue du Temple (p 115)*

Best **Souk Escape**
★ Café des Épices $ *75 Rahba Qedima (p 21)*

Kasbah & Around Dining

Casa Lalla **1**
Chez Bahia **2**
Jardins de la Medina **3**
La Sultana **4**
Nid' Cigogne **5**

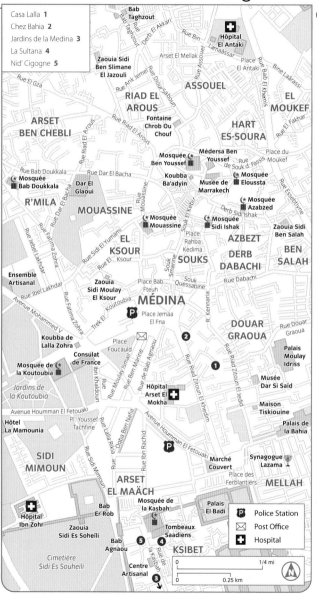

Bab Taghzout
Bab Taghzout
Derb El Akkari
Rue Bin
Hôpital El Antaki
Rue Bin Lamaassar
Arset El Mellak
Rue Ank Jemel
Rue Doukkalabouin
Rue El Gza
Zaouia Sidi Ben Slimane El Jazouli
Place El Antaki
Bine Laârassi
Bab El Khemis
ASSOUEL
EL MOUKEF
Rue El Fakhar
RIAD EL AROUS
Rue Riad El Arous
Fontaine Chrob Ou Chouf
HART ES-SOURA
Place du Souk d. Moukef
ARSET BEN CHEBLI
Médersa Ben Youssef
Rue de Souk d. Fassi
Mosquée Ben Youssef
Rue Bab Doukkala
Rue Dar El Bacha
Koubba Ba'adyin
Mosquée Eloussta
Rue Essebtiyne
Mosquée Bab Doukkala
Dar El Glaoui
Musée de Marrakech
Mosquée Azabzed
R'MILA
MOUASSINE
Rue Mouassine
Mosquée Sidi Ishak
Mosquée Azabzed
Rue Jebel Lakhdar
Rue Fatima Zohra
Mosquée Mouassine
Place Rahba Kedima
AZBEZT
Zaouia Sidi Ben Salah
EL KSOUR
Souk El Kebir
Rue Sidi El Yamani
Rue El Ksour
SOUKS
DERB DABACHI
BEN SALAH
Ensemble Artisanal
Avenue Jbel Lakhdar
Souk Smarine
Rue Dabachi
Avenue Mohammed V
Zaouia Sidi Moulay El Ksour
Place Bab Fteuh
Souk Quessabine
R. Kennaria
Trek El Koutoubia
MÉDINA
Koubba de Lalla Zohra
Place Jemaa El Fna
2
DOUAR GRAOUA
Rue Douar Graoua
Mosquée de la Koutoubia
Place Foucauld
Rue de Bab Agnaou
Rue Riad Zitoun El Jedid
1
Palais Moulay Idriss
Consulat de France
Rue Moulay Ismaïl
Rue Bab Marine
Musée Dar Si Said
Jardins de la Koutoubia
Ibn Khaldoun
Hôpital Arset El Mokha
Maison Tiskiouine
Avenue Houmman El Fetouaki
Pl. Youssef Tachfine
Rue Riad Zitoun El Kedim
Palais de la Bahia
Hôtel La Mamounia
Rue Lalla Rkia
Rue Orba Ben Nafia
Avenue Houmman El Fetouaki
Synagogue Lazama
SIDI MIMOUN
Rue Sidi Mimoun
Rue Ibn Rachid
Marché Couvert
MELLAH
ARSET EL MAÄCH
Place des Ferblantiers
Hôpital Ibn Zohr
Bab Er Rob
Mosquée de la Kasbah
Palais El Badi
P — Police Station
Zaouia Sidi Es Soheïli
Tombeaux Saadiens
✉ — Post Office
Bab Agnaou
5
4
KSIBET
✚ — Hospital
Cimetière Sidi Es Souheïli
Centre Artisanal
3
0   1/4 mi
0   0.25 km

Jemaa el Fna, Souks & Mouassine Dining

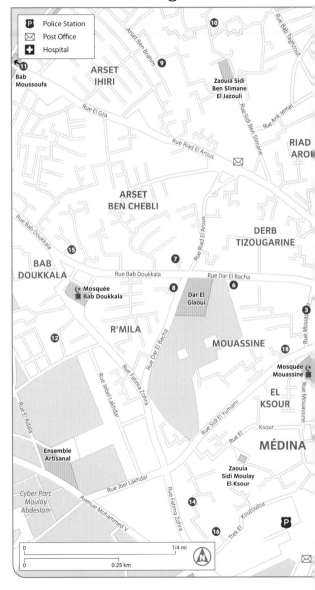

🅿	Police Station
✉	Post Office
➕	Hospital

ARSET IHIRI

Arset Ben Brahim

⑩

⑨

Bab Moussoufa

⑪

Zaouia Sidi Ben Slimane El Jazouli

Rue El Gza

Rue Sidi Ben Slimane

Rue Ank Jemel

RIAD AROU

Rue Riad El Arous

✉

ARSET BEN CHEBLI

Rue Riad El Arous

DERB TIZOUGARINE

Rue Bab Doukkala

⑮

BAB DOUKKALA

Rue Bab Doukkala

⑦

Rue Dar El Bacha

⑥

⑧

★ Mosquée Bab Doukkala

Dar El Glaoui

⑫

R'MILA

Rue Dar El Bacha

Rue Fatima Zohra

MOUASSINE

③

Rue Mouassine

⑱

Mosquée Mouassine ★

Rue Jebel Lakhdar

EL KSOUR

Rue Sidi El Yumami

Rue El

Ksour

MÉDINA

Rue El Adala

Ensemble Artisanal

Cyber Parc Moulay Abdeslam

Rue Jbel Lakhdar

Rue Fatima Zohra

Zaouia Sidi Moulay El Ksour

Avenue Mohammed V

⑭

⑯

Koutoubia

Trek El

🅿

✉

0	1/4 mi
0	0.25 km

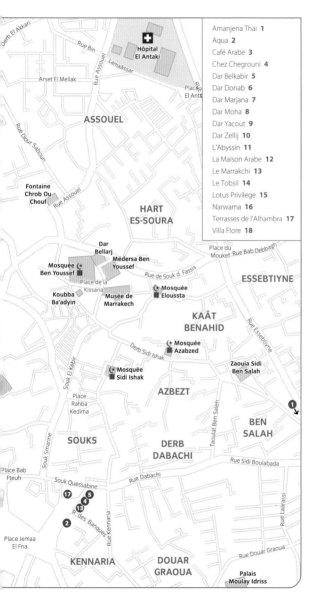

Derb El Akkari

Rue Bin
Lamaâssar

Hôpital
El Antaki

Rue Assoul

Arset El Mellak

Place
El Ants

ASSOUEL

Rue Diour Saboun

Fontaine
Chrob Ou
Chouf

Rue Assouel

**HART
ES-SOURA**

Dar
Bellarj

Mosquée
Ben Youssef

Médersa Ben
Youssef

Rue de Souk d. Fassis

Place du
Moukef Rue Bab Debbagh

Place de la
Kissaria

Koubba
Ba'adyin

Musée de
Marrakech

Mosquée
Eloussta

ESSEBTIYNE

Rue Essebtiyne

**KAÂT
BENAHID**

Derb Sidi Ishak

Mosquée
Azabzed

Mosquée
Sidi Ishak

Zaouia Sidi
Ben Salah

Souk El Kebir

Place
Rahba
Kedima

AZBEZT

Taoulat Ben Saleh

**BEN
SALAH**

1

SOUKS

Souk Smarine

**DERB
DABACHI**

Rue Sidi Boulabada

Place Bab
Fteuh

Souk Quessabine

Rue Dabachi

R. des Banques

Rue Kennaria

17
5
4
13
2

Rue Laarassi

Place Jemaa
El Fna

KENNARIA

**DOUAR
GRAOUA**

Rue Douar Graoua

Palais
Moulay Idriss

Amanjena Thai **1**
Aqua **2**
Café Arabe **3**
Chez Chegrouni **4**
Dar Belkabir **5**
Dar Donab **6**
Dar Marjana **7**
Dar Moha **8**
Dar Yacout **9**
Dar Zellij **10**
L'Abyssin **11**
La Maison Arabe **12**
Le Marrakchi **13**
Le Tobsil **14**
Lotus Privilege **15**
Narwama **16**
Terrasses de l'Alhambra **17**
Villa Flore **18**

Ville Nouvelle Dining

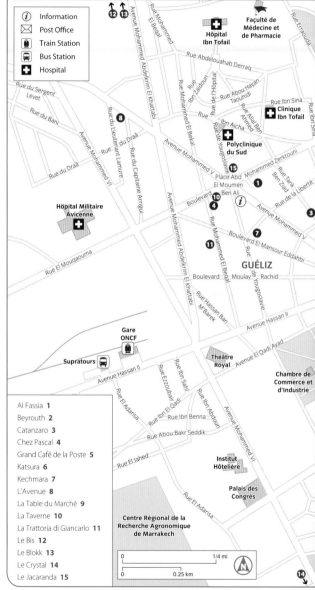

Symbol	Label
ⓘ	Information
✉	Post Office
🚆	Train Station
🚌	Bus Station
✚	Hospital

Al Fassia **1**
Beyrouth **2**
Catanzaro **3**
Chez Pascal **4**
Grand Café de la Poste **5**
Katsura **6**
Kechmara **7**
L'Avenue **8**
La Table du Marché **9**
La Taverne **10**
La Trattoria di Giancarlo **11**
Le Bis **12**
Le Blokk **13**
Le Crystal **14**
Le Jacaranda **15**

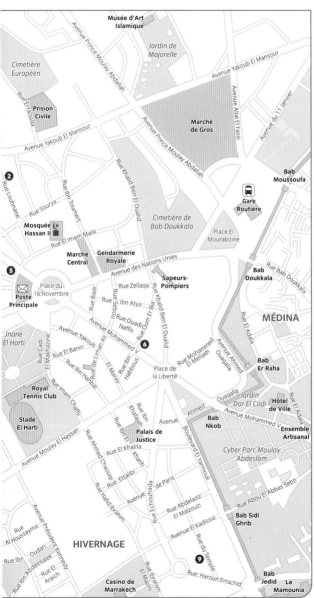

Musée d'Art Islamique
Jardin de Majorelle
Cimetière Européen
Avenue Prince Moulay Abdallah
Avenue Yakoub El Mansour
Rue Errauda
Prison Civile
Avenue du 11 Janvier
Avenue Allal El Fassi
Avenue Yakoub El Mansour
Marché de Gros
❷
Rue Loubnane
Rue Ibn Toumert
Rue Sourya
Bab Moussoufa
Rue Khalid Ben El Ouald
Avenue Prince Moulay Abdallah
Gare Routière
Mosquée Hassan II
Rue El Imam Malik
Cimetière de Bab Doukkala
Place El Mourabitine
❺
Poste Principale
Marché Central
Gendarmerie Royale
Place du 16 Novembre
Avenue des Nations Unies
Bab Doukkala
Rue Bab Doukkala
Rue Zellaqa
Sapeurs-Pompiers
Rue El Adala
MÉDINA
Rue Badr
Rue Ibn Atya
Rue Sebou
Rue Khalid Ben El Ouald
Jnane El Harti
Avenue Yakoub
Rue Ouadi Naffis
Rue Oum El
❻
Rue Mohammed El Mellakh
Avenue Ahmed Ouaqala
Bab Er Raha
Rue Cadi
Rue El Makhzine
Rue El Banin
Avenue Mohammed V
Rue de Liman Ali
Rue El Marini
Rue Ben Habbous
Place de la Liberté
Ouaqala
Jardin Dar El Cadi
Hôtel de Ville
Rue El Adala
Royal Tennis Club
Rue Imam Chafii
Rue Ibn El Harbal
Ahmed
Avenue Mohammed V
Ensemble Artisanal
Stade El Harti
Rue Ibn Khallah
Bab Nkob
Cyber Parc Moulay Abdeslam
Avenue Moulay El Hassan
Rue Ibn El
Avenue
Boulevard El Yarmouk
Rue Ahmed Chaoui
Palais de Justice
Rue El Khalifa
Rue El Khatib
Rue Ettalibi
Rue Halid Ibrahim
Avenue
Rue Echouhada
de Paris
Rue Abdelaziz El Malzouzi
Bab Sidi Ghrib
Rue
Al Houssaymma
Avenue Président Kennedy
Rue Ibn Abdelmalek
Rue Ibn Oudari
Rue El Araich
HIVERNAGE
Avenue El Kadissia
Rue du Temple
Rue Ibrahim El Mazini
❾
Casino de Marrakech
Rue Haroun Errachid
Bab Jedid
La Mamounia

Marrakech **Dining A to Z**

★★ Al Fassia VILLE NOUVELLE *MOROCCAN* Quality as well as quantity is what makes this female-run restaurant one of Marrakech's best. Bring an enormous appetite for slow cooked lamb, crisp pigeon *pastilla*, or chicken tagine with caramelized pumpkin—it's all delicious. *55 Boulevard Zerktouni.* ☎ *0524-43-40-60. Entrees 95–140dh. AE, MC, V. Lunch and dinner daily. Map p 108.*

★ Amanjena Thai PALMERAIE *INTERNATIONAL* A palatial hideaway fringed by olives and palms, this renowned Thai-Spanish restaurant is well worth the taxi ride out of town. Bangkok chef Khun Narongsak's seasonally changing menu might include sea bass in spicy red curry sauce and stir-fried king prawn. Alternatively, try Xavier Arnaud Gili's flavorsome tapas and paellas. Dine on a terrace overlooking the pool and golf course. *Route de Ouarzazate 12km.* ☎ *0524-40-33-53. Entress 180–400dh. AE, MC, V. Lunch and dinner daily. Map p 106.*

kids Aqua JEMAA EL FNA, SOUKS & MOUASSINE *PIZZA* Star-shaped lanterns illuminate the indigo ceiling at this hip pizzeria. Young waiters bring good-value pizza, tagines, and salads to the terrace, which affords superb views over the action on Jemaa el Fna below. Ask for a table at the front. *68 Place Jemaa el Fna.* ☎ *0524-38-13-24. Snacks and entrees 25–60dh. No credit cards. Lunch and dinner daily. Map p 106.*

Beyrouth VILLE NOUVELLE *LEBANESE* When tagine fatigue kicks in, this informal Middle Eastern restaurant makes a refreshing change. Herbs and spices shine through in dishes such as Lebanese *tabbouleh* salad, crisp falafel, and *mouhalabieh* (milk flan infused with orange

A strikingly lit alcove at Café Arabe.

Star-shaped lanterns illuminate Aqua pizzeria.

water). The mezze plates are great for sharing. *9 Rue Loubnane* ☎ *0524-42-35-25. Entrees 80–150dh. Lunch and dinner daily. MC, V. Map p 108.*

Café Arabe JEMAA EL FNA, SOUKS & MOUASSINE *ITALIAN* Luca from Milan runs this Mediterranean-style café with midday snacks served in the serene courtyard. The vibe is more upbeat after dark when flavors such as veal in white-wine sauce and octopus salad are served in the crimson-walled restaurant. Afterwards, head up to the terrace for decadent cocktails (see p 124). *184 Rue Mouassine.* ☎ *0524-42-97-28. www.cafearabe.com. Entrees 120–190dh. AE, MC, V. Lunch and dinner daily. Map p 106.*

★ **Casa Lalla** KASBAH & AROUND *FRENCH* Keep your eyes open for the sign pointing down a narrow alley to this chic, romantic riad with room for just 18 diners. Here French chef, Pierre Olivier, cooks inventive, market-fresh menus with seasonal-inspired delicacies such as sesame-encrusted tuna and succulent

steaks with cardamom. Take a seat in the candle-lit courtyard among the citrus fruit trees. *16 Derb Jamaa, Riad Zitoun el-Kedim.* ☎ *0524-42-97-57. www.casalalla.com. Tasting menu 400dh. MC, V. Dinner Mon–Sat. Map p 105.*

kids Catanzaro VILLE NOUVELLE *ITALIAN* When Marrakchis get cravings for thin-crust pizza from a wood oven they head to this family-run Italian restaurant in Guéliz, where the decor is rustic and the ambience buzzy. Grilled meats, pasta dishes, and classic desserts such as tiramisu also feature on the menu. *42 Rue Tariq Ibn Ziad.* ☎ *0524-43-37-31. Pizza 50–65dh. No credit cards. Lunch and dinner daily. Map p 108.*

Chez Bahia KASBAH & AROUND *MOROCCAN* You can't miss this place with its rows of tagines steaming away out front. Locals and all-comers pile in for inexpensive lunches. *206 Riad Zitoun el-Kedim.* ☎ *0661-31-78-20. Entrees 25–40dh. No credit cards. Lunch and dinner daily. Map p 105.*

For intimate riad dining, book a table at Casa Lalla.

Feast on French cuisine at classic brasserie Chez Pascal.

★ **Chez Chegrouni** JEMAA EL FNA, SOUKS & MOUASSINE *MOROCCAN* Simple, tasty Moroccan fare and big-top views of the circus antics on Jemaa el Fna are on the menu at affable Chegrouni. Scribble down your order for thick *harira* (lentil and chickpea) soup, nicely spiced tagines, or vegetarian couscous. *4-6 Place Jemaa el Fna. No phone. Entrees 40–60dh. Lunch and dinner daily. No credit cards. Map p 106.*

★ **Chez Pascal** VILLE NOUVELLE *FRENCH* Take an eccentric French chef with a passion for fresh produce and seasonal flavors and you know tables will soon be at a premium. Bedecked with vintage curios and candelabras, this brasserie has a Paris-worthy menu with dishes such as Gabon-style crab and butter-tender lamb medallions, followed by gooey chocolate fondant. *32 Boulevard Zerktouni.* ☎ *0524-44-72-15. www.chezpascal-marrakech.com.*

Entrees 90–160dh. MC, V. Lunch and dinner daily. Map p 108.

Dar Belkabir JEMAA EL FNA, SOUKS & MOUASSINE *MOROCCAN* Fuchsia-purple walls, cushioned nooks, and filigree lanterns give this relaxed restaurant a glamorous twist. The fragrant Moroccan salads are among the best I've ever tried and the perfect prologue to a tangy chicken tagine with preserved lemons. Nice touch: the bill is presented in a mini treasure chest. Mercifully, it's never a fortune. *12 Place Jemaa el Fna.* ☎ *0661-15-85-36. Entrees 60–120dh. MC, V. Lunch and dinner daily. Map p 106.*

★ **Dar Donab** JEMAA EL FNA, SOUKS & MOUASSINE *MOROCCAN* In-the-know Marrakchis and celebrities whisper quietly about this ornate retreat next to Dar el Bacha Palace. Through fruit tree-shaded gardens, you reach a domed restaurant warmed by an open fire. Dress up to feast like Moroccan royalty on classics such as lamb *tanjia* with almonds. *53 Rue Dar el-Bacha, Bab Doukkala.* ☎ *0524-44-18-97. www.dardonab.com. Entrees 95–200dh. MC, V. Lunch and dinner daily. Map p 106.*

★ **Dar Marjana** SOUKS & MOUASSINE *MOROCCAN* Lanterns light the passage to this venerable riad, where aperitifs are served in the cypress-fringed patio. Traditionally attired waiters then usher diners across to the salon for dish after irresistible dish of salads, *pastillas*, and tagines. Stay for live Moroccan music and belly dancing where audience participation is part of the fun. *15 Derb Sidi Ali Tair, Bab Doukkala.* ☎ *0524-38-51-10. Five-course menu including drinks 726dh. MC, V. Dinner Wed–Mon. Map p 106.*

Dar Moha JEMAA EL FNA, SOUKS & MOUASSINE *MOROCCAN* Gold drapes and chandeliers adorn this opulent 19th-century riad. The menu is a fixed-priced feast of dishes such as flaky lobster *pastilla* with coriander jus and melon couscous with thyme honey. The salons can feel stuffy in summer, so ask for a table in the courtyard, where Gnaoua musicians serenade diners under the banana fronds. Reservations essential. *81 Rue Dar el-Bacha.* ☎ *0524-38-62-64. www.darmoha. ma. Tasting menu lunch 220dh, dinner 530dh. AE, MC, V. Lunch and dinner daily. Map p 106.*

★ **Dar Yacout** JEMAA EL FNA, SOUKS & MOUASSINE *MOROCCAN* Revamped by imaginative American architect Bill Willis, this palatial riad is pure fantasy with its soaring arches, chandeliers, and bathrooms with *tadelakt* (polished plaster) fireplaces. Brace yourself for a marathon of too-good-to-leave salads, tagines, lamb, couscous, and pastries. Yacout draws celebrities, royals, and affluent locals so reservations can be difficult to organize. Book well ahead. *79 Derb Sidi Ahmed Soussi.* ☎ *0524-38-29-29. Set menu including aperitif and wine 700dh. AE, MC, V. Dinner Tues–Sun. Map p 106.*

★ **Dar Zellij** SOUKS & MOUASSINE *MOROCCAN* Ideal for intimate tête-à-têtes, this 17th-century riad is hidden in the Sidi Ben Slimane neighborhood in the northern medina. Lanterns illuminate graceful arches and tables sprinkled with rose petals in the courtyard, where

You say Tagine, I say Tanjia

Beghrir: Light, spongy Moroccan pancakes served with butter and honey; a staple on every riad breakfast table.

Bisara: Rich bean soup drizzled with olive oil.

Briouatte: Filo pastry pocket with sweet or savory filling.

Cornes de Gazelle: Horn-shaped, almond paste-filled cookies.

Harira: Thick lentil and garbanzo bean (chickpea) soup flavored with herbs and spices; traditionally eaten to break fasting during Ramadan.

Kefta: Lamb or beef meatballs seasoned with Moroccan spices.

Mechoui: Lamb slow-roasted on a spit or over a charcoal fire and infused with cumin and lemon; served with bread and olives.

Pastilla: Sweet flaky pigeon or chicken pie. The dessert version is with cream and almonds.

Tagine: Tender chicken or lamb casserole, slow-cooked over charcoal in a glazed earthenware pot with a conical lit; additions include preserved lemons, olives, prunes, and almonds.

Tanjia Succulent jugged beef or lamb, slow-braised in a clay pot and infused with saffron, cumin, and garlic.

Tagine.

Moroccan salads, lamb tagines with figs, and crispy *pastillas* are brought to the table. *1 Kssour Sidi Ben Slimane.* ☎ *0524-38-26-27. Tasting menu 600dh. MC, V. Lunch Sat and Sun, dinner Wed–Mon. Map p 106.*

★ Grand Café de la Poste

VILLE NOUVELLE *FRENCH* Be catapulted back to the colonial 1920s at this Marrakchi institution, a picture of French grandeur with its high ceilings, sweeping marble staircase, and terrace. By night, the candlelit restaurant is an elegant setting for dishes such as monkfish carpaccio and tender lamb shank, washed down with a nice glass of *vin rouge*. *Avenue Imam Malik cnr Boulevard el-Mansour Eddahbi.* ☎ *0524-43-30-38. Entrees 115–195dh. Lunch and dinner daily. AE, MC, V. Map p 108.*

★ Jardins de la Medina

KASBAH & AROUND *INTERNATIONAL* Relax in a courtyard perfumed by jacaranda trees at this Kasbah hideaway. The menu blends Moroccan with international flavors. Try signatures such as Atlantic oysters followed by monkfish tagine with argan oil or a coconutty Thai beef curry. Sweet-toothed diners rave

Dine alfresco at La Sultana.

about the pumpkin soufflé. Sunday brunch served by the pool is a highlight. *21 Derb Chtouka.* ☎ *0524-38-18-51. www.lesjardinsdelamedina. com. Entrees 120–220dh. MC, V. Lunch and dinner daily. Map p 105.*

Katsura VILLE NOUVELLE *SUSHI* Marrakchi hipsters nibble sushi here before shimmying over to Diamant Noir (p 126) or African Chic (p 133) next door. Thai curries and wok dishes can be ordered mild, medium, or spicy. The bamboo, monochrome prints, glass walls, and funky orange alcoves are an adventure in pan-Asian cool. *Rue Oum Errabia.* ☎ *0524-43-43-58. Entrees 70–100dh. AE, MC, V. Lunch and dinner Tues–Sun. Map p 108.*

★ Kechmara

VILLE NOUVELLE *INTERNATIONAL* Glass walls, spindly lights, and molded chairs—retro Kechmara (a word play on Marrakech) is one of Guéliz's trendiest haunts. Go for light bites such as tapas or well-prepared pasta, as you mull over the latest contemporary art exhibition. As the night wears on, the vibe becomes upbeat with live music and DJs (p 124). *3 Rue de la Liberté.* ☎ *0524-43-43-58. www. kechmara.com. Entrees 90–170dh. MC, V. Lunch and dinner Mon–Sat. Map p 108.*

★ L'Abyssin

PALMERAIE *INTERNATIONAL* Like a mirage in the date palm oasis of La Palmeraie, Palais Rhoul's slinky restaurant centers on a Zen-style garden with water features, candles, and white Egyptian cotton tents. Palate-awakening starters such as zucchini (courgette)-mint soup are followed by mains such as fruity duck breast with blackberry sauce. Reservations recommended. *Palais Rhoul, Route de Fès 6 km.* ☎ *0524-32-85-84. www.restaurant-labyssin.com. Entrees 150–180dh. MC, V. Dinner Wed–Mon. Map p 106.*

L'Avenue VILLE NOUVELLE *INTERNATIONAL* Decked out with striking chandeliers, shimmering fabrics, and potted palms, this chic Guéliz brasserie attracts a well dressed crowd. Tables draped in white linen set the scene for flavors such as lemon-coconut gambas (prawn or shrimp) soup, signature rib eye steaks, and chocolate melting cake. *Cnr Route de Targa and Rue du Capitaine Arrigui.* ☎ *0524-45-89-01. Entrees 120–230dh. MC, V. Lunch and dinner daily. Map p 108.*

★★★ La Maison Arabe JEMAA EL FNA, SOUKS & MOUASSINE *MOROCCAN* Since the 1940s, La Maison Arabe has stayed true to its promise of authentic Moroccan cuisine and polished service. Dishes such as melt-in-your-mouth *pastillas*, and flavorsome lamb *tanjia* strike a perfect balance. An open fire crackles and Andalusian musicians strum in the dining room. *1 Derb Assehbe, Bab Doukkala.* ☎ *0524-38-70-10. www.lamaison arabe.com. Set menu 400dh. AE, MC, V. Dinner daily. Map p 106.*

★★★ La Sultana KASBAH & AROUND *MOROCCAN* La Sultana offers one of the most bewitching settings in Marrakech, with crisp white linen, live lute music, and service as polished as the golden platters you eat from. Full-bodied Siroua wines pair nicely with succulent beef *tanjia* braised in a clay pot and honey-glazed leg of lamb. *403 Rue de la Kasbah.* ☎ *0524-38-80-08. Entrees 140–220dh. AE, MC, V. Lunch and dinner daily. Map p 105.*

★ La Table du Marché VILLE NOUVELLE *FRENCH* French chef Christophe Leroy puts a Moroccan spin on the market-fresh flavors of Saint-Tropez at his sleek Hivernage restaurant. Enticing whiffs of garlic and grilled fish lure foodies into the elegant, flower-bedecked dining

Refined surrounds at La Maison Arabe's restaurant.

room, where you might start with crunchy salade Niçoise, and then move on to bouillabaisse-style monkfish tagine. *4 Rue du Temple.* ☎ *0524-42-41-00. www.christophe-leroy.com. Entrees 160–210dh. AE, MC, V. Lunch and dinner daily. Map p 108.*

La Taverne VILLE NOUVELLE *MOROCCAN* A blast from the colonial past, La Taverne has dapper waiters in dickie bows and one of Marrakech's prettiest gardens, strewn with ivy, roses, and trees lit by moon-and-star lanterns. Pull up a chair by the fountain to dine on Franco-Moroccan staples from tagines to tender veal. *22 Boulevard Zerktouni.* ☎ *0524-44-61-26. Entrees 70–110dh. MC, V. Lunch and dinner daily. Map p 108.*

★ La Trattoria di Giancarlo VILLE NOUVELLE *ITALIAN* Red brick arcades frame a lantern-lit pool at this authentic trattoria. Start

Savor local cuisine and Jemaa views at Le Marrakchi.

with smoked trout from the Atlas Mountains, followed by beef medallions with parmesan, washed down with a full-bodied Meknès merlot. There's a fireplace for chilly winter evenings. *179 Rue Mohammed el Bekal.* ☎ *0524-43-26-21. Entrees 120–150dh. AE, MC, V. Dinner daily. Map p 108.*

★★★ **Le Bis** VILLE NOUVELLE *FRENCH* Stark and stylish describe the space and fare at Laurent Bocca's Guéliz restaurant. The affordable French menu focuses on light, fresh ingredients, including crisp salads, fish, and creative accompaniments such as pumpkin risotto. An outdoor patio makes for romantic dining, and inside, a palette of white, black, and gray is accented by an entire wall of ornamental plaster. *6–7 Rue Sakia el Hamra, Semlalia.* ☎ *0524-44-66-34. Entrees 140–190dh. MC, V. Lunch and dinner Mon–Sat. Map p 108.*

★ **Le Blokk** PALMERAIE *INTERNATIONAL* Be transported back to 1960s Manhattan at this glamorous monochrome lounge, sporting leather walls and photos of jazz legends. Jazz singers croon on the stage as a stylish crowd tucks into grilled langoustine and the recommended Rossini beef with *foie gras. Ennakhlil, Propriété Farah, La Palmeraie.* ☎ *0674-33-43-34. www. leblokk.com. Entrees 75–190dh. DC, MC, V. Dinner daily. Map p 108.*

★★ **Le Crystal** VILLE NOUVELLE *FRENCH* Cylindrical lanterns cast a soft glow on bare wood floors and cream walls at colonial-chic Le Crystal, part of mega club Pacha (p 126). Foodies come for the Michelin-starred Pourcel brothers' Italian-infused flavors such as creamy *gambas*-mascarpone risotto and shellfish tagliatelle. *Zone Hôtelière de l'Aguedal, Boulevard Mohammed VI.* ☎ *0524-38-84-00. Entrees 180–290dh. AE, MC, V. Lunch and dinner daily. Map p 108.*

Le Jacaranda VILLE NOUVELLE
FRENCH Philippe Coustal mans the
stove at this art-slung French bistro,
going strong since 1950. Cream *tadelakt* walls and an open fire create a
warm, intimate atmosphere for signatures such as garlicky *escargots*,
foie gras, and butter-soft filet
mignon with Roquefort. *32 Boulevard Zerktouni.* ☎ *0524-44-72-15.
Entrees 140–200dh. AE, MC, V.
Lunch and dinner daily. Map p 108.*

★★ **Le Marrakchi** JEMAA EL FNA,
SOUKS & MOUASSINE *MOROCCAN*
Dark and seductive, Le Marrakchi
is a kind of 21st-century Berber
tent, with incredible wrap-around
windows overlooking Jemaa el
Fna. The 'greatest hits' menu stars
classics such as *tanjia. 52 Jemaa
el Fna.* ☎ *0524-44-33-77. Entrees
100–170dh; set menu 260dh.
MC, V. Lunch and dinner daily.
Map p 106.*

★★ **Le Tobsil** JEMAA EL FNA,
SOUKS & MOUASSINE *FRENCH*
Buried deep in the medina, this riad
is lauded for its waistline-expanding
diffa (feast) of vegetarian meze, flaky
pastillas, tagines, couscous, fruit,
and pastries, served up in a romantic candle-lit setting. Reservations
recommended. *22 Derb Abdellah
Ben Hessaïen, Bab Ksour.* ☎ *0524-
44-40-52. Set menu 600dh. MC, V.
Dinner Wed–Mon. Map p 106.*

★★ **Lotus Privilege** JEMAA EL
FNA, SOUKS & MOUASSINE *MOROC-
CAN* Inventive Moroccan cuisine
served in an eclectic, imperial-style
space. The menu changes every
three months, and offers diners a
six-course set menu that may
include quail tagine, burbot *pastilla*,
and salmon *briouattes. 9 Derb Sidi
Ali ben Hamdouch, Bab Doukkala.*
☎ *0524-38-73-18. Set menu 500dh.
AE, MC, V. Dinner daily. Map p 106.*

★ **Narwama** JEMAA EL FNA,
SOUKS & MOUASSINE *THAI* Take a

*Glimpse the storks on the Kasbah's walls
from Nid' Cigogne.*

palatial 19th-century riad, add
lounge beats, top with a Moroccan-
Thai menu, and you have Narwama.
Marrakchi trendies sip mint mojitos
and gaze up to cedar ceilings, monumental chandeliers, and a fountain
of flames, as waiters bring authenti-
cally spicy Thai curries to the table.
30 Rue Koutoubia. ☎ *0524-44-08-
44. Entrees 115–225dh. MC, V. Dinner daily. Map p 106.*

kids Nid' Cigogne KASBAH &
AROUND *MOROCCAN* Bid the
storks *bonsoir* at this unpretentious
place, perched above the Kasbah
and with close-ups of the nests dot-
ting the battlements of the Saâdian
Tombs. Dusk is primetime viewing
on the fairy-light filled terrace. The
pastillas and tagines are average,
but the vistas are anything but.
60 Place des Tombeaux Saâdians.
☎ *0524-38-20-92. Entrees 40–60dh.
Lunch and dinner daily. No credit
cards. Map p 105.*

Terrasses de l'Alhambra
JEMAA EL FNA, SOUKS & MOUASS-
INE *MOROCCAN* Stylish and modern with deep wine-red walls and a
tent-like ceiling, this lively haunt has

Dine on elegant French-Moroccan cuisine at Villa Flore.

a heated terrace with views across Jemaa el Fna. Yet prices remain low for salads, pizzas, and cream-topped fruit sundaes. The Alhambra salad with hummus and black olives is recommended. *Place Jemaa el Fna.* ☎ *0524-42-75-70. Entrees 65–130dh. Lunch and dinner daily. No credit cards. Map p 106.*

★★★ **Villa Flore** JEMAA EL FNA, SOUKS & MOUASSINE *FRENCH*

This unsung riad gem boasts an effortlessly chic ambience and a passion for market fresh produce. Whether you choose the tranquil patio or the classy salon, the spider crab bisque or the saffron-infused couscous, you won't be disappointed. See also p 16. *4 Derb Azzouz.* ☎ *0524-39-17-00. Entrees 90–160dh. MC, V. Lunch and dinner daily. Map p 106.* ●

Brains, Snails & Gastro Tales

At dusk, white-aproned chefs set up makeshift eateries on Jemaa el Fna, their flaming grills sending wisps of smoke into the night sky. Dine at least once at these open-air food stands; if not for the food, for the electric atmosphere. Pick the busiest stall with the freshest produce, and choose from the buffet (make sure you get only what you order). Feeling daring? How about a bowl of snails, brains, or mutton head and fries? Despite hygiene horror stories, stalls here are regulated and mostly clean. Tummy troubles are usually water related, and so drink the bottled stuff and bring your own cutlery.

7 The Best **Nightlife**

Nightlife Best Bets

Best Clubbing Temple
★★★ Pacha, *Zone Hôtelière de l'Aguedal, Avenue Mohammed VI* (p 126)

Best Place to Rock the Kasbah
★★ Kosybar, *47 Place des Ferblantiers* (p 124)

Best Souk Terrace
★ Terrasse des Épices, *15 Souk Cherifia* (p 125)

Best Belly Dancing
★★★ Le Comptoir Darna, *37 Avenue Echouhada* (p 128)

Best Lounge Bar
★ Café Extrablatt, *Cnr Avenue Echouhada and Rue Alquadissia. 61* (p 124)

Best Sunbathe and Party
★ La Plage Rouge, *Route de l'Ourika 10km* (p 128)

Best High-Octane Club
★★ Théâtro, *Es Saadi Gardens & Resort, Avenue El Quadissia* (p 127)

Best Garden Party
★ Bô-Zin, *Route de l'Ourika 3.5km* (p 127)

Best Rooftop Lounging
Amentis, *Cnr Avenue Echouhada and Rue Alkadissia* (p 127)

Best Avant-Garde Café
Kechmara, *3 Rue de la Liberté* (p 124)

Best Jemaa el Fna Balcony
Grand Balcon du Café Glacier, *Jemaa el Fna* (p 124)

Best Club for People-Watching
New Feeling, *Palmeraie Golf Palace, Palmeraie* (p 126)

Best Swift Medina Beer
Grand Hotel Tazi, *Cnr Rue Bab Agnaou and Avenue el-Mouahidine* (p 124)

Best Cuba Feeling
Montecristo, *20 Rue Ibn Aicha* (p 126)

Best Oriental Beats
★ Diamant Noir, *Hotel Marrakech, Avenue Mohammed V* (p 126)

Best 1001 Nights Supper Club
★ Le Tanjia, *14 Derb Jdid* (p 128)

The stylish bar of Kosybar.

Medina Nightlife

Café Arabe **1**
Grand Balcon du Café Glacier **2**
Grand Hotel Tazi **3**
Kosybar **4**
Le Tanjia **5**
Terrasse des Épices **6**

Bab Taghzout
Rue Bab Taghzout
Derb El Akkari
Rue Bin
Hôpital El Antáki
Rue Assouil Lamaássar
Place El Antaki
Rue Bab El Khemis
Bine Ladrassi
Arset El Mellak
Rue Ank Jemel
Rue Diour Saboun
ASSOUEL
EL MOUKEF
Rue El Fakhar
RIAD EL AROUS
Rue Riad El Arous
Fontaine Chrob Ou Chouf
HART ES-SOURA
Place du Moukef
ARSET BEN CHEBLI
Médersa Ben Youssef
Rue de Souk d' Fassis
Rue Bab Doukkala
Rue Dar El Bacha
Mosquée Ben Youssef
Mosquée Eloussta
Rue Essebtiye
Mosquée Bab Doukkala
Dar El Glaoui
Koubba Ba'adyin
Musée de Marrakech
Mosquée Azabzed
R'MILA
MOUASSINE
Derb Sidi Ishak
Mosquée Mouassine
Mosquée Sidi Ishak
Zaouia Sidi Ben Salah
Rue Jebel Lakhdar
Rue Fatima Zohra
Rue Sidi El Yamami
EL KSOUR
Place Rahba Kedima
AZBEZT
BEN SALAH
Rue El Ksour
Souk Smarine
SOUKS
DERB DABACHI
Rue El Kebir
Ensemble Artisanal
Rue Joel Lakhdar
Avenue Mohammed V
Zaouia Sidi Moulay El Ksour
Souk Quessabine
Rue Dabachi
Place Bab Fteuh
MÉDINA
Trek El Koutoubia
R. Kennaria
Place Jemaa El Fna
DOUAR GRAOUA
Rue Douar Graoua
Place Foucauld
Koubba de Lalla Zohra
Consulat de France
Rue Ben Marine
Rue de Bab Agnaou
Hôpital Arset El Mokha
Rue Riad Zitoun El Kedim
Palais Moulay Idriss
Rue Ibn Khaldoun
Rue Moulay Ismaïl
Musée Dar Si Said
Mosquée de la Koutoubia
Jardins de la Koutoubia
Rue Bab Agnaou
Maison Tiskiouine
Avenue Houmman El Fetouaki
Pl. Youssef Tachfine
Rue Lalla Rkia
Palais de la Bahia
Hôtel La Mamounia
Rue Sidi Mimoun
Rue Oqba Ben Nafia
Avenue Houmman El Fetouaki
SIDI MIMOUN
Rue Ibn Rachid
Marché Couvert
Synagogue Lazama
ARSET EL MAÄCH
Mosquée de la Kasbah
Place des Ferblantiers
MELLAH
Hôpital Ibn Zohr
Bâb Er Rob
Palais El Badi
Zaouia Sidi Es Soheili
Bab Agnaou
Tombeaux Saadiens
Rue de la Kasbah
KSIBET
Cimetière Sidi Es Souheili
Centre Artisanal

P Police Station
⊠ Post Office
✚ Hospital

0 .... 1/4 mi
0 .... 0.25 km

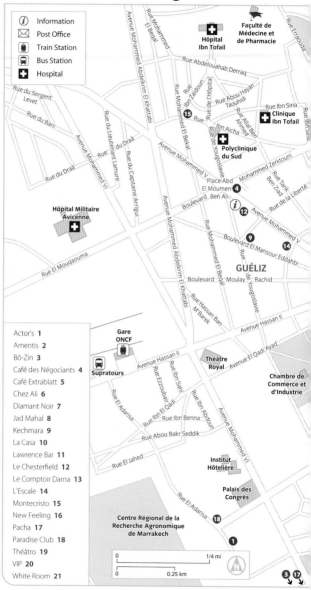

(i) Information
⊠ Post Office
🚉 Train Station
🚌 Bus Station
✚ Hospital

Actor's **1**
Amentis **2**
Bô-Zin **3**
Café des Négociants **4**
Café Extrablatt **5**
Chez Ali **6**
Diamant Noir **7**
Jad Mahal **8**
Kechmara **9**
La Casa **10**
Lawrence Bar **11**
Le Chesterfield **12**
Le Comptoir Darna **13**
L'Escale **14**
Montecristo **15**
New Feeling **16**
Pacha **17**
Paradise Club **18**
Théâtro **19**
VIP **20**
White Room **21**

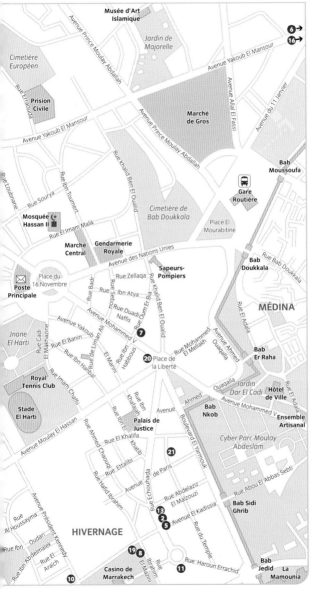

Marrakech Nightlife A to Z

Bars, Cafés & Lounges

Café Arabe MEDINA   Ideal for souk-side imbibing, this sleek café-lounge is a great spot to watch the sun set over the medina. Nab a sofa on the romantic, lantern-lit terrace for chill-out tunes and an aperitif. The mood is relaxed and the views are enchanting. *184 Rue el-Mouassine.* ☎ *0524-42-97-28. www.cafe arabe.com. Map p 121.*

Café des Négociants VILLE NOUVELLE   This buzzy French-style café is perennially popular for its pavement terrace. Pull up a chair to people-watch and converse over an orange juice or mint tea. No alcohol is served. *Place Abdelmoumen Ben Ali, off Avenue Mohammed V.* ☎ *0524-43-57-82. Map p 122.*

★ **Café Extrablatt** VILLE NOU-VELLE   More than Teutonic in name, this slick lounge bar sports a streamlined German design with caramel leather sofas, glass walls, and spiral chrome lights. Yet the grown-up vibe and international menu wouldn't be out of place in New York City. Hipsters come here to drink, converse, and enjoy lounge grooves till 3am. *Cnr Avenue Echou-hada and Rue Alquadissia.* ☎ *0524-43-50-43. www.extrablatt-marrakech.com. Map p 122.*

Grand Balcon du Café Glacier MEDINA   Service isn't great here and drinks magically change price with the mood of the bartender, but wow what a view! Snap-happy visitors flock to the roof terrace for a balcony over the dusk mayhem on Jemaa el Fna against the photogenic backdrop of the illuminated Koutoubia. *Jemaa el Fna* ☎ *0524-44-21-93. Map p 121.*

Grand Hotel Tazi MEDINA   This hotel bar may have the ambience of a railway station waiting room, but its comparatively cheap beer (25dh) and handy location near Jemaa el Fna ensure its perennial popularity. The crowd is a mix of locals and tourists. *Cnr Rue Bab Agnaou and Avenue el-Mouahidine.* ☎ *0524-44-27-87. Map p 121.*

Kechmara VILLE NOUVELLE   Über-cool 'Kech', as regulars call it, is an avant-garde café-lounge with rotating art exhibitions and a tasty menu (p 114). The Foltran brothers' razor-sharp eye for design shows in the minimalist snow-white and chrome interior. Come for the jazzy music, stiff drinks on the terrace, and Wednesday night gigs at 7pm. *See p 114. Map p 122.*

★★ **Kosybar** MEDINA   This hip lounge-restaurant (see also p 13) boasts a stunning roof terrace where you come eye-to-eye with Kasbah's resident storks. It's a bewitching place to watch sunset over a glass of full-bodied Moroccan

Unwind over drinks at Café Extrablatt.

Kechmara is a cool haunt for sipping cocktails and conversing.

wine. Stay for intimate chats by the fire in the lounge downstairs and, at the weekend, superb live jazz and soul music. *47 Place des Ferblantiers.* ☎ *0524-38-03-24-72. Map p 121.*

La Casa VILLE NOUVELLE   The decor is nouveau Berber chic, the crowd an image-conscious mix of Marrakchis and tourists, and the music a fusion of hot Latino and RnB at this hotel bar. Come for tapas and stay for salsa. A 2-for-1 happy hour from 7pm to 10pm fuels the party. *Hotel El Andalous, Avenue Président Kennedy.* ☎ *0524-44-82-26. Map p 122.*

Lawrence Bar VILLE NOUVELLE A jazz pianist creates an intimate atmosphere in this softly-lit hotel bar, with comfortable armchairs for conversing and quaffing. The terrace is inviting on warm evenings. *Sofitel Marrakech, Rue Harroun Errachid.* ☎ *0524-42-56-00. Map p 122.*

Le Chesterfield VILLE NOUVELLE This pseudo-English pub is nowhere near as raucous as a British watering hole. Still, the dimly lit, wood-paneled bar draws locals and all-comers with draft beer, cozy

armchairs, and a lantern-lit terrace for summertime drinking. *Hotel Nassim, 115 Avenue Mohammed V.* ☎ *0524-44-64-01. Map p 122.*

L'Escale VILLE NOUVELLE   This rowdy drinking den is always full of (mostly male) Marrakchis. It's a real local joint with cheap beer, a lively buzz, tasty bar snacks (particularly the grilled chicken), and good people-watching on the pavement terrace. *Rue Mauritanie. No phone. Map p 122.*

★ **Terrasse des Épices** MEDINA Hidden away in the souks, this is one of my favorite roof terraces for mint tea at sundown. Charcoal-hued walls, wicker lanterns, and Moroccan *bhous* (alcoves) with scatter cushions set the scene for relaxed drinks with fabulous views. *See p 53. Map p 121.*

Clubs

Actor's VILLE NOUVELLE   Actor's is like stepping into a black-and-white B movie, with shots of pouting divas on the walls, and DJs working the decks. Nightly soirées range from Cuban salsa and funky disco to ladies' night on a Wednesday. It's

Superstar DJs entertain the crowds at Marrakech's megaclub, Pacha.

busy at the weekend but less so on weekdays. *Hotel Medina, Avenue Mohammed VI.* ☎ *0524-33-99-99. www.actorsmarrakech.com. Cover 150dh. Map p 122.*

Diamant Noir VILLE NOUVELLE
Sure it's a bit of a dive, but this rough diamond has the right ingredients for a fun night out: groovy house, *raï* (Algerian folk music), and oriental beats; voyeuristic mirrors and balconies overlooking the dance floor; and an easy-going attitude. A word of warning for men: the girls fluttering their lashes at the upstairs bar may just have their eyes on your wallet. *Hotel Marrakech, Avenue Mohammed V.* ☎ *0524-43-43-51. Cover 100–150dh. Map p 122.*

Montecristo VILLE NOUVELLE
Fashionistas and, it must be said, the odd call girl prop up the bar at this lounge-club hybrid. Cuba is the theme downstairs, where soul and funk bands play to an enthusiastic cigar-smoking crowd. More appealing still is the candlelit roof terrace for drinks under the stars. The party kicks off after 11pm. *20 Rue Ibn Aicha.* ☎ *0524-43-90-31. Map p 122.*

New Feeling VILLE NOUVELLE
A 100dh taxi ride out of town in the Palmeraie, this hot-spot is a magnet for affluent Moroccans. The decor is slick with curvaceous seating, Pop Art on the walls, and a funky glass bar. Dress up to join shimmying locals on the dance floor or—if you dare—the podium. Get's going after midnight. *Palmeraie Golf Palace, Palmeraie.* ☎ *0524-30-10-10. Cover 200dh. Map p 122.*

★★★ Pacha VILLE NOUVELLE
The mega club that took Ibiza by storm now shakes Marrakech with a cocktail of electro and deep house, plus superstar guest DJs such as Roger Sanchez and David Guetta. Billed as Africa's biggest club and accommodating 3,000, Pacha heaves at the weekend. Come during the day in summer for DJs working the decks and trendies working their tans and hangovers by the swimming pool. *Zone Hôtelière de l'Aguedal, Boulevard Mohammed VI.* ☎ *0524-38-84-00. www.pacha marrakech.com. Cover 100–250dh. Map p 122.*

Paradise Club VILLE NOUVELLE
Lights flash and the dance floor thuds to RnB, hip-hop, and house at this über-glam Guéliz nightclub.

Despite the five-star prices of the drinks, the vibe is attitude-free and the crowd becomes more sociable as the night wears on. Dress to impress the doormen. *Hotel Mansour Eddahbi, Avenue Mohammed VI.* ☎ *0524-33-91-00. Cover 150–200dh. Map p 122.*

★★ **Théâtro** VILLE NOUVELLE Pacha's only serious rival for the Marrakchi clubbing crown is this pulsating venue at Es Saadi (p 141). Hedonists lounge on four-poster beds, sweaty 20-somethings gyrate to techno, house, and RnB on the packed dance floor, and bar staff impress clubbers with Tom Cruise-style cocktail mixing. *Es Saadi Gardens & Resort, Avenue El Quadissia. www.theatromarrakech.com. Cover 150dh. Map p 122.*

VIP VILLE NOUVELLE You can't miss the neon sign announcing this club opposite Diamant Noir. Despite seedy 'call girl' undertones, VIP is worth a look for its oriental cabaret acts, live music, and bass-loaded dance floor pumping out techno. *Place de la Liberté.* ☎ *0524-43-45-69. Cover 100–150dh. Map p 122.*

White Room VILLE NOUVELLE A glamorous crowd frequents this sleek hotel disco, with a compact dance floor and white sofas for lounging and sipping well-mixed cocktails. *Hotel Royal Mirage Deluxe, Rue de Paris.* ☎ *0524-42-54-00. No cover. Map p 122.*

Supper Clubs

Amentis VILLE NOUVELLE Behind the theatrical red curtains lies a decadent scene of illuminated palm columns, scarlet ceilings, and flickering candles. Moroccan fusion food is served, as DJs play oriental lounge grooves and a troupe of dancers keep the vibe upbeat. After dinner, head up to the roof terrace for cocktails and lounging in Berber-style

tents. *Cnr Avenue Echouhada and Rue Alkadissia.* ☎ *0524-43-48-43. www.amentis-marrakech.com. Entrees 150–230dh. Map p 122.*

★ **Bô-Zin** VILLE NOUVELLE You can't help but feel as decadent as the Queen of Sheba lounging beside flickering torches in the lush gardens of Bô-Zin. DJs spin soulful tunes as the glammed-up crowd feast on Thai-style *gambas* (prawn or shrimp) curries and sip cocktails such as the Jungle Jô (vodka, tequila, lime, and ginger) at 110dh a pop. It's worth the expense and the taxi ride at the weekend. *Route de l'Ourika 3.5km.* ☎ *0524-38-80-12. www.bo-zin.com. No cover; entrees 150–390dh. Map p 122.*

Chez Ali VILLE NOUVELLE Sure, it's folksy, touristy, and extravagant, but bring a sense of humor and a childish love of the bizarre and you'll have a fun night at Chez Ali. While diners feast Moroccan-style in *caidals* (canvas tents), Berber horsemen in white robes and turbans ride bareback and perform stunts.

Look out for the distinctive sign to VIP club.

Filigree lanterns cast an enticing glow over Le Tanjia.

Further entertainment is delivered by jugglers, belly dancers, musicians, acrobats, fireworks, and even Aladdin on a flying carpet. *Route de Casablanca, Palmeraie.* ☎ *0524-30-77-30. Set menu including drinks 400dh. Map p 122.*

Jad Mahal VILLE NOUVELLE & AROUND The entertainment at this flamboyant haunt is quite spectacular. Look forward to belly

dancing and fire-breathing displays followed by cocktails in the chandelier-lit bar, where Bruno Cheno and his band bash out jazzy classics. As the night wears on, diners shuffle over to the club to bop till 2am. *10 Rue Haroun Errachid, Fontaine de la Mamounia, Bab Jdid.* ☎ *0524-43-69-84. Entrees 160–260dh. Map p 122.*

★★★ **Le Comptoir Darna** VILLE NOUVELLE & AROUND Hands down Marrakech's best supper club, this Art Deco villa is a pure Arabian Nights fantasy, with fire-whirling dervishes and glittering belly dancers. Head upstairs to the lantern-lit terrace for exotic cocktails, electro beats, and sheesha. Attracts a fashionable clientele. *37 Avenue Echouhada.* ☎ *0524-43-77-02. www.comptoirdarna.com. Map p 122.*

★ **Le Tanjia** MEDINA Experience an Ali Baba's cave of twinkly lanterns at this supper club in the Medina. Enjoy a flavorsome *tanjia* (jugged beef or lamb) and a show of shimmying belly dancers hoping to entice blushing gents up to dance. DJs and hookah pipes await you downstairs after dinner. *14 Derb Jdid.* ☎ *0524-38-38-36. Tasting menu 700dh, entrees 140–180dh. Map p 121.* ●

Beach Party

As chilled as champagne on ice during the day, Marrakech's urban beaches heat up as day spills into night. A short taxi ride from the center, **La Plage Rouge** (Route de l'Ourika 10km; ☎ 0524-37-80-86) is one of Marrakech's slickest and sandiest party hotspots, where revelers bask on loungers under the palms, splash in an 80m-long lagoon-style pool, and shimmy on the beach as DJs spin upbeat anthems. Join the bronzed Marrakchis jet-set for fusion cuisine and clubbing till 1am. Rival **Nikki Beach** (see p 34) draws a chic crowd to the date palm oasis of the Palmeraie. Here cabana beds frame an azure pool, DJs play electro beats, and a supper club revives hungry partygoers.

Arts & Entertainment
Best Bets

Best for **Glitzy Gambling**
★ La Mamounia Casino, *Avenue Bab Jdid (p 133)*

Best **Sunset Circus**
★★★ Jemaa el Fna, *Jemaa el Fna (p 134)*

Best **Blockbuster Movies**
★ Cinéma Le Colisée, *Boulevard Mohammed Zerktouni (p 133)*

Best **Live Latino**
★ African Chic, *6 Rue Oum Errabia (p 133)*

Best **Culture Fix**
★ Institut Français, *Route de Targa (p 134)*

Best **Piano Bar**
La Maison Arabe, *1 Derb Assehbe, Bab Doukkala (p 134);* and Hotel Les Jardins de la Koutoubia, *26 Rue de la Koutoubia (p 134)*

Best for **Weekend Gigs**
★ Kosybar, *47 Place des Ferblantiers (p 134)*

Best **Bollywood Flicks**
Cinéma Eden, *Derb Dabbachi (p 133)*

Best **Theater**
★ Théâtre Royal, *40 Avenue de la France (p 134)*

Best **Pre-Clubbing Poker**
Casino de Marrakech, *Rue Ibrahim el-Mazini (p 133)*

The ritzy Casino de Marrakech at Es Saadi.

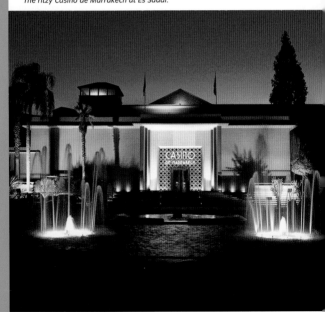

Medina Arts & Entertainment

Cinéma Eden 1
Cinema Mabrouka 2
Hotel Les Jardins de la Koutoubia 3
Jemaa el Fna 4
Kosybar 5
La Maison Arabe 6
La Mamounia Casino 7

Ville Nouvelle Arts & Entertainment

African Chic 1
Casino de Marrakech 2
Cinéma Le Colisée 3
Institut Français 4
Théâtre Royal 5

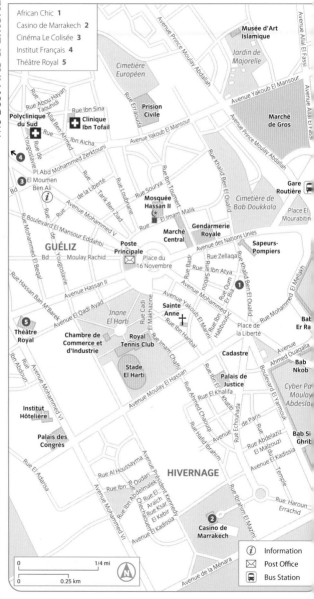

Arts & Entertainment **A to Z**

Casinos

Casino de Marrakech VILLE NOUVELLE Dress to impress the doormen at this plush 1950s casino in the luxurious Es Saadi hotel. The Marrakchi jet-set and well-heeled tourists come here for blackjack and poker before spending their winnings (or drowning their sorrows) in Théâtro (p 127). *Hotel Es Saadi, Rue Ibrahim el-Mazini.* ☎ *0524-44-88-11. www.casinodemarrakech.com. Map p 132.*

★ **La Mamounia Casino** VILLE NOUVELLE Try your hand at poker, blackjack, or roulette (gaming tables 8pm–4am) at Marrakech's glitziest casino. Even if your luck is down, the 1920s setting is sublime. The dress code is strictly no jeans or sneakers. *Hotel La Mamounia, Avenue Bab Jdid.* ☎ *0524-44-45-74. www.grandcasino mamounia.com. Map p 131.*

Film

Cinéma Eden MEDINA It's looking a little tatty with dog-eared Bollywood posters plastering the walls, but that doesn't bother the all-male cinema-goers in the slightest; they are here for kung-fu, gangsters, and gore. Even made-in-Mumbai Hindi romances can be riotous affairs at Eden. Screenings are at 3pm, 6pm, and 9pm. *Derb Dabbachi.* ☎ *0524-63-62-99. Tickets 15dh. Map p 131.*

★ **Cinéma Le Colisée** VILLE NOUVELLE Smarter and less rowdy than medina cinemas, Le Colisée is the principal host of the Marrakech International Film Festival (p 39). Here women can watch flicks in peace without having to dodge male advances and flying peanuts. The cinema shows mostly Hollywood blockbusters dubbed in French. Screenings are at 3pm,

The façade of Cinéma Le Colisée in Ville Nouvelle.

7pm, and 9pm. *Boulevard Moham-med Zerktouni.* ☎ *0524-44-88-93. Tickets 25–35dh. Map p 132.*

Cinema Mabrouka MEDINA Like Eden, this testosterone-filled cinema can be a lot of fun (unless you're a woman alone). Housed in a splendid old building, Mabrouka is loud, popular, and central. Expect a line-up of Hong Kong action flicks and Hindi comedies. Screenings are in Arabic and French. *Rue Bab Agnaou.* ☎ *0524-44-33-03. Tickets 15–25dh. Map p 131.*

Live Music & Street Entertainment

★ **African Chic** VILLE NOUVELLE A vibrant Afro-Brazilian bar with a Moroccan twist. African Chic oozes cult kitsch, with elephant paintings, zebra-print sofas, banana palms, and a giant pot-bellied Buddha lording it over the dance floor. Grab a caipirinha, nibble tapas, and do your best Patrick Swayze impression to live Latino music (nightly from 10pm). *6 Rue Oum Errabia.* ☎ *0524-43-14-24. www.african-chic.com. Map p 132.*

Cobra on Jemaa el Fna.

Hotel Les Jardins de la Koutoubia MEDINA This five-star hotel is shortly due a revamp, but in the meantime it's *the* place for a quiet drink, a conversation, and live piano music. Place your order at the bar, your request with the pianist, and recline in a red velvet armchair in sophisticated, dimly lit surrounds. *26 Rue de la Koutoubia.* ☎ *0524-38-88-00. www.lesjardinsdela koutoubia.com. Map p 131.*

★★★ **Jemaa el Fna** MEDINA Bag a ringside seat to observe the oboe-playing snake charmers, gyrating transvestites, acrobats turning back flips to riotous applause, and fire breathers spouting flames into the night sky. Look out for bizarre one-offs such as banjo players balancing cockerels on their heads. Gnaoua musicians in sky-blue robes fuel the party with their spinning tassels, castanets, and drums. *See p 8. Map p 131.*

★ **Kosybar** MEDINA Cozy up by the fire in a candlelit alcove, order a glass of Moroccan wine, and sit back to enjoy heartfelt jazz and soul performances. There's live music from Thursday to Sunday at 10.30pm. *See p 124. Map p 131.*

La Maison Arabe MEDINA Slip into a comfortable leather armchair by the fire in La Maison Arabe's exotic bar, decked out with African art. Piano melodies rise above the hum of chatter in this 1930s colonial-style lounge, where well-dressed guests linger over an aperitif or nightcap. *See p 142. Map p 131.*

Theatre & Cultural Venues
★ **Institut Français** VILLE NOU-VELLE Marrakech's cultural linch-pin, the Institut Français covers a diverse array of events: from innovative dance performances to art-house film screenings, readings, concerts, and exhibitions of local and international art. See the website for the latest listings. *Route de Targa.* ☎ *0524-44-69-30. www.ifm. ma. Ticket prices vary. Map p 132.*

★ **Théâtre Royal** VILLE NOU-VELLE Charles Boccara's iconic Théâtre Royal (p 76) is the latest addition to Marrakech's cultural scene. If your French or Arabic is up to scratch, check out the program, which spans comedy, opera, and dance performances. *40 Avenue de la France.* ☎ *0524-43-15-16. Ticket prices vary. Map p 132.* ●

Théâtre Royal illuminated after dark.

9

The Best **Lodging**

Lodging Best Bets

Best **Medina Indulgence**
★★★ Riad Farnatchi $$$$$ *Derb el Farnatchi, Rue Souk el Fassis (p 144)*

Best **Five-Star Welcome**
★★★ Dar Charkia $$$–$$$$ *49–50 Derb el-Halfaoui, Rue de Bab Doukkala (p 144)*

Best **Berber Chic**
★★★ Riyad El Cadi $$$$$ *87 Derb Moulay Abdelkader (p 146)*

Best **Rooftop Views**
★★ Riad L'Orangerie $$$ *61 Rue Sidi el-Yamani (p 145)*

Best **Intimate Dining**
★★ Villa Flore $$ *4 Derb Azzouz. (p 146)*; and ★ Casa Lalla $$$ *16 Derb Jamaa, Riad Zitoun-el-Kedim (p 140)*

Best **Oriental Fantasy**
★★★ La Sultana $$$$$ *403 Rue de la Kasbah (p 142)*

Best **Italian Chic**
★ Riad 72 $$$ *72 Arset Awsel, Dar el-Bacha (p 143)*

Best **Moroccan Elegance**
★★★ La Maison Arabe $$$$–$$$$$ *1 Derb Assehbé, Bab Doukkala (p 142)*

Best **Royal Treatment**
★★ Dar Donab $$$–$$$$$ *53 Rue Dar el-Bacha (p 140)*

Best **Palmeraie Escape Act**
★★★ Caravanserai $$$–$$$$ *264 Ouled Ben Rahmoune (p 140)*

Best **Enchanted Garden**
★★★ Riad Enija $$$$ *9 Derb Mesfiouni, Rahba Qedima (p 144)*

Best **Hidden Gem**
★★ Dar Sholmes $$ *82 Derb Sidi M'Barek, Quartier Sidi Mimoun (p 141)*

Best **A-list Hideaway**
★★★ Jnane Tamsna $$$$$ *Douar Abiad, La Palmeraie (p 141)*

Best **Homestyle Riad**
★ Riad Davia $$–$$$ *Derb Aarab, Bab Aylen (p 143)*; and ★ Riad Mabrouka $$$ *56 Derb el-Bahia, Riad Zitoun el-Jedid (p 145)*

Best **Resort for Hivernage Hipsters**
★ Es Saadi Gardens & Resort $$$$–$$$$$ *Avenue El Quadissia. (p 141)*

Best **Bird's-Eye View**
★ Dar Les Cigognes $$$–$$$$ *108 Berima (p 141)*

Best **Affordable but Stylish**
★ Jnane Mogador $–$$ *Fasanenstrasse 69 (p 141)*; and ★ Riad Dar Attajmil $$–$$$ *23 Rue Laksour (p 143)*

Best **Family Retreat**
★ Le Caspien $–$$ *12 Rue Loubnane (p 142)*

An oasis in the sultry heart of the medina - Riyad el Cadi.

Ville Nouvelle & Palmeraie
Lodging

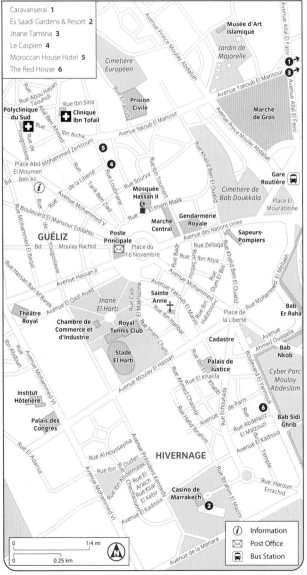

Caravanserai **1**
Es Saadi Gardens & Resort **2**
Jnane Tamsna **3**
Le Caspien **4**
Moroccan House Hotel **5**
The Red House **6**

Medina Lodging

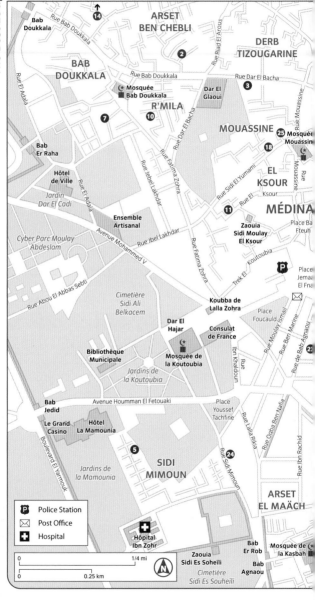

ARSET BEN CHEBLI

DERB TIZOUGARINE

Bab Doukkala

Rue Bab Doukkala

↑ 14

2

Rue Riad El Arous

3

Rue Dar El Bacha

BAB DOUKKALA

Rue El Adala

Rue Bab Doukkala

Mosquée Bab Doukkala

Dar El Glaoui

Rue Dar El Bacha

R'MILA

7

10

Rue Mouassine

MOUASSINE

25 Mosquée Mouassine

Rue Mouassine

18

Bab Er Raha

Rue Jebel Lakhdar

Rue Fatima Zohra

Rue Sidi El Yunnami

EL KSOUR

Hôtel de Ville

Jardin Dar El Cadi

Rue El Adala

Ensemble Artisanal

11

Rue El Ksour

MÉDINA

Place Ba Fteuh

Avenue Mohammed V

Rue Jbel Lakhdar

Rue Fatima Zohra

Zaouia Sidi Moulay El Ksour

Trek El Koutoubia

Cyber Parc Moulay Abdeslam

Rue Abou El Abbas Sebti

P Place Jemaa El Fna

Cimetière Sidi Ali Belkacem

Koubba de Lalla Zohra

Place Foucauld

Rue Moulay Ismail

Rue Ben Marine

Rue de Bab Agnaou

✉

22

Bibliothèque Municipale

Dar El Hajar

Mosquée de la Koutoubia

Consulat de France

Rue Ibn Khaldoun

Jardins de la Koutoubia

Avenue Houmman El Fetouaki

Place Youssef Tachfine

Rue Lalla Rikia

Rue Oqba Ben Nafia

Rue Ibn Rachid

Bab Jedid

Le Grand Casino

Hôtel La Mamounia

5

SIDI MIMOUN

24

Rue Sidi Mimoun

Boulevard El Yarmouk

Jardins de la Mamounia

ARSET EL MAÄCH

P Police Station

✉ Post Office

✚ Hospital

0 _____ 1/4 mi

0 _____ 0.25 km

Ⓝ

✚ Hôpital Ibn Zohr

Zaouia Sidi Es Soheïli

Cimetière Sidi Es Souheïli

Bab Er Rob

Bab Agnaou

Mosquée de la Kasbah

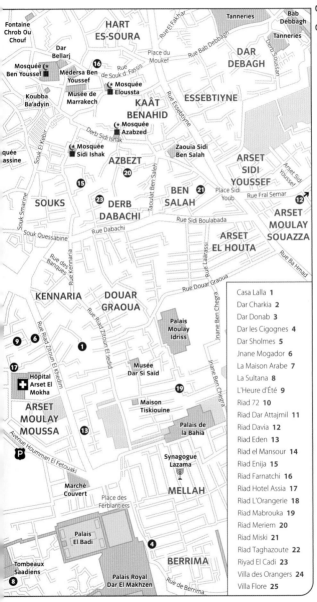

Fontaine Chrob Ou Chouf

HART ES-SOURA

Rue El Fakhar

Tanneries

Bab Débbagh

Tanneries

Rue Bab Debbagh

Dar Bellarj

Place du Moukef

DAR DEBAGH

Derb Soussan

Mosquée Ben Youssef

Médersa Ben Youssef

Rue de Souk d. Fassis

Mosquée Eloussta

Musée de Marrakech

Rue Essebtiyne

ESSEBTIYNE

Koubba Ba'adyin

KAÂT BENAHID

Souk El Kebir

Derb Sidi Ishak

Mosquée Azabzed

quée assine

Mosquée Sidi Ishak

AZBEZT

Zaouia Sidi Ben Salah

ARSET SIDI YOUSSEF

Arset Sidi Youssef

Taoulat Ben Saleh

SOUKS

Souk Smarine

DERB DABACHI

BEN SALAH

Place Sidi Youb

Rue Fral Semar

Souk Quessabine

Rue Dabachi

Rue Sidi Boulabada

ARSET MOULAY SOUAZZA

Rue Ba Hmad

Rue des Banques

Rue Kennaria

ARSET EL HOUTA

Rue Laârassi

KENNARIA

DOUAR GRAOUA

Rue Douar Graoua

Jnane Ben Chegra

Rue Riad Zitoun El Jedid

Palais Moulay Idriss

Hôpital Arset El Mokha

Musée Dar Si Saïd

Jnane Ben Chegra

ARSET MOULAY MOUSSA

Maison Tiskiouine

Avenue Houmman El Fetouaki

Palais de la Bahia

Synagogue Lazama

Marché Couvert

Place des Ferblantiers

MELLAH

Palais El Badi

Tombeaux Saadiens

Palais Royal Dar El Makhzen

BERRIMA

Rue de Berrima

Casa Lalla **1**
Dar Charkia **2**
Dar Donab **3**
Dar les Cigognes **4**
Dar Sholmes **5**
Jnane Mogador **6**
La Maison Arabe **7**
La Sultana **8**
L'Heure d'Été **9**
Riad 72 **10**
Riad Dar Attajmil **11**
Riad Davia **12**
Riad Eden **13**
Riad el Mansour **14**
Riad Enija **15**
Riad Farnatchi **16**
Riad Hotel Assia **17**
Riad L'Orangerie **18**
Riad Mabrouka **19**
Riad Meriem **20**
Riad Miski **21**
Riad Taghazoute **22**
Riyad El Cadi **23**
Villa des Orangers **24**
Villa Flore **25**

Marrakech **Lodging A to Z**

★ **Caravanserai** PALMERAIE
Renowned architect, Charles Boccara, transformed a caravanserai into this Houdini-worthy escape near the Palmeraie, complete with tranquil gardens, pool, and hammam. Nouveau rustic rooms feature playful textures such as bark and canvas, and eggshell-smooth *tadelakt* (polished plaster) bathrooms. *264 Ouled Ben Rahmoune.* ☎ *0524-30-03-02. www.hotel-caravanserai. com. 17 units. Doubles 1200–1800dh; suites 1550–2400dh w/breakfast. AE, MC, V. Map p 137.*

★ **Casa Lalla** MEDINA Pared-down Moroccan chic describes this French-run riad, where sleek rooms kissed with crimson and gold are jazzed up with *tadelakt* and chiffon drapes. Foodies flock to the serene courtyard for Pierre Olivier's taste sensations (p 111). Spend lazy afternoons lolling on the patio and drifting off in the sultry hammam. *16 Derb Jamaa, Riad Zitoun el-Kedim.* ☎ *0524-42-97-57. www.casalalla. com. 8 units. Doubles 1200–1500dh w/breakfast. AE, MC, V. Map p 138.*

★★★ **Dar Charkia** MEDINA Personal shopping trips, hassle-free city tours, belly dancing lessons—just say the word and charismatic owners Lisa and Michael grant your wish. Each individually decorated suite reveals loving detail with richly embroidered fabrics, bursts of hot color, and huge *tadelakt* showers. A delicious breakfast is served on the roof terrace with Atlas Mountain views or in the orange tree-shaded courtyard. *49–50 Derb el-Halfaoui, Rue de Bab Doukkala.* ☎ *0524-37-64-77. www.darcharkia.com. 6 units. Suites 1650–2400dh w/breakfast. AE, MC, V. Map p 138.*

★★ **Dar Donab** MEDINA Snuggling up to Dar el-Bacha, this *petit* palace is astonishing. Suites are exquisitely decorated with stuccowork, canopy beds, and sunken bathtubs. Top that with impeccable service and gardens lush with grapefruit trees and bougainvillea to see why Dar Donab is beloved by celebrities—George Clooney and Uma Thurman included. *53 Rue Dar el-Bacha.* ☎ *0524-44-18-97. www.dardonab.*

The ultimate escape act - Caravanserai.

Dar Charkia offers a warm welcome and creatively designed rooms.

com. 6 units. Doubles 1440–1800dh; suites 2240–5000dh w/breakfast. MC, V. Map p 138.

★ **Dar les Cigognes** MEDINA Wake up to views of the *cigognes* (storks) on the Badi Palace walls at this revamped 17th-century merchant's home. Bearing the imprint of architect Charles Boccara, each of the 11 rooms is unique: whether you snooze in a tent-like bed in the blue-*tadelakt* Sahara room or in a gilt four-poster in the ruby-red Harem room. The citrus-scented courtyard and domed hammam induce relaxation. *108 Berima.* ☎ *0524-38-27-40. www.lescigognes. com. 11 units. Doubles 1600–2400dh w/breakfast. AE, MC, V. Map p 138.*

★★ **Dar Sholmes** MEDINA Hidden in a labyrinth of alleys near Koutoubia, Dar Sholmes is a gem. French owner André painstakingly renovated the riad with a traditional meets contemporary approach— think gray *tadelakt* walls, graceful arches, hand-carved doors, and vivid Moroccan artwork. Rooms feature ethnic touches such as *kélims* and lanterns, plus mod cons like

WiFi and flat-screen TVs. Step up to the terrace for sweeping views over the city. *82 Derb Sidi M'Barek, Quartier Sidi Mimoun.* ☎ *0524-38-39-54. www.darsholmes.com. 6 units. Doubles 750–1550dh w/breakfast. MC, V. Map p 138.*

★ **kids Es Saadi Gardens & Resort** VILLE NOUVELLE The Rolling Stones dodged the paparazzi at this ritzy Hivernage retreat in the 1960s. Set in tropical gardens, the resort is every bit as photogenic today, with its palm-fringed pool, Atlas Mountain views, spa, and casino. For the rock-star treatment, book a domed palace suite or a villa with private pool. All fruit, vegetables, and herbs served at mealtimes are home-grown on Es Saadi's nearby farm. *Avenue El Quadissia.* ☎ *0524-44-88-11. www.essaadi. com. 150 units. Doubles 1950–2300dh; suites 3700–4700dh; villas 9000–27,000dh w/breakfast. MC, V. Map p 137.*

★ **Jnane Mogador** MEDINA The medina bustle fades as you step into the mosaic-tiled courtyard centered on a trickling fountain. This funky riad is great value for your dirham, offering clean, colorful quarters with satellite TV. Chill in the Berber-style tent or with a top-to-toe scrub in the hammam (125dh). Breakfast costs an extra 40dh. It's popular, so book well ahead. *116 Riad Zitoun el-Kedim.* ☎ *0524-42-63-24. www.jnanemogador.com. 17 units. Doubles 380–480dh. MC, V. Map p 138.*

★★★ **Jnane Tamsna** PALMERAIE Brad Pitt, Hugh Grant, and David Bowie are among the A-listers fond of this serene Palmeraie retreat, set in jasmine-scented gardens. Keyhole arches and adobe passageways lead to chic Moroccan rooms, decorated with natural fabrics, bold artworks, and warm colors. Savor

Moneysaving Tips

Booking ahead for accommodation is essential year-round in Marrakech, because the best places fill up fast and many riads only have half a dozen rooms. Most places offer a 10–20% discount on rates in **low season** (January–February and June–August), and you can pick up great deals if you're prepared to stay in a lesser-known corner of the medina. If traveling with a group of friends, consider **renting a riad** in its entirety (see p 164). For discount hotels and last-minute deals, try **Priceline** (www.priceline.com), **Ebookers** (www.ebookers.com), and **Late Rooms** (www.laterooms.com).

home-grown treats in the garden, pamper yourself in the spa, join a cookery class, or slip on the Gucci shades to indulge in a little star-gazing by the pool. *Douar Abiad, La Palmeraie.* ☎ *0524-32-84-84. www. jnanetamsna.com. 24 units. Doubles 3300–4650dh. MC, V. Map p 137.*

★★★ La Maison Arabe
MEDINA   A gourmet haunt since the 1940s, La Maison Arabe has all the right riad ingredients: an enviable medina location, attentive service, a sultry hammam (p 16), decadent dining (p 115), and all the five-stars trappings. With ivy-strewn courtyards, antique-slung corridors, and open fires crackling in cedarwood salons, this is the epitome of Moroccan elegance. Stylish rooms welcome guests with complimentary wine and roses. Moroccan pancakes are made in front of you at breakfast. *1 Derb Assehbé, Bab Doukkala.* ☎ *0524-38-70-10. www. lamaisonarabe.com. 17 units. Doubles 1500–2500dh; suites 2500–6000dh w/ breakfast. MC, V. Map p 138.*

★★★ La Sultana
MEDINA   Like the film set for 1,001 Arabian Nights, this cluster of palatial riads is pure oriental fantasy, complete with a dreamy spa (p 33) and roof terrace overlooking the Kasbah. You'll be

dazzled by opulent rooms with marble bathrooms and lavish suites such as the safari-themed 'Elephant Suite' with bejeweled Indian bedding, fireplace, and Jacuzzi. *403 Rue de la Kasbah.* ☎ *0524-38-80-08. www.lasultanamarrakech.com. 28 units. Doubles 2800–5200dh; suites 5100–7800dh w/breakfast. AE, MC, V. Map p 138.*

★ kids Le Caspien
VILLE NOUVELLE   After a splurge in the boutiques of Guéliz, Le Caspien is a calm retreat. The modern, air-conditioned rooms feature balconies and satellite TV, unexpected perks considering the low rates. Chipper staff, a sunny pool area, and tasty Franco-Moroccan cuisine sweeten the deal. Breakfast costs an extra 50dh. *12 Rue Loubnane.* ☎ *0524-42-22-82. www.lecaspien-hotel.com. 38 units. Doubles 550dh. MC, V. Map p 137.*

L'Heure d'Été
MEDINA   The cracking location near Jemaa el Fna is the big draw at this simple, well-kept riad. Rooms are bright and secure with decent beds, modern bathrooms, and WiFi. Enjoy breakfast on the sunny roof terrace. *96 Rue Sidi Bouloukat.* ☎ *0524-39-17-27. www.lheure-dete.com. 14 units. Doubles 450–750dh w/breakfast. Cash only. Map p 138.*

kids Moroccan House Hotel
VILLENOUVELLE Moroccan maximalism describes this cheerful Guéliz hotel—frills, four-poster beds, and over-the-top plasterwork. Whether you find this place trendily kitsch or out-dated, it's certainly good value, with clean air-conditioned rooms, a pool for afternoon dips, a central location, and a terrace where generous breakfasts are served. *3 Rue Loubnane.* ☎ *0524-42-03-05. www.moroccanhouse hotels.com. 14 units. Doubles 584–964dh w/breakfast. AE, MC, V . Map p 137.*

★ **Riad 72** MEDINA Intimate and exclusive with just three rooms and one suite, this slinky Italian-run riad is a temple to minimalist chic with its monochrome hues, Zen-style simplicity, and banana-tree shaded courtyard. On clear days, the roof terrace affords incredible Atlas Mountain views. Revive with a hammam or a delicious meal made with seasonal produce. *72 Arset Awsel, Dar el-Bacha.* ☎ *0524-38-76-29. www.riad72.com. 4 units. Doubles 1250–2250dh w/breakfast. AE, MC, V. Map p 138.*

★ **Riad Dar Attajmil** MEDINA The tabby cat dozing by the entrance has the right idea; there is a kind of hush about this bijou riad, where banana fronds shade the courtyard. Rooms reveal Moroccan flourishes such as Atlas carpets, buffed *tadelakt*, and wood ceilings. Anything you want, just ask the friendly staff—from a pre-dinner hammam to a Med-style feast on the roof terrace by candlelight. *23 Rue Laksour.* ☎ *0524-42-69-66. www.darattajmil. com. 4 units. Doubles 990–1200dh w/breakfast. MC, V. Map p 138.*

★ **Riad Davia** MEDINA Expect a heartfelt welcome at this homely riad, squeezed down a quiet alley in

A tadelakt bathroom at Riad Davia.

an authentic part of town near Bab Aylen. Framing a whitewashed courtyard with a plunge pool, each of the open-plan rooms has its own flair—from star-lit Dawiya with its four-poster bed, *tadelakt* fireplace, and private patio to ethnic-style Cheikh. Book a hammam, or learn tagine tricks with free cookery classes. *Derb Aarab, Bab Aylen.* ☎ *0524-39-18-01. www.riaddavia. com. 5 units. Doubles 880–1550dh; suites 1550–1750dh w/breakfast. MC, V. Map p 138.*

★ **Riad Eden** MEDINA Escape the Medina hubbub at this color-charged riad, glammed up with zebra stripes, bold artworks, and *zellij* tilework. The individually designed rooms in warm reds and oranges feature *tadelakt* walls, striped bedding, and ethnic touches. Owners Emmanuel and Hélène will fine-tune your stay, whether you plan to venture into the desert or dine in the hip salon. *25 Derb Jdid, Riad Zitoun el-Kedim.* ☎ *0672-04-69-10. www.riadeden-marrakech.com. 6 units. Doubles 550–1500dh w/breakfast. MC, V. Map p 138.*

Riad Fever

The medina is honeycombed with riads, the traditional court-yard houses that have become hot property over the past decade, with Europeans giving them boutique makeovers. Italian chic, rose-petal romance, nouveau Moroccan—whatever your style, there's a riad with your name on it. Nearly all offer fragrant patios, roof ter-races, a family welcome, and home cooking. Before you venture down the riad route, though, remember that most are buried deep in the medina and tricky to find, so ask someone to collect you from a nearby landmark. To be near the sights opt for the Kasbah or Jemaa el Fna; for neighborhood charm and style, try Mouassine. Families and first-timers may prefer the space and modern creature comforts of hotels in Ville Nouvelle or villas in the Palmeraie.

★ Riad el Mansour MEDINA

This elegant riad prides itself on attentive, but not intrusive service. Rooms are decked out in Moroccan and European pieces, and have extras such as an mp3 docking sta-tion, WiFi, extra bedding, fresh fruit, and plenty of lighting. There's also an in-house hammam, spa, and gym. *227 Derb Jdid, Bab Doukkala.* ☎ *0524-38-15-77. www.riadel mansour.com. 6 units. Doubles 1600–2960dh. AE, MC, V. Map p 138.*

★★ Riad Enija MEDINA Down a

twisty *derb* (alley) off Rahba Qedima and behind a heavy wooden door, you'll find this 280-year-old riad. Relax in tropical gardens full of swaying palms, cypress trees, bab-bling fountains, and dozing turtles. The illusion is complete in artfully designed rooms—some with four-poster boat beds, others with ornately carved ceilings and mosaic-tiled bathrooms. Breakfast is served in the vaulted surrounds of a former hammam. *9 Derb Mesfiouni, Rahba Qedima.* ☎ *0524-44-09-26. www. riadenija.com. 12 units. Doubles 3200dh; suites 4650dh w/breakfast. AE, MC, V. Map p 138.*

★★★ Riad Farnatchi

MEDINA   Canadian manager Lynn Perez and her expert team attend to your every whim 24/7—be it break-fast on the Majorelle-blue roof ter-race, dinner à deux by the fire in the theatrical 'Marococo' salon, or an invigorating gommage in the ham-mam. The nine suites come with pri-vate living rooms with fireplaces, fossil bathtubs, and handmade beds (where you'll find your complimen-tary *jellabah* (robes) and *babouches* (slippers). All-important touches include Molton Brown toiletries, WiFi, and iPod decks. *Derb el Farnat-chi, Rue Souk el Fassis.* ☎ *0524-38-49-10. www.riadfarnatchi.com. 9 units. Suites 3100–4750dh. MC, V. Map p 138.*

Riad Hotel Assia MEDINA Right

in the thick of things, this is a great budget find with its quiet red brick courtyard, smiley English-speaking staff, and warm, spotless rooms. Satellite TV, air conditioning, and a panoramic roof terrace with Koutou-bia views seal the deal. *32 Rue de la Recette.* ☎ *0524-39-12-85. www. hotel-assia-marrakech.com. 26 units. Doubles 420dh w/breakfast. MC, V. Map p 138.*

★★ Riad L'Orangerie MEDINA A smooth blend of French finesse and Moroccan craftsmanship, this boutique riad has high-ceilinged rooms with attention-grabbing details such as Berber rugs, silky *tadelakt* walls, and monochrome shots of Marrakech. The mosaic-tiled pool and hammam are first rate, and the roof terrace affords sweeping views over the city's rooftops. *61 Rue Sidi el-Yamani.* ☎ *0661-23-87-89. www.riadorangeraie.com. 7 units Doubles 1450–1550dh; suites 1900dh w/breakfast. MC, V. Map p 138.*

★ Riad Mabrouka MEDINA Make yourself at home at this riad near Dar Si Said, where high-ceilinged, stucco salons warmed by fireplaces, create a feeling of space and grandeur. Every room is different, from the Berber-chic Bamako to the purple-blue Tangier with its charcoal *tadelakt* bathroom. The roof terrace is a quiet escape with padded loungers and straw hats for guest use. *56 Derb el-Bahia, Riad Zitoun el-Jedid.* ☎ *0524-37-75-79. www.riad-mabrouka.com. 5 units. Doubles 1450–2100dh w/breakfast. AE, MC, V. Map p 138.*

★ Riad Meriem MEDINA New York designer Thomas Hays has created a romantic riad with original artwork, themed rooms (some with large soaking tubs), inviting courtyards, and attentive and friendly staff. Be warned that the ambient lighting is a bit dark, which can be a positive or negative, depending on your needs. *97 Derb el Cadi, Azbezt.* ☎ *0524-38-77-31. www.riadmeriem. com. 5 units. Doubles 1950–2900dh w/breakfast. V. Map p 138.*

★ kids Riad Miski MEDINA Near Ali Ben Youssef Medersa, this tiny riad is a delight with light-filled, citrus-hued rooms overlooking a serene patio. But it's the service that takes it to another level: owner Francis pleases youngsters with magic tricks and grown-ups with argan-oil massages, while his partner Christine will help you get your bearings. Raja rustles up superb Moroccan food (dinner 200dh). Check the website for courses from calligraphy to belly dancing. *6 Derb Sidi Abdelouassaa, Ben Saleh.* ☎ *0524-39-16-29. www. riadmiski.com. 5 units. Doubles 500–1500dh w/breakfast. AE, MC, V. Map p 138.*

Be bewitched by Riad Enija.

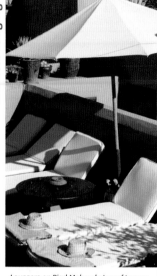

Loungers on Riad Mabrouka's roof terrace.

Riad Taghazoute MEDINA This simple riad offers great value, with air-conditioned rooms in warm hues, a plant-filled patio, and a terrace with 360-degree views over the medina. It's conveniently just around the corner from Jemaa el Fna. *39 Derb Kabada.* ☎ *0524-38-75-84. www.riad-taghazout.com. 9 units. Doubles 400–500dh w/breakfast. Cash only. Map p 138.*

★★★ Riyad El Cadi MEDINA Like a mirage in the medina's sultry heart, El Cadi refreshes the senses. Corridors graced with antique Berber kélims lead to light-filled rooms with heavenly beds, Middle Atlas carpets, and objets d'art. My favorite is the oblong Berber Suite with its coffered ceiling, fireplace. and sky-lit bathtub for lathering up with zingy essential oil cosmetics. The roof terrace and hammam invite total relaxation. *87 Derb Moulay Abdelkader.* ☎ *0524-37-86-55. www. riyadelcadi.com. 12 units. Doubles*

1320–2200dh; suites 2750–3600dh w/breakfast. MC, V. Map p 138.

★ The Red House VILLE NOUVELLE European imperialism adds grandeur to the Moroccan mix at this 19th-century mansion in Hivernage, sumptuously decorated with *zouak* (finely-painted wood) ceilings and stucco. Service is attentive, suites are lavish organza, velvet, and four-poster affairs, and the garden pool is ideal for summertime chilling. *Avenue el-Yarmouk.* ☎ *0524-43-70-40. www.theredhouse-marrakech.com. 8 units. Doubles 2200–3100dh; suites 2600–4200dh w/breakfast. AE, MC, V. Map p 137.*

★ Villa des Orangers MEDINA Facing the Royal Palace, this is a handsome hideaway, where corridors adorned with richly carved stucco and *zellij* tilework lead to a courtyard perfumed by namesake orange trees. The olive tree-fringed pool is a refreshing tonic after a morning in the souks. Rooms are decorated in *tadelakt* and rich fabrics. Rates include airport transfers, light lunches, soft drinks, and WiFi. *6 Rue Sidi Mimoune.* ☎ *0524-38-46-38. www.villadesorangers.com. 19 units. Doubles 3400–7400dh w/ breakfast. AE, V. Map p 138.*

★★ Villa Flore MEDINA Suave and sociable, this boutique riad marries oriental warmth with French sophistication. The aesthetic would be minimalist were it not for accents of color, antiques, and glam flourishes such as zebra stripes. Rooms are fresh and light, with marble bathrooms and flat-screen TVs. Book a massage, admire mountain views from the terrace, and enjoy dinner at the restaurant (p 118). *4 Derb Azzouz.* ☎ *0524-39-17-00. www.villa-flore.com. 5 units. Doubles 900–1650dh w/breakfast. MC, V. Map p 138.* ●

10 The Best Day Trips & Excursions

Essaouira

① Cooperative Assouss Argane
② Skala du Port
③ Port
④ Fish Auction
⑤ Place Moulay El Hassan
⑥ Place Orson Welles
⑦ Ramparts
⑧ Coopérative Artisanal des Marqueteurs
⑨ Skala de la Ville
⑩ Medina
⑪ Galerie d'Art Damgaard
⑫ Essaouira Bay
⑬ Camel Rides
⑭ Borj el-Berod

Where to Stay
Dar Liouba **15**
Dar Ness **16**
Madada Mogador **17**
Maison des Artistes **18**
Riad Baladin **19**
Where to Dine
After Five **20**
Chez Sam **21**
Crêperie Mogador **22**
Fish Souk **23**
Pâtisserie Driss **24**
Silvestro **25**
Taros Café **26**

Romans, pirates, Portuguese explorers, and blissed-out hippies and rock stars—they all fell for this dazzling coastal town, where gold-tinged ramparts create an amphitheatre between sea and sky. Today the easy-going spirit lives on in Essaouira's medina, a tangle of whitewashed houses, quirky riads, and sunny cafés; all washed in that dreamy Atlantic light.

① ★★ Cooperative Assouss Argane. Approaching Essaouira, you will pass numerous women's cooperatives producing argan oil, including Assouss. Here, in the courtyard, you can watch the traditional method used from cracking open the pits to roasting the bitter kernels, sweetening them for culinary oil. Give something back to this hard-working community by visiting the shop, selling organic argan oil (around 150dh per 50ml bottle), creams, and *amlou* or Berber peanut butter, a thick spread made from argan-oil residue and honey. ⏱ *30 min. Douar Chihimate, 3km from El Hanchane.* ☎ *0661-18-03-44. Daily 8am–6pm. MC, V.*

② ★ Skala du Port. The tang of salt catches your nostrils at this sea bastion, lined with brass canons. The strategic lookout guards the entrance to Essaouira's harbor and affords fine views over the fishing

See argan oil made using traditional Berber methods at Cooperative Assouss Argane.

port and across to the Île de Mogador, an island home to a fort, a derelict prison, and Eleanora's falcons

Argan Oil from the Source

Prized by Berbers for its culinary and cosmetic uses for centuries, **argan oil** derives from the gnarled, thorny argan tree, a hardy species indigenous to southwest Morocco. Although cooperatives wax lyrical about its health benefits (it's high in vitamin E, anti-oxidants, and essential fatty acids), the most fascinating thing about the oil is how it's produced. Argan oil is *the* ultimate green food. Nimble-footed goats climb the trees, eat the oval fruits, and excrete the almond-shaped pits, which are then collected, cracked open, and the kernels ground and pressed. It's a long process from goat digestion to glowing complexion, however; 15 hours work for just one liter of the precious golden oil!

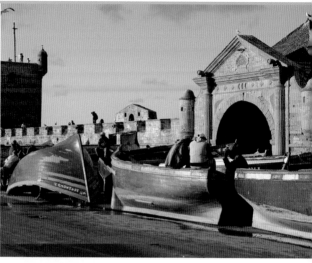

Fishing boats in front of the ramparts of Essaouira.

(bring binoculars to spot them). 🕐 *15 min. Essaouira Port. Admission: 10dh adults, 3dh children under 12. Daily 8:30am–12pm and 2:30–6pm.*

❸ ★ Port. Get up with the gulls to catch the action at Essaouira's vibrant fishing port, where every morning fleets of colorful boats bring in the day's catch. Observe the crates of flapping fish as they're unloaded to sell at auction, while fishermen working opposite build boats and repair nets. If you're going to wander here, be sure to wear old shoes—it can get slippery and mucky. 🕐 *30 min. Essaouira Port.*

❹ Fish Auction. For the freshest fish, locals flock to the cavernous auction hall opposite the port, where the catch is weighed and sold to the highest bidder. The hall is jam-packed during the auction, which lasts around an hour and takes place twice daily. 🕐 *15 min. Opposite the port. Daily 7am and 3pm.*

❺ Place Moulay El Hassan. Pass through the harbor gate to Essaouira's bustling, tree-fringed main square. It's an attractive plaza for strolling, people-watching, and sipping a freshly squeezed orange juice (5dh) from one of the carts. Wafts of grilled fish lure you over to the seafood stalls in the eastern corner of the square, where chefs sing their own praises as they grill squid and shrimps. The food is good and cheap (10–40dh per item), but personally I prefer the less touristy stalls in the medina (p 152). The square is lined with pavement cafés and bars ideal for watching the world go by. 🕐 *20 min. Place Moulay el Hassan.*

❻ Place Orson Welles. Framed by crenellated walls, this grassy square has a bust paying homage to Academy award-winning American director, producer, and actor Orson Welles (1915–1985), because scenes from *Othello* (1952) were filmed by Essaouira's ramparts. 🕐 *10 min. Place Orson Welles.*

Surf's Up

Thrashed by Atlantic waves and blessed with constant winds and broad sands, Essaouira has carved out its reputation as a **surfing**, **windsurfing**, and **kite-surfing** hotspot. The coastal city has hosted several international championships in recent years. If you're itching to ride or skim those big rollers, you can hire equipment or take lessons in and around Essaouira. **Magic Fun Afrika** (☎ 0524-47-38-56; www.magicfunafrika.com) rents out kite boards and windsurfing boards in Essaouira, Sidi Kaouki (20km south) and Moulay Bouzerktoun (20km north) for around 500dh per day. May through September are the best months. Wetsuits are recommended year-round.

7 ★ **Ramparts.** Walking along Essaouira's imposing sand-hued fortifications, thrashed by Atlantic waves, you can timeline the fascinating history of one of Morocco's most important ports. Formerly called Mogador, this city has been a trade hub since Roman times when it produced purple dye for imperial togas. In the 16th century, the seafaring Portuguese built a fortress here and the harbor became a magnet to pirates and molasses exporters. Today's sturdy ramparts date from the 18th century and are the handiwork of French military architect and slave Théodore Cornut, whose creation was dubbed 'Es-Saouira' (the beautiful designed). Film directors seem to agree and

Gaze out to sea from clifftop bastion Skala de la Ville.

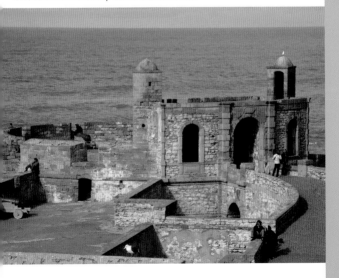

several blockbusters have been shot here including *Kingdom of Heaven* (2005). 🕐 *20 min.*

⑧ Coopérative Artisanal des Marqueteurs. Nip into this carpenters' cooperative for fixed-price fragrant thuya woodcarvings and marquetry. Particularly pretty are the photo frames, vases, and trinket boxes inlaid with mother of pearl, light lemon wood, and dark acacia wood. 🕐 *10 min. 6 Rue Khalid ben Oualid. No phone. MC, V.*

⑨ ★★ Skala de la Ville. Follow the ramparts until you reach this cliff top sea bastion. With waves pummeling the shore and crashing spectacularly on the rocks below and gulls circling above, the setting is pure drama. Nowhere in Essaouira is the lure of the sea more powerful. Sit astride one of the 19th-century canons at sunset, or venture down to the hobbit-like thuya woodcarving workshops. Opposite, look for the man who knits brightly colored beanies; his needles are some of the swiftest I've ever seen and you might need a hat for those bracing Atlantic breezes. 🕐 *20 min. Rue de la Skala. Admission free. Daily during daylight hours.*

⑩ ★ Medina. It's a joy to roam the laid-back, traffic-free streets of Essaouira's UNESCO-listed medina, formerly Mogador. Unlike Marrakech, the narrow streets here are grid-like and easy to navigate. Wander at your leisure to find pavement cafés, tiny galleries, and tree-shaded squares. It's also great for shopping—cheaper than Marrakech and without the hard sell. Top buys include thuya marquetry, argan oil, basketwork, paintings, *babouches* (slippers), and colorful throws. In the center, mosey around the **Spice Souk** for spices, herbs, and hammam essentials, and the **Jewelry Souk** for Berber beads and silver. Find a shady spot to sip a mint tea and soak up the atmosphere. 🕐 *1 hr.*

⑪ Galerie d'Art Damgaard. Essaouira's dreamy sea views and Atlantic light have inspired many artists. This spacious gallery, founded by Danish art dealer Frederic Damgaard, exhibits and sells paintings and sculptures by locals. Look out for creative works such as Ali Maimoune's abstract collages and Said Ourzaz's bright Pollock-inspired pieces. 🕐 *15 min. Avenue Oqba Ibn Nafia. ☎ 0523-78-44-46. Admission free. Daily 9am–1pm and 3–7pm.*

Gnaoua Time

In late June, Essaouira reverberates to the hypnotic rhythms of drums, castanets, and chanting at the free four-day **Gnaoua & World Music Festival** (☎ 0522-27-26-02; www.festival-gnaoua.net). Descendents of Black African slaves, the Gnaoua are musicians, clairvoyants, and dancers, who work themselves into a ritual trance of mystical beats and spinning fez tassels to drive away *djinn* (evil spirits). Alongside mesmerizing Gnaoua performances, the festival also stages top-drawer jazz, rock, and world music concerts on stages throughout the city. If you plan on joining the 500,000 revelers, book accommodation well in advance.

Practical Matters

Essaouira is situated 170km west of Marrakech. Frequent public buses (p 163) ply the route between the main bus station at Bab Doukkala and Essaouira; the journey takes three-and-a-half hours and costs 50dh. More comfortable are the air-conditioned **Supratours** (p 163) coaches, which depart near Marrakech's main train station, take three hours and cost 65dh. The route is a straight, easy drive from Marrakech, but if you'd rather not do the honking, enlist the services of a reputable driver and guide, such as **Authentic Morocco** (see p 158).

⑫ ★ Essaouira Bay. A relentless wind generally rules out sunbathing on this long, sandy beach, but the bay is ideal for strolling, surfing, camel rides, and fresh fish lunches at one of the beachfront shacks. When the tide is out, locals play soccer on the sand. My favorite time is when the setting sun paints the sea and sky gold, magenta, and purple. ⏲ *45 min.*

⑬ Camel Rides. You won't have to walk far along the beach to find a camel ride. Expect to pay 120–150dh per hour. Sunset is the most atmospheric time for a dromedary trek. ⏲ *1 hr. Essaouira Bay.*

⑭ ★★ Borj el-Berod. 'And so castles made of sand fall in the sea, eventually.' So sang Jimi Hendrix in 1967. Whether he was referring to these extraordinary 18th-century fortress ruins is a matter of heated debate, because the song was

A camel ready to take you for a ride on Essaouira Bay.

released a year before he visited Essaouira. The idiosyncratic sandcastle-like ruins that appear to topple and spill into the sea are at their most atmospheric silhouetted at sunset. ⏲ *15 min. Essaouira Bay.*

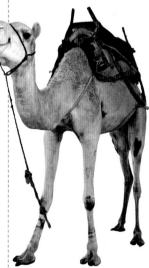

Where to Stay

Dar Liouba MELLAH You'll feel *chez vous* (at home) at this stylish, intimate riad. The spotless white-washed rooms are accentuated with bold colors: from zesty green in the argan tree room to cobalt blue in the ocean room. Keyhole arches, *tadelakt* (polished plaster) fireplaces, and cedarwood screens add Moroccan authenticity. *28 Impasse Moulay.* ☎ *0524-47-62-97. www.darliouba.com. 7 units. Doubles 600–900dh w/breakfast. MC, V.*

★ **Dar Ness** MEDINA The breezy blue-and-white hues and terracotta tiles evoke Andalusia, while the arches, lanterns, and rich rugs say Morocco at this friendly 18th-century gem. There's a patio for summer lounging and an open fire for chilly nights. High ceilings and minimal fuss create an aura of space

Maison des Artistes.

and tranquility. *1 Rue Khalid ben Oualid.* ☎ *0524-47- 68-04. www.darness-essaouira.com. 9 units. Doubles 750–850dh w/breakfast. MC, V.*

★ **Madada Mogador** MEDINA Expect a warm *bienvenue* at this ultra-hip riad, where terrace vistas sweep from the fishing port to Essaouira's sandy bay (sunset is prime-time viewing). Rooms reveal an eye for detail: from rosewood furnishings to smooth *tadelakt* and age-old brass basins from Fez. Other major draws include the delicious breakfasts, massages, and cookery courses. *5 Rue Youssef el-Fassi.* ☎ *0524-47-55-12. www.madada.com. 7 units. Doubles 1110–1150dh, suites 1650dh, w/breakfast. MC, V.*

Maison des Artistes MEDINA Go boho at this chilled retreat run by Parisian Cyril Ladeuil. Perched above the ramparts, with dazzling Atlantic views from the terrace, it has an eccentric beach house vibe. The bright rooms are filled with quirky artworks and tantalizing sea breezes. Ask for the suite with surround ocean views. *19 Rue Laâlouj.* ☎ *0524-47-57-99. www.lamaisondesartistes.com. 7 units. Doubles 600–1350dh w/breakfast. MC, V.*

★★ **Riad Baladin** MEDINA Swiss owner Nicole knows exactly what guests crave at this gorgeous medina riad: Moroccan-style romance with a personalized service, a mere stone's throw from the sea. Whether you're reclining on a canopy bed, stepping up to a *tadelakt* bathtub, or sipping a glass of home-brewed beer by the fire, it's a winning formula. *9 Rue Sidi Magdoul.* ☎ *0524-24-48-136. www.riad baladin.com. 6 units. Doubles 700dh w/breakfast. Cash only.*

Where to Dine

★ **After Five** MEDINA *FRENCH-MOROCCAN* Essaouira hipsters dine under the stone arches at this chic lounge restaurant beneath Madada Mogador (p 154). Purple tones and soft lighting create a contemporary setting for Franco-Moroccan fusion cuisine. The seafood—especially the stuffed crab—is superb. *Madada Mogador, 5 Rue Youssef el-Fassi.* ☎ *0524-47-33-49. Menu 150dh. MC, V. Dinner Wed–Mon, lunch Sat and Sun.*

Chez Sam PORT *SEAFOOD* Grab a dockside table and savor a plate of garlicky John Dory or fresh sardines at this laid-back shack. The borderline tacky decor detracts nothing from the harbor views and lip-smacking seafood. *Fishing Port.* ☎ *0524-47-65-13. Entrees 85–220dh. MC, V. Lunch and dinner daily.*

Crêperie Mogador MEDINA *CREPES* The Bretons running this sunny, boho-style haunt have a way with a frying pan. Whether you go for sweet or buckwheat, their light, fluffy crêpes are uniformly delicious. Toppings range from Camembert to sardine and green pepper. *4 Rue Lâalouj.* ☎ *0524-78-30-96. Crêpes 20–45dh. Cash only. Lunch and dinner Sat–Thurs.*

★★ **Fish Souk** MEDINA *SEAFOOD* The courtyard setting is humble, but I've rarely had a better meal in Morocco than at Essaouira's fish souk. Here your seafood will be weighed, grilled, and served with bread, salad, lime wedges, and spicy sauce. Around 50dh buys you a tasty fish lunch, while for 100dh you'll eat like a king—prawns, seabass, squid—the works. Bring your cutlery or eat like the locals with your fingers. *Avenue de l'Istiqlal. No phone. Entrees 20–50dh. Cash only. Lunch daily.*

★ **Pâtisserie Driss** MEDINA *PASTRIES* Step back to the 1920s at this poster-plastered, mosaic-tiled Essaouira institution, where an arty crowd gathers for 19dh breakfasts of strong coffee and croissants. The hum of chatter and rustling of newspapers fills the relaxed café, justly famed for its *cornes de gazelle* (crescent-shaped cookies filled with almond paste). *9 Rue El Hajjali.* ☎ *0524-47-57-93. Light meals and pastries 10–40dh. Cash only. Breakfast, lunch, and dinner daily.*

Silvestro MEDINA *ITALIAN* Marvel at Giuseppe preparing the pasta in the show kitchen of this cheerful, lemon-hued Italian bistro. Go for wood-fired pizza or appetizing entrees such as swordfish with capers and olives or saffron-infused shrimp tagliatelle. *70 Rue Lâalouj.* ☎ *0524-47-35-55. Entress 70–110dh. MC, V. Breakfast, lunch, and dinner daily.*

★ **Taros Café** MEDINA *FRENCH-MOROCCAN* Probably the funkiest hangout in town, the breezy ocean-facing terrace is perfect for gazing out to sea. Menu treats include Oualidia oysters, flavorful monkfish stew, and cinnamon-dusted *tarte aux pommes*. Come here in the evening for cocktails and rhythms from Gnaoua music to electro. *Place Moulay el-Hassan.* ☎ *0524-47-64-07. www.taroscafe.com. Entress 90–140dh. MC, V. Lunch and dinner Mon–Sat.*

Ourika Valley & Oukaïmeden

Little more than an hour from Marrakech, you can explore rural villages in the High Atlas or pound the slopes in Oukaï-meden, Morocco's only ski resort. The Ourika Valley cuts a path through a patchwork of gorges, terraces, and mud-brick villages to Setti Fatma, where the cool mountain air, waterfalls, and vistas of 3000m peaks are invigorating after a stint in the city.

❶ ★ Nectarome. If you're a fan of botanical gardens, make the short, bumpy detour to Nectarome, situated 35km southeast of Marrakech at the entrance to the Ourika Valley. There are guided tours (mostly in French) providing some background on the varieties of aromatic and medicinal plants and flowers grown here. Otherwise, wander at your leisure through gardens fragrant with citronella, mint, geranium, and thyme. The shop stocks a wide range of homegrown organic teas, essential oils, and hammam

gear. 🕐 *45 min. Tnine de l'Ourika.* ☎ *0524-48-24-47. www.nectarome. com. Admission 15dh adults, 10dh children under 12, guided tour 60dh. Daily 9am–5pm, Aug closed.*

❷ ★ Setti Fatma. At the head of the valley, this tumbledown Berber village, is as far as you can go without a 4x4 or mule. Heavy floods devastated many homes in 1995, so what you see today is a curious mishmash of traditional mud-built and new breeze-block houses. Still, the backdrop is striking: Canyon-like

Exploring the Souks

Almost every Berber village in the valley, no matter how small, has a weekly souk. By far the biggest and most popular is the Monday roadside souk in **Tnine Ourika**, a sociable affair where neighbors gather for a chit-chat amid mountains of fresh vegetables, herbs, and sacks of rice and pulses. Other souks in the valley sell a mix of second-hand clothing, spices, and meat. Expect a few humorous surprises such as dentists, barbers, and donkey shoeing. Unless you want your tooth extracted with rusty pliers or your moustache trimmed, you're better off browsing than buying.

slopes speckled with cacti and walnut trees rise above a fast flowing river, affording views of the snowy Atlas Mountains beyond. The village is the starting point for some stunning treks, including North Africa's highest peak **Jbel Toukal** (4167m) in the Toubkal National Park. Setti Fatma itself draws day-trippers in search of fresh air and rejuvenating summer strolls. There's little to see except some souvenir shops in the center. In August, the religious festivities of *moussem* bring feasting, music and jollity to the village. ⏱ *1 hr.*

3 ★ Setti Fatma Waterfalls. The seven-tiered waterfall is the main draw in Setti Fatma. It's a rocky 20-minute ascent past ramshackle mountain cafés to the first cataract. Reaching the higher falls involves some boulder scrambling, and so it's advisable to hire one of the local guides often found touting for business in the area. Surefootedness and sturdy footwear are essential. Despite rather persistent vendors trying to sell you honey/fossils/a carpet, this is an attractive ramble shadowing a cascading stream, with views to jagged mountains. The thundering waterfalls are particularly striking after heavy rain. Take good care if you follow the

locals in for a refreshing summer dip. ⏱ *45 min–1 hr. Setti Fatma. Admission free. Daylight hours.*

4 Riverfront Cafés. All of Setti Fatma's restaurants are geared towards tourists, but you'll find slightly lower prices and a more authentic atmosphere in those perched above the river, where

Mules by the stream in Setti Fatma.

around 50dh buys you a tagine and mint tea. I like to sit at one of the sunny terraces to watch the women washing clothes, children playing, and animals roaming on the river banks below. *Setti Fatma. $.*

❺ ★★ **Oukaïmeden.** A fork in the Ourika Valley road, 43km from Marrakech, leads to the serpentine road up to Oukaïmeden, Africa's highest ski resort at 2,600m (8,533 feet). The looping road passes Berber villages where children stand by the roadside selling bags of walnuts and apples. En route, you'll notice dramatic shifts in the landscape—from sheep grazing rocky red-tinged slopes to pine trees and mountain goats at higher altitudes. The resort draws trekkers in summer and skiers on snowy winter weekends from Marrakech and Casablanca. From December to March, a chairlift (one way 25dh, day pass 100dh) rises to Jbel Attar (3,258m (10,693 feet)) and

Hike up to the cool waterfalls of Setti Fatma.

five mogul-dotted runs. You can rent skis by the lifts or in local shops (50–100dh per day). 🕐 *2 hrs.* ●

Practical Matters

The easiest way to reach the Ourika Valley and/or Oukaïmeden is to charter a **grand taxi** from Marrakech (around 300dh each way, up to six persons) or arrange a tour. A good bet is the reputable UK-based company **Authentic Morocco** (☎ 0044-117-373-91-45 www.authentic-morocco.com), whose tailor-made itineraries mean you can combine a morning exploring Setti Fatma with an afternoon skiing in Oukaïmeden. If you prefer to join a group, **Sahara Expedition** (☎ 0524-42-79-77; www.saharaexpe.ma) arranges day trips to the Ourika Valley for around 200dh per person. If you decide to drive, be aware that some of the smaller roads are little more than bumpy dirt tracks and only accessible by a 4x4 vehicle.

The
Savvy Traveler

Before You Go

Government Tourist Offices

For pre-travel enquiries, contact the Moroccan National Tourist Office (☎ 0537-67-40-13; www.visit-morocco.org) with their headquarters in Rabat. Their website has information in English to help plan your stay.

Moroccan National Tourist Offices:

In the US: 104 West, 40th Street, Suite 1820, Manhattan, New York (☎ 0013-477-915-640).
In Canada: 1800, McGill College, Suite 2450, Montreal, Quebec H3A 3J6 (☎ 01-514-842-8111).
In the UK: 205 Regent Street, London W1B 4HB (☎ 020-74-37-00-73).

The Best Times to Go

There is no 'wrong' season to visit Marrakech because the sun shines virtually year-round. March to May and September to October are the best months to avoid the extreme heat. You can wander the souks without wilting but nights are still warmer than in winter. Summer is ideal for open-air festivals, lazy days spent beside riad pools, and partying under the stars. The city swelters in July and August, so be sure to wear sunscreen and carry bottled water wherever you go, or escape to the cooler climes of the Ourika Valley (p 156) and Essaouira (p 148). Visit from November to February for fewer crowds and great deals on riads, but be prepared for chilly nights.

Festivals & Special Events

SPRING. Women get behind the wheel in the ultimate off-road rally through the Sahara to Essaouira, the **Aïcha des Gazelles** (www.rallye aichadesgazelles.com), in March. The same month casts a marvelous

spell over Marrakech at the **Marrakech International Magic Festival** (p 23), nine days of juggling, conjuring, and all-round hocus pocus. Fans of strings and symphonies make for the Théâtre Royale (p 76) in March for the **Rencontres Musicales de Marrakech** (www. maghrebarts.ma), staging everything from Bach to Andalusian concerts. If you're intrigued how Marrakech's garden grows, come in April for the **Jardin'Art** (www. jardinsdumaroc.com/festival), comprising green-fingered events, workshops, exhibitions, and concerts in Cyber Park (p 16). Fashionistas, meanwhile, flock to **Caftan** (www. moroccofestivals.co.uk) in May to see the latest styles on the catwalk at the Palmeraie Golf Palace. May is also the month to make new *amis* at the **Friendship Festival** (www. friendshipfest.com), with bass-loaded gigs on Jemaa el Fna to bridge cultures and celebrate religious tolerance.

SUMMER. Gnaoua musicians work crowds into a trance-like frenzy with pulsating drum and castanet beats at Essaouira's **Gnaoua & World Music Festival** (p 152) in June. It's summer's biggest shindig with non-stop revelry and hypnotic African rhythms. Practice your belly dancing before shimmying over to the free **Marrakech Popular Arts Festival** (www.marrakechfestival.com), a made-in-Morocco folk extravaganza, welcoming acts from Berber musicians to High Atlas dancers. Some concerts are staged in the enigmatic surrounds of the Badi Palace. Jazz aficionados should check out the concert line-up at the **Montreux Jazz Festival Morocco** (www. montreuxjazz.com), which rocks the beautiful Bahia Palace in June.

MARRAKECH TEMPERATURE & RAINFALL

	JAN	FEB	MAR	APR	MAY	JUNE
Daily Temp. (°F)	64	66	71	73	80	87
Daily Temp. (°C)	18	19	22	23	27	31
Rainfall (in.)	1	1.1	1.3	1.2	0.6	0.3
Rainfall (cm)	2.5	2.8	3.3	3.1	1.5	0.8

	JULY	AUG	SEPT	OCT	NOV	DEC
Daily Temp. (°F)	97	97	89	80	71	66
Daily Temp. (°C)	36	36	32	27	22	19
Rainfall (in.)	0.1	0.1	0.3	0.9	1.2	1.2
Rainfall (cm)	0.3	0.3	1.0	2.3	3.1	3.1

FALL. If you love nothing better than a good wedding, make the pilgrimage west to the High Atlas for the **Imilchil Marriage Festival** in August, where around 40 couples tie the knot and others try to meet their match in a kind of tribal speed dating. Clubbers won't want to miss October's hottest event, **Puro Desert Lounge** (www.purodesert lounge.com), a mammoth weekend-long party at Pacha (p 126), which has starred big names such as Momo, Café del Mar Ibiza, and DJs Scream and Costa in recent years.

WINTER. The major draw on December's cultural calendar is the **Marrakech International Film Festival** (p 39), where avid filmgoers are glued to big screens on Jemaa el Fna and across the city. Expect a mix of independent and pan-African movies, plus the Bollywood flicks that drive the crowds wild. In January, the medina resonates to the patter of 5,000 sprightly feet competing in the 42km **Marrakech Marathon** (www.marathon-marrakech.com) from Jemaa el Fna to the Palmeraie and back. In late February, 4L Renaults make a dusty dash across the Sahara in the **4L Trophy** rally (www.4ltrophy.com), with pit-stops to deliver 50kg of essential supplies, such as clothes and schoolbooks, to desert children. The awards ceremony is held in Marrakech.

The Weather

Marrakech is Morocco's sunshine city, blessed with a minimum of seven hours sunlight daily. Spring brings balmy days and sporadic light showers, with temperatures hovering around 25°C (77°F)—just right for leisurely strolls. Summers are sizzling hot (particularly July and August), with temperatures sometimes peaking at 45°C (113°F), making a sunbed and mint tea preferable to a walk in the souks! Autumn is still warm enough to catch rays on the medina rooftops and explore with no sweat. Sunny days here are an antidote to the winter gloom elsewhere, with days warming up nicely to 20°C (68°F). Night temps, however, can dip as low as 6°C (43°F), so check the heating and blanket situation with your riad.

Cell (Mobile) Phones

To use your mobile in Morocco, it needs to be compatible with the GSM 900 band. Call your operator to check your international roaming agreement. Two major operators cover the country: Maroc Telecom (www.iam.ma) and Méditel (www.meditel.ma). You can buy SIM cards (30–50dh) and top-up cards from any of their stores and from the

Useful Websites

www.ilovemarrakesh.com: The lowdown on riads, restaurants, sights, hammams, and more.

www.speakmoroccan.com: Handy vocabulary lessons in Darija (Moroccan Arabic) to improve your haggling in the souks.

www.map.ma/eng: Moroccan news in English.

www.marrakechpocket.com: French language site with info on dining and cultural events, plus maps and weather.

www.moroccofestivals.co.uk: Line-up of annual festivals and one-off events in Morocco.

www.visitmorocco.org: Tourist office website with info on sights, events, themed tours, accommodation, and transport.

ubiquitous téléboutiques, including those around Rue Bab Agnaou and in Guéliz. Remember you will pay for receiving, as well as making, calls in Morocco.

Car Rentals

Unless you're heading out to the High Atlas for several days, there is little need to rent a car in Marrakech,

because it's cheaper and easier to negotiate the center on foot or by taxi. All major international car-rental companies operate here, with branches at the airport. Among them are Avis (☎ 0524-43-31-69; www.avis.com), Hertz (☎ 0524-43-13-94; www.hertz.com), and Budget (☎ 0524-43-11-80; www.budget.com).

Getting **There**

By Plane

Located 6km southwest of the medina, Menara Airport (☎ 0524-44-78-65; www.onda.org.ma) is the main gateway to Marrakech. The airport is served by a number of national and European airlines such as Royal Air Maroc and low-cost carriers Ryanair, Atlas Blue, and easyJet, flying to destinations including Casablanca, Paris, London, Madrid, and Brussels. Major airlines fly to the Mohammed V International Airport in Casablanca.

If you want to pay taxi drivers in dirham, there are ATMs and currency exchange offices in Arrivals, but many also accept euros.

Taxis pull up in front of Arrivals. The 15-minute journey to the

medina should cost roughly 60dh for a petit taxi and 80dh for a grand taxi, slightly more for trips to Guéliz and the Palmeraie. Alternatively, take the shuttle bus, which departs hourly from 6am to midnight, costs 20dh and stops in Hivernage, Jemaa el Fna, Bab Doukkala, and Guéliz. If you're staying in the medina for the first time, it's worth arranging a transfer through your riad (100–150dh) to avoid getting lost.

By Car

Driving in Morocco can be a breeze or a nightmare, depending on the road and traffic conditions. Marrakech is notorious for its congestion and reckless road hogs, some at the wheel without a license or insurance. The national speed limit is 40km/h (25mph) in urban areas and 100km/h (62mph) outside towns. Driving is on the right and seat belts are obligatory, though you would never believe it! Major routes from Marrakech include the P7 to Casablanca, the P24 to Fez, the P10 to Essaouira, and the P10/P40 to Agadir.

By Train
Morocco's railway network is run by Office National des Chemins de Fer or ONCF (☎ 0524-44-77-68; www.oncf. ma). National trains pull into the sleek new station (Gare de Marrakech, corner of Avenue Hassan II and Avenue Mohammed VI, Guéliz), which is worth a visit even if you're not planning a journey—see p 77. There are frequent services to Rabat (112dh; 4 hrs), Casablanca (84dh; 3 hrs), Fez (180dh; 7 hrs), and Tangiers (190dh;

9 hrs); these are 2nd-class fares. You can pre-book tickets at the station.

By Bus
The national coach company CTM (☎ 0524-43-44-02) provides an efficient, inexpensive service between Marrakech and destinations including Fez, Ouarzazate, Casablanca, and Essaouira. Coaches depart from Marrakech's Gare Routière or central bus station (☎ 0524-43-39-33) at Bab Doukkala. You can book tickets in advance here or at the CTM office (12 Boulevard Mohammed Zerktouni, Guéliz). Near the central train station, Supratours (Avenue Hassan II; ☎ 0524-43-55-25; www.supratours. ma) runs comfortable, air-conditioned coaches to cities including Essaouira and Agadir.

Eurolines (www.eurolines.co.uk) operates long-distance services to Paris and London.

Getting **Around**

By Bus
Public buses trundle across the city from morning to night. They are cheap (3–5dh) and frequent, though avoid them at rush hour when they're packed. Pay the driver your fare as you board. Useful routes include: Nos 1 and 20 Place de la Foucauld–Guéliz; Nos 2 and 10 medina–central bus station at Bab Doukkala; Nos 3 and 8 medina–central train station; No 6 Avenue Mohammed V–Agdal Gardens; and No 11 medina–Menara Gardens.

For a stork's-eye view of the city, ride the bright red double-decker City Sightseeing (☎ www.city-sightseeing.com) bus. A 24-/48-hour pass costs 130dh/200dh for adults, 65dh/100dh for children. The pass gives you unlimited use of two hop-on-hop-off tours: the 90-minute Marrakech 'Monumental' route,

departing half hourly and covering the medina and Guéliz, and the 60-minute 'Romantic' route to the Palmeraie, departing at 1pm, 2.10pm, 3.20pm, and 4.30pm. Tours begin at the tourist office (p 167).

By Calèche
The most relaxed and romantic way to get around Marrakech is by horse-drawn carriage. Old-style calèches line up for custom along Place de la Foucauld, slightly southwest of Jemaa el Fna. They also wait outside major attractions such as Jardin Majorelle and the Menara Gardens. To see the Atlas Mountains, cajole a driver to take you on an anti-clockwise tour of the medina. Official government rates are 80dh per hour, but realistically you'll have to use your bargaining power to reach a fair rate

(100–150dh per hour). Be sure to fix a price in advance.

By Taxi

Yes, the stories are true about conniving taxi drivers with broken meters and no change, but there are exceptions. Bear in mind that if you say you're staying at one of Marrakech's plush hotels, your driver may charge you over the odds (even double), so ask him to stop nearby. For short trips, flag down a petit taxi (typically a Fiat Uno or Peugeot hatchback). They can take three passengers and are equipped with a meter, which they are supposed to use. Pay a maximum 20dh by day and 40dh by night (half that for short journeys).

Accommodating up to six persons, grand taxis (usually cream Mercedes) have no meter and can effectively charge, or overcharge, as they choose. They stop near major hotels and transport hubs such as Jemaa el Fna and Bab Doukkala. Be prepared to haggle.

By Car

Traffic jams, near misses with overladen donkey carts, a distinct lack of parking, and improvised roundabout rules make driving in Marrakech only for the brave or foolhardy. I only recommend hiring a car if you plan to venture farther afield (for instance to Essaouira, Imlil, or the Ourika Valley) for more than a few days. Within the city itself, it's cheaper and easier to walk or use taxis. There are no parking meters in Marrakech, but gardiens de voitures attend parking areas such as the one next to Koutoubia; expect to pay around 5dh for a few hours, 10dh overnight.

On Foot

Unless you manage to slip your donkey past customs, you're going to be doing a fair bit of walking in Marrakech. The derbs (winding alleys) are so narrow in the maze-like medina and its bamboozling heart (the souks) that they are largely off limits to all forms of transport, bar mule-driven carts and kamikaze moped drivers. Bring a pair of flat, comfy shoes that don't mind the mud and prepare to explore on foot. Sure, you can cover distance by skirting around the ramparts, but you would be missing half of the fun and all of the details. From Jemaa el Fna, Kasbah and Mouassine are a 15-minute stroll, and you can walk to Guéliz in less than half an hour.

Nearly every traveler has a tale about getting lost. Just take a look at a Marrakech map and you'll see why: the medina is an indecipherable web of blind alleys. Applying Western logic (signs, street names, etc.) is unlikely to work. I try to make a mental map of landmarks such as Jemaa el Fna, Souk Semmarine, Kasbah Mosque, and Koutoubia. If you're desperate, there are probably at least 10 unofficial guides willing to show you the way for a few dirham.

Take care when crossing roads such as Avenue Mohammed V, where zebra crossings seem to be superfluous. I find the best way is to tag onto some friendly locals.

Fast **Facts**

APARTMENT & RIAD RENTALS   Visit **www.holidaylettings.co.uk**, **www.iha.com**, **www.homelidays.** **co.uk**, and **www.holiday-rentals.** **co.uk** for vacation apartments in Marrakech, which are often great value for longer stays. Many riads can also be rented in their entirety; approach them directly or check out **www.riadsmorocco.com** and **www.lodgis.com**.

ATMS/CREDIT CARDS Many banks, including Crédit du Maroc, Société Générale Maroc, and Banque Populaire, have ATMs for withdrawing cash 24/7. Try Rue Bab Agnaou and Rue Moulay Ismail in the medina and Avenue Mohammed V in Guéliz. Visa, Cirrus, and MasterCard are widely accepted, but your bank may charge a fee for the service. You can exchange currency at banks, post offices, some hotels, and at the airport. Be sure to ask whether riads, shops, and restaurants accept plastic payment; not all do. Some restaurants play the credit card game, where they pretend payment has been refused, so you'll pay them in cash instead.

BUSINESS HOURS Banks generally open 8:30am–11.30am and 2:30–5pm Monday through Friday. Shopping hours vary dramatically, but as a guide most souks open daily 9am–7pm, with some closing early on Fridays. Shops in Guéliz usually open 9:30am–1pm and 3–7:30pm Monday through Saturday.

CONSULATES AND EMBASSIES **US Consulate**, 8 Boulevard Moulay Youssef, Casablanca 20000 (☎ 0522-20-41-27); **Canadian Embassy**, 13 bis Rue Jaafa-as-Sadik, Agdal Rabat (☎ 0537-68-74-00); **British Consulate**, 55 Boulevard Zerktouni, Guéliz (☎ 0524-42-08-46); **Irish Consulate**, Boulevard Moulay Ismail, Route de Rabat, Casablanca (☎ 0522-66-03-06).

CUSTOMS AND TAXES You're allowed to import one liter of spirits or wine and 200 cigarettes. Sales tax, value added tax (VAT), is 20%. Travelers are entitled to a refund. For details see **www.globalrefund.com**.

DENTISTS & DOCTORS The private hospital **Polyclinique du Sud** (2 rue de Yugoslavie; ☎ 0524-44-79-99) can treat medical and dental emergencies 24/7 and has English-speaking doctors. Another recommended doctor is **Dr Hamid Laraqui** (203 Ave Mohammed; ☎ 0524-43-32-16).

ELECTRICITY Morocco has 220V, cycle AC, frequency 50Hz. European two-pin plugs are standard.

EMERGENCIES Dial ☎ 19 for the police or ☎ 15 for the fire service. To report a theft or crime, call the brigade touristique (tourist police) ☎ 0524-38-46-01. See 'Dentists & Doctors', above.

GAY AND LESBIAN TRAVELERS Marrakech is tolerant for a Muslim city, yet still somewhat 'in the closet' when it comes to homosexuality, which remains taboo. That said, there are a few gay-friendly places in town including **Diamant Noir** (p 126). Gay sex is illegal, though most people adopt the attitude that what goes on behind closed doors isn't their concern.

HEALTH Immunizations are not a prerequisite to enter Morocco, but your doctor may recommend boosters for hepatitis A and typhoid. Most travel complaints concern upset stomachs, and so pack those anti-diarrheals. Avoid tap water (stick to bottled water), ice, and street food cooked in unhygienic conditions; take a peek at the kitchen if you can, and eat where the locals do. Year-round it's advisable to wear sunscreen and drink plenty of water to prevent dehydration.

HOLIDAYS The Islamic calendar determines when religious holidays fall each year, which include: Islamic New Year (7th December, 2010; 26th November, 2011); Mawlid al-Nabi or Prophet's Birthday (26th February, 2010; 15th February, 2011); beginning of Ramadan (11th August 11, 2010; 1st August, 2011); end of Ramadan or Eid al-Fitr (10th October, 2010; 30th August, 2011); and Festival of Sacrifice or Eid al-Adha (15th November, 2010; 6th November, 2011). **Moroccan state holidays** include: 1st January (New Year's Day), 11th January (Manifesto of Independence), 1st May (Labor Day), 30th July (Feast of the Throne), 14th August (Allegiance Day), 20th August (Feast of the King and the People's Revolution), 21st August (King Mohammed's Birthday), 6th November (Anniversary of the Green March) and 18th November (Independence Day).

INSURANCE It's essential to have an adequate insurance policy before traveling to Marrakech, covering cancellation, lost luggage, and medical emergencies (Morocco has no reciprocal health care agreements with other countries). Try the following in the US: **Access America** (☎ 866/807-3982; www.access america.com); **Travel Guard International** (☎ 800/826-4919; www. travelguard.com); **Travel Insured International** (☎ 800/243-3174; www.travelinsured.com); and **Travelex Insurance Services** (☎ 888/457-4602; www.travelex-insurance. com). Recommended in the UK are **Money Supermarket** (☎ 0845/345-5708; www.moneysupermarket. com) and **Atlas Direct** (www.atlas direct.net). For additional medical insurance in the US, contact **MEDEX Assistance** (☎ 410/453-6300; www. medexassist.com) or **Travel Assistance International** (☎ 800/821-2828; www.travelassistance.com).

INTERNET Internet cafés generally open 10am–11pm and charge

around 7–12dh for an hour. You'll find them around Jemaa el Fna, Rue Bab Agnaou, and Avenue Mohammed V. Computers can be slow, particularly in the evening when locals are online. The best place for speedy connections is the modern **Cyber Park** (p 16), charging 5dh per hour. Numerous riads, bars, and cafés now offer free WiFi including **Café des Épices** (p 21) and **Café du Livre** (p 74).

LOST PROPERTY Should your wallet wander off, call your credit company immediately and contact the police ☎ 19. **Visa**'s toll-free emergency number in the US is ☎ 800/847-2911, or ☎ 002-11-00-11, then enter 8066-654-0163 in Morocco. **American Express** cardholders and traveler's check holders should call ☎ 800/221-7282 in the US, or reverse-charge phone number ☎ 5336/393-1111 in Morocco. **MasterCard** holders should call ☎ 800/627-8372 in the US, or reverse-charge phone number ☎ 5636/722-7111 overseas.

MAIL & POSTAGE Poste Maroc (☎ 0524-33-09-50; www.bam.net. ma) provides postal services in Morocco. Post offices are identified by a yellow-and-blue sign. Most open from 8:30am–6:30pm Monday through Friday, and Saturday 8:30am–12pm. The main post office is on Place du 16 Novembre (p 75), where you can buy stamps and pick up *poste restante* (general delivery) mail. There is another central branch on Jemaa el Fna. As one riad owner put it: Moroccan mail makes its way across the Atlantic on the back of a swimming donkey, so don't expect your postcards to get home before you do!

MONEY Morocco's currency is the **dirham.** At the time of writing, the exchange rate was approximately 10dh = $1.24 (or £0.77; £0.89). For up-to-date rates, check the currency converter website **www.xe.com**.

PASSPORTS & VISAS Nationals of the US, UK, Australia, Canada, New Zealand, and EU countries don't require a visa for stays of less than 90 days. Your passport should be valid for at least six months from the date of entry.

PHARMACIES There's a 24-hour pharmacy on Jemaa el Fna (☎ 0524-43-04-15), next to the Commissariat, which posts a list of *pharmacies de garde* (late-opening pharmacies). Other useful addresses include the **Pharmacie de la Liberté** (☎ 0524-44-69-51) on Place de la Liberté and **Pharmacie Dar El Bacha** (☎ 0524-38-69-88) on Rue Fatima Zohra.

POLICE The brigade touristique (p 165) on Rue Sidi Mimoun are geared up to assist tourists. For local police, dial ☎ 19.

SAFETY Marrakech is overall a safe city, particularly since the plain-clothes tourist police began patrolling the medina. You're more likely to be a victim of petty theft or carpet-shop scams than violent crime. Pickpockets prowl Jemaa el Fna by night. A few common-sense precautions—not walking down dark *derbs* alone (particularly women), hiding your cash in a money belt, and watching your valuables—should minimize any risk. Unofficial guides in the souks are more annoying than dangerous.

TELEPHONES Call ☎ 160 for local directory enquiries and ☎ 120 for the international operator. If you're making an international call, dial ☎ 00, wait for the tone, and then enter the country code, area code, and number. The country code for Morocco is ☎ 212. Marrakech's area code is ☎ 0524.

TIPPING Tip waiters at restaurants and tour guides roughly 10%. Round up the bill if you've just had tea or a snack. Tip porters around 10dh and riad staff about the same per day. Keep a few dirham handy for doormen, washroom attendants, street entertainers posing for photos on Jemaa el Fna, and anyone else who performs a service for you. Taxi drivers don't expect a tip (they often overcharge anyway), but I often reward their honesty if they switch on the meter!

TOILETS Public toilets are extremely rare in Marrakech, though you find facilities at most major attractions. If you get stuck in the souks, your best bet is to order a drink in a café or riad where you can use the (generally clean) toilets.

TOURIST INFORMATION The **ONMT** tourist office (Place Abdel Moumen ben Ali, ☎ 0524-43-61-79) is open Monday through Friday 8:30am–12pm and 2:30–6:30pm, and Saturday 9am–12pm and 3–6pm. It has a small selection of brochures and can recommend official guides.

TRAVELERS WITH DISABILITIES Narrow *derbs* in the medina, heavy traffic, and riads without lifts don't make Marrakech the most accessible of destinations, but don't be discouraged. With a little extra planning it's possible for travelers with disabilities to discover the city. Book a ground-floor hotel room in a part of town reachable by taxi such as Guéliz or the Palmeraie. Marrakchis are a flexible lot and will do everything they can to accommodate your needs. **Access-Able Travel Source** (☎ 303/232-2979; www.access-able.com) has access information for people traveling worldwide.

Marrakech: **A Brief History**

1062 Marrakech is a military camp until Almoravid leader Youssef ben Tachfine 'the Wise and Shrewd' makes the strategic trading post the capital of Morocco. He oversees the construction of the medina ramparts and the irrigation network.

1106 Tachfine's pious son, Ali ben Youssef ascends to throne and reigns until 1142. The new sultan further develops Marrakech's architecture and irrigation systems. The *medersa* (p 8) is named in his honor.

1147 A rival Berber tribe, the Almohads, seize control of Marrakech, demolishing nearly every Almoravid monument, including Koutoubia. Under Almohad rule, Marrakech thrives as a trade hub on the trans-Saharan caravan route.

1150 Construction begins on the new Koutoubia (p 7) mosque with a magnificent minaret added as a final flourish.

1184 Sultan Yacoub el-Mansour, rises to the throne, creating the Kasbah (p 54), the monumental city gate Bab Agnaou (p 57), and the Agdal and Menara gardens (p 101). His 15-year reign marks the start of a golden age, attracting scholars, poets, philosophers, and great thinkers to the city.

1269 The Merenids oust the Almohads and make the capital of Morocco Fez, pushing Marrakech into a spiral of decline. The city falls into shambles and famine.

1521 Saâdian leaders seize control of Marrakech and work architectural wonders, using the money gained from trading sugar to employ some of Morocco's top artisans to restore the city to its former glory.

1558 Saâdian Sultan Malay Abdullah bankrolls the Jewish quarter (Mellah) and is paid back tenfold in tax. He uses his newfound wealth to rebuild Ali ben Youssef Medersa (p 8).

1578 Malay Abdullah's powerful successor Ahmed el-Mansur (the Golden), who reigns until 1603, trades in sugar and slaves, and pours his riches into the opulent Badi Palace (p 33) and the Saâdian Tombs (p 43). Marrakech prospers under his Midas touch.

1672 The Saâdis are conquered by the Arab Alouites, who plunder the Badi Palace, seal up the Saâdian Tombs, and move the capital of Morocco to Meknès, dealing a hefty blow to Marrakech. Moulay Ismail 'the Bloodthirsty' (1672–1727) instills terror, with an insatiable appetite for slavery.

1750 Sultan Sidi Mohammed III decides to restore Marrakech, which has fallen into a terrible state of disrepair.

1792 Mad Sultan Moulay Yazid is the last to be buried in the Saâdian Tombs.

1866–7 Sultan Moulay Hassan builds the sublime Bahia Palace (p 44) for his grand vizier (similar to a prime minister) Si Moussa.

1890s Si Moussa's son, Bou Ahmed, extends the Bahia Palace, adding a garden and a hammam for his four wives, 24 concubines, and countless offspring. When he dies, the palace is ransacked and his family expelled.

1912 Saharan chieftain El Hiba captures Marrakech, but his triumph is short lived. French forces soon occupy the city establishing a 'protectorate', (lasting until 1956) and during this period build Ville Nouvelle.

1918 The French colonialists appoint Berber warlord Thami el-Glaoui as Pasha of Marrakech, giving him power to do as he pleases, namely torturing dissidents. He also finds time to schmooze with royalty and play golf with Winston Churchill.

1953–5 Thami el-Glaoui conspires with the French to overthrow Morocco's rightful king, Mohammed V; bloody nationalist riots mark the beginning of the end for the French occupation.

1956 Morocco gains independence under King Mohammed V. Thami el-Glaoui begs for forgiveness on his deathbed. Rabat remains the capital of Morocco.

1961 King Mohammed V dies and his son, Hassan II, ascends the throne in an unstable political and economic climate.

1967–9 The Summer of Love (1967) draws hippies and rock stars seeking kif, exotic climes, and spiritual enlightenment to Marrakech. Crosby, Stills, and Nash release 'Marrakech Express' in 1969.

1975 Hassan II arranges the Green March, a mass protest where 350,000 civilians march to the Western Sahara to lay claim to the Spanish colony and its lucrative phosphate industry.

1999 King Hassan II dies and Mohammed VI breaths fresh life into the monarchy, pledging to 'reign over a state of law not of fear'.

2000s King Mohammed VI's vision to attract 10 million tourists to Morocco by 2010.

Marrakech **Culture Savvy**

SOCIAL GRACES Before you pack the beachwear, consider that Morocco is a **Muslim** country, and so a few social graces will go a long way.

Dress conservatively in loose clothing such as long-sleeved tops and baggy skirts or trousers—skimpy skirts and tight tops often draw unwanted attention. Women may also wish to cover their hair. Solo women travelers sometimes feel harassed, but if you dress appropriately, appear confident, and ignore the cat calls of *salut la gazelle!*, you should be fine.

Greet locals warmly with a handshake and touch your heart with your right hand to show sincerity. If you're invited to a home, remove your shoes as you enter. Take a small gift for the host, such as sweets or figs. Eat with your right hand (the left is considered 'unclean'). Drinking alcohol or displaying affection—hand holding and kissing in public is considered disrespectful. Finally, don't assume that everyone in Marrakech is out to cheat you; most locals are genuinely friendly. Never make a Moroccan lose honor (face) by being rude. If a situation gets heated, walk away.

FAITH Faith is everywhere you look in Marrakech: the muezzin's piercing call at 5am, slender minarets rising above the medina, and inscriptions from the Koran adorning palaces.

Spa Speak

Gommage: An invigorating scrub using *savon noir* (see below) and an exfoliating *kessa* glove, which removes layers of dead skin, cleanses the pores, and improves circulation.

Kessa: The Brillo-like mitt used for the gommage, featuring a grainy texture to remove impurities and leave skin radiant.

Rhassoul: Mineral-rich clay from the Atlas Mountains said to improve skin texture and leave hair glossy. The powder is mixed into a paste with water and applied from head to toe in the hammam.

Savon Noir: Gloopy black soap made from olive oil and crushed olive pits, and often scented with eucalyptus. It's left to work for a few minutes, and then removed with a *kessa* glove during the gommage.

Non-Muslims aren't admitted to mosques, where locals pray five times a day. Be particularly sensitive during **Ramadan**—try not to eat, drink, or smoke in public during the day.

PHOTOGRAPHY If you want to take a photo, it's respectful to ask permission first as many Muslims—especially women—feel uncomfortable in front of the lens. Others, such as the Gnaoua musicians, acrobats and snake charmers on Jemaa el Fna, earn a living in tips from posing for photos.

HAMMAM ETIQUETTE Visiting a hammam is a must-have Marrakech experience. With a little know-how

even your first time to a public hammam can be enjoyable instead of bewildering. It may sound like a cliché, but go with the flow: take a mat to avoid sitting in the sludge, a rough kessa mitt, toiletries, and a change of underwear. Leave modesty at the door, your clothes and towel in the changing room, and then venture into the warren of tiled chambers with gushing faucets. The closer you get to the wood fire, the hotter and steamier it becomes. For the uninitiated, it's easier to pay the *tayeba* (hammam attendant) to perform the gommage, apply the *rhassoul* clay, and throw buckets of warm and ice-cold water at you.

Useful Phrases & Menu Terms

Useful Words & Phrases

ENGLISH	FRENCH	PRONUNCIATION
Hello (good day)	Bonjour	bohn-jhoor
Good evening	Bonsoir	bohn-swahr
Goodbye	Au revoir	o ruh-vwahr
How are you?	Comment ça va?	kuh-mahn sah-vah?
I'm (very) well	Ça va (très) bien	sah-vah treh bee-ahn
Thank you	Merci	mair-see

ENGLISH	FRENCH	PRONUNCIATION
You're welcome	De rien	duh ree-ehn
Please	S'il vous plaît	seel voo play
Yes/No	Oui/Non	wee/noh
Pleased to meet you	Enchanté(e) (m/f)	ahn-shahn-tai
What's your name?	Comment vous appelez-vous?	kuh-mahn voo za-pel-ay-voo?
My name is	Je m'appelle	jhuh-ma-pel
I'm sorry/excuse me	Pardon	pahr-dohn
Do you speak English?	Parlez-vous anglais?	par-lay-voo zahn-glay?
I don't understand	Je ne comprends pas	jhuh ne kohm-prahn pas
Where is...?	Où est...?	ooh eh...?
the train station	la gare	lah gar
the bus station	la gare routière	lah gar roo-tee-air
the bank	la banque	lah bahnk
the market	le marché	luh mahr-shay
the police station	le commissariat	luh koh-mee-sah-ree-a
the toilets	les toilettes	lay twa-let
the pharmacy	la pharmacie	lah far-ma-see
the main square	la place	lah plass
here/there	ici/llà	ee-see/lah
left/right	à gauche/à droite	a gohsh/a drwaht
straight ahead	tout droit	too drwah
a ticket	un billet	uh bee-yay
one-way ticket	aller simple	ah-lay sam-pluh
return ticket	aller-retour	ah-lay re-toor
How much is it?	Ça, c'est combien?	Sah, seh kom-bee-an?
It's too expensive	C'est trop cher	Seh troh sh-air
I will give you...	Je vous donne...	jhuh voo dohn...
Do you have a room for...?	Avez-vous une chambre pour...?	Avay-voo ewn shawm-bruh poor...?
with a shower/ a bath	avec une douche/ avek ewn dooch/	une baignoire ewn bay-nwar
Is breakfast included?	Petit déjeuneur inclus?	peh-tee day-jheun-ay ehn-klu?
air-conditioning	climatisation	klee-ma-tee-sa-see-on

Numbers

ENGLISH	FRENCH	PRONUNCIATION
1	un	uhn
2	deux	duh
3	trois	twah
4	quatre	kah-truh
5	cinq	sank
6	six	seess
7	sept	set
8	huit	weet
9	neuf	nuhf
10	dix	deess

ENGLISH	FRENCH	PRONUNCIATION
11	onze	ohnz
12	douze	dooz
13	treize	trehz
14	quatorze	kah-torz
15	quinze	kanz
16	seize	sez
17	dix-sept	deez-set
18	dix-huit	deez-weet
19	dix-neuf	deez-noof
20	vingt	vehn
30	trente	trahnt
40	quarante	kah-rahnt
50	cinquante	sang-kahnt
100	cent	sahn
1,000	mille	meel

Days of the Week

ENGLISH	FRENCH	PRONUNCIATION
Monday	lundi	luhn-dee
Tuesday	mardi	mahr-dee
Wednesday	mercredi	mair-kruh-dee
Thursday	jeudi	jheu-dee
Friday	vendredi	vawn-druh-dee
Saturday	samedi	sahm-dee
Sunday	dimanche	dee-mahnsh
Today	aujourd'hui	o-jhor-dwee
Tomorrow	demain	de-man
Tonight	ce soir	suh swahr
Yesterday	hier	ee-air

Menu Savvy

ENGLISH	FRENCH	PRONUNCIATION
I would like	Je voudrais	jhe voo-dray
To book a table for…at…	réserver une table pour… à…	reh-zher-vay ewn ta-bleh poor…a…
Please give me…	Donnez-moi… s'il vous plaît	doe-nay-mwah… seel voo play
the menu (wine list)	la carte (des vins)	la cart (day van)
the check/bill	l'addition	la-dee-see-ohn
a fork	une fourchette	ewn four-shet
a spoon	une cuillère	ewn kwee-air
a knife	un couteau	uh koo-toe
a napkin	une serviette	ewn sair-vee-et
a bottle of	une bouteille de	ewn boo-tay duh
a cup of	une tasse de	ewn tass duh
a glass of	un verre de	uh vair duh
appetizer	une entrée	ewn en-tray
main course	un plat principal	uh plah pran-see-pahl
breakfast	petit déjeuner	peh-tee day-jheun-ay
lunch	déjeuner	day-jheun-ay

ENGLISH	FRENCH	PRONUNCIATION
dinner	dîner	deen-eh
service/tip included	service compris	sehr-vees cohm-pree
waiter/ waitress	Monsieur/ Mademoiselle	muh-syuh/ mad-mwa-zel

Toll-Free Numbers & Websites

AER LINGUS
☎ 800/474-7424 in the US
☎ 01/886-8844 in Ireland
www.aerlingus.com

AIR CANADA
☎ 888/247-2262
www.aircanada.com

AIR FRANCE
☎ 800/237-2747 in the US
☎ 0820-820-820 in France
www.airfrance.com

AIR NEW ZEALAND
☎ 800/262-1234 or -2468 in the US
☎ 800/663-5494 in Canada
☎ 0800/737-000 in New Zealand
www.airnewzealand.com

ALITALIA
☎ 800/223-5730 in the US
☎ 8488-65641 in Italy
www.alitalia.com

AMERICAN AIRLINES
☎ 800/433-7300
www.aa.com

AUSTRIAN AIRLINES
☎ 800/843-0002 in the US
☎ 43/(0)5-1789 in Austria
www.aua.com

BMI
No US number
☎ 0870/6070-222 in Britain
www.flybmi.com

BRITISH AIRWAYS
☎ 800/247-9297 in the US
☎ 0870/850-9-850 in Britain
www.british-airways.com

CONTINENTAL AIRLINES
☎ 800/525-0280
www.continental.com

DELTA AIR LINES
☎ 800/221-1212
www.delta.com

EASYJET
No US number
www.easyjet.com

IBERIA
☎ 800/772-4642 in the US
☎ 902/400-500 in Spain
www.iberia.com

ICELANDAIR
☎ 800/223-5500 in the US
☎ 354/50-50-100 in Iceland
www.icelandair.is

KLM
☎ 800/374-7747 in the US
☎ 020/4-747-747 in the Netherlands
www.klm.com

LUFTHANSA
☎ 800/645-3880 in the US
☎ 49/(0)-180-5-838426 in Germany
www.lufthansa.com

NORTHWEST AIRLINES
☎ 800/225-2525
www.nwa.com

QANTAS
☎ 800/227-4500 in the US
☎ 612/131313 in Australia
www.qantas.com

SCANDINAVIAN AIRLINES
☎ 800/221-2350 in the US
☎ 0070/727-727 in Sweden
www.scandinavian.net

SWISS INTERNATIONAL AIRLINES
☎ 877/359-7947 in the US
☎ 0848/85-2000 in Switzerland
www.swiss.com

UNITED AIRLINES
☎ 800/241-6522
www.united.com

US AIRWAYS
☎ 800/428-4322
www.usairways.com

VIRGIN ATLANTIC AIRWAYS
☎ 800/862-8621 in continental US
☎ 0870/380-2007 in Britain
www.virgin-atlantic.com

Index

See also Accommodations and Restaurant indexes, below.

A

Access-Able Travel Source, 167
Acrobats, 63
Actor's (club), 125–126
Adhan, 3, 21, 61
African Chic (bar), 114, 133
Agafay Desert, 98
Agdal Gardens, 59, 101, 168
Ahmed el-Mansour, 12, 33, 43, 57, 58, 69, 168
Aïcha des Gazelles (festival), 160
Air travel, 162
Ali Ben Youssef Medersa, 3–4, 8, 46, 67–68, 145, 168
Ali Ben Youssef Mosque, 67, 68
Allegiance Day, 166
Almohads, 168
Almoravid monument, 8
Alouites, 168
Amentis (supper club), 120, 127
Amir, Noureddine, 91
Amlou, 149
Andalusian gardens, 11
Antiques, 80, 86–87
Apartment rentals, 164–165
Architecture
    Ali Ben Youssef Mosque, 68
    Gare de Marrakech, 77, 163
    Koubba Ba'adyin, 8, 45, 46, 68
    Koubba Fatima Zohra, 61
    Koutoubia, 3, 7, 21, 43, 61, 77, 168
    Théâtre Royal, 76, 134, 160
    tour of, 42–46
Argan oil, 80, 87, 88, 89, 149
Art galleries and museums
    Dar Si Said, 11, 27–28, 32–33, 44, 45, 55, 145
    in Essaouira, 152
    Galerie 127, 76, 86

Galerie Noir Sur Blanc, 76, 86
    in Guéliz, 76
    Islamic Art Museum, 15, 26, 74
    Khalid Art Gallery, 38, 70, 80, 86
    La Qoubba Galerie, 69, 80, 86
    Matisse Art Gallery, 76, 86
    Ministerio del Gusto, 38, 39
    Musée de Marrakech, 8, 29, 32, 45, 68–69
Arts and crafts tour, 24–29
Assalam aleikum, 49
Assouss Argane, 80, 87–88, 149
Atika (store), 75, 89
Atlas Karting, 98
Atlas Mountains, 99, 101, 157, 163
ATMs, 165
Au Fil D'Or, 39, 50, 80, 90
Authentic Morocco, 153, 158
Avenue Mohammed V, 77
Aya's (store), 27, 90

B

Bab Agnaou, 13, 43, 57, 168
Bab Debbagh, 66
Bab Doukkala mosque, 71
Bab Hmar, 97
Bab Jdid, 101
Babouches, 7, 26, 28, 51, 80, 90, 91, 144, 152
Badi Palace, 33, 57, 160, 168
Bahia Palace, 4, 11–12, 44, 55, 160, 168
Balloon flights, 98
Banks, 165
Bars, 124, 125
Bartering, 51
Bathhouses, 22. See also Hammams
Bazar Ben Allal, 87
Beaches
    at Essaouira, 151, 153
    La Plage Rouge, 4, 40, 120, 128
    Nikki Beach, 4, 34–35, 128
Beach parties, 128
Beghrir, 113
Benacher, Mustapha, 16

Ben Rahal (store), 75, 80, 87
Bergé, Pierre, 26, 40
Bhous, 45, 125
Biking, quad, 98
Birkemeyer, Frédérique, 91
Bob Music, 40, 80, 94
Boccara, Charles, 76, 140, 141
Borj el-Berod, 153
Botanical gardens
    Jardin Majorelle, 4, 15, 26, 40, 74, 101, 102
    Nectarome, 156
Bou Ahmed, 11, 168
Bô-Zin (supper club), 120, 127
Brahim, Ahamed, 87
Briouatte, 113
Brisara, 113
Bristow, Joanna, 90
Buggy raiding, 98
Buses, 153, 163
Business hours, 165

C

Café Arabe, 111, 124
Café des Épices, 166
Café des Négociants, 124
Café du Livre, 166
Café Extrablatt, 16, 120, 124
Cafés, 124, 125
Caftan (festival), 160
Caidals, 127
Calèches, 7, 12, 61, 163–164
Calligraphy, 45
Calling codes, 167
Camel rides, 4, 22, 23, 97, 153
Caravan routes, 168
Carpets, 71, 75, 80, 87
Carpet Souk (Criée Berbere), 7, 20, 28, 50
Car rentals, 162
Carriages, horse-drawn, 102, 163–164
Casino de Marrakech, 78, 133
Casinos, 78, 133
Celebrity Marrakech tour, 36–41
Cell phones, 161–162
Ceramics, 28, 55
Chamber of the Twelve Pillars, 43, 58
Chater, Nourredine, 76
Cheno, Bruno, 128
Cherakaoui, Larbi, 76
Chez Ali (supper club), 127–128

Children
camel rides for, 22, 23
gardens for, 7, 32, 34, 76, 78
in Green Marrakech, 101
hotels catering to, 141–143, 145
at Koutoubia, 21, 61
restaurants for, 110, 111, 117
shopping with, 20, 80, 89, 91, 93
water parks for, 99
Chouf, 69
Chouf Fountain, 46, 69
Churchill, Winston, 169
Ciel d'Afrique, 98
Cigognes, 141
Cinema, 39, 133, 161
Cinéma Eden, 133
Cinéma Le Colisée, 39, 133
Cinema Mabrouka, 133
Circuit de la Palmeraie, 102
Circus, open-air. *See* Jemaa el Fna
City Hall (Hôtel de Ville), 77
Climate, 160, 161
Clubs, 125–127
Consulates, 165
Coopérative Artisanal des Marqueteurs, 152
Cornes de gazelle, 62, 75, 94, 113, 155
Cornut, Théodore, 151
Cosmetics, 87–89
Côté Sud, 75, 91
Coustal, Philippe, 117
Crafts, 92–93, 152
arts and crafts tour, 24–29
best bets, 28, 80
at Ensemble Artisanal, 15–16, 26, 77, 80, 91
at foundouks, 20, 29, 38, 53, 70, 80, 92
in foundouks, 20, 29, 53, 70
at Place des Ferblantiers (Tinsmith's Square), 13, 21–22, 26–27, 56–57
in Ville Nouvelle neighborhood, 75
Credit cards, 165
Criée Berbère (Carpet Souk), 7, 20, 28, 50
Crosby, Stills, and Nash, 169
Currency, 162, 166–167
Customs, 165

Cyber cafés, 101, 166
Cyber Park, 16, 26, 77, 78, 101, 160, 166

D
Damgaard, Frederic, 152
Dancers, High Atlas, 160
Dar al Baida pavilion, 101
Dar Charkia, 90
Dar Chérifa, 32
Dar el Bacha Palace, 70, 112
Darj w ktarf motifs, 7, 43, 58, 61
Dar M'Nebhi Palace, 29
Dars, 27
Dar Si Said, 11, 27–28, 32–33, 44, 45, 55, 145
Day trips and excursions, 148–158
Essaouira, 148–155
Oukaimeden, 156, 158
Ourika Valley, 156–158
Dentists, 63, 165
Derbs, 13, 144, 164
Derb Zaouiat Lakhdar, 67
Diamant Noir (club), 114, 120, 126, 165
Diffa, 29, 97
Dining. *See also* Restaurant Index
best bets, 104
in Essaouira, 150, 155
in Jemaa el Fna, 4, 63, 118
maps, 105–109
in Setti Fatma, 157–158
at supper clubs, 127–128
Dirham, 166–167
Disabilities, travelers with, 167
Djinn, 152
Dobry, Yann, 89
Doctors, 165
Doors, decorative, 44
Dress, appropriate, 169
Dried-fruit carts, in Jemaa el Fna, 63
Drinking water, 118, 165
Driving, 153, 158, 162–164
Dromedary rides, 4, 22, 23, 97, 153
Dune buggies, 98
Dyer's Souk (Souk Sebbaghine), 7–8, 52–53, 87

E
Ebookers (website), 142
Église des Saints-Martyrs, 78
Eid al-Adha, 166
Eid al-Fitr, 166
Electricity, 165
Electronics, 51–52
El Hiba, 169
Embassies, 165
Emergencies, 165
Ensemble Artisanal, 15–16, 26, 77, 80, 91
Entertainment. *See* Jemaa el Fna
Es Saadi Gardens and Resort, 41, 127
Essaouira, 4, 29, 99, 148–155, 160
Essaouira Bay, 153
Eurolines, 163
Exchange rate, 166–167

F
Faith, 169, 170
Fashion, 38, 39, 50, 75, 80, 89–91, 160
Fatima hand, 46
Feast of the King and the People's Revolution, 166
Feast of the Throne, 166
Festivals, 152, 160–161
Fez, 168
Film, 39, 133, 161
Fish auction, 150
Flint, Bert, 27, 55
Foundouk al Mizane, 29, 53, 80, 92
Foundouks, 20, 70
Foundouk Sarsar, 38, 53
Foundouk Tiwtiw, 29
Fountains, 46, 53, 69
4L Trophy rally, 161
Fragrances, 89
French language, 170–173
French occupation, 169
Friendship Festival, 160
Fruit and Nut Souk (Souk Kchacha), 49
Full-day tours
one day, 6–9
two day, 10–13
three day, 14–16
Furans, 4, 56, 67

G
Galerie 127, 76, 86
Galerie d'Art Damgaard, 152
Galerie Noir Sur Blanc, 76, 86

Garden of Paradise, 102
Gardens
    Agdal Gardens, 59,
      101, 168
    Andalusian gardens, 11
    at Bahia Palace, 55
    Cyber Park, 16, 26, 77,
      78, 101, 160, 166
    Dar Si Said, 11, 27–28,
      32–33, 44, 45, 55,
      145
    Es Saadi Gardens and
      Resort, 41, 127
    Jardin el Harti, 76
    Jardin Majorelle, 4, 15,
      26, 40, 74, 101, 102
    Koutoubia Gardens,
      7, 32, 61, 101
    Menara Gardens, 12,
      34, 101, 168
    Nectarome, 156
    at riads, 4, 35
Gare de Marrakech, 77, 163
Gay and lesbian travelers,
  165
Gifts, 28, 71, 80, 91–93, 152
Gili, Xavier Arnaud, 110
Ginseng, 88
Glaoui, Hassan El, 76
Gnaoua and World Music
  Festival, 152, 160
Gnaoua musicians, 62, 63
Golf, 97
Gommage, 170
Grand Balcon du Café
  Glacier, 63, 120, 124
Grand Hotel Tazi (bar), 62,
  120, 124
Grand taxis, 158, 164
Green March, 169
Green Marrakech, 100–102
Guéliz, 4, 15, 71, 75, 76,
  165
Guelsa, 22
Guetta, David, 126
Guides, 13, 66

H
Haggling, 51
Hammam Ben Youssef, 67
Hammams, 8. *See also* Spas
    Es Saadi Gardens and
      Resort, 41, 127
    etiquette and services,
      22, 170
    at hotels, 140–146
    La Maison Arabe, 16,
      38, 134
Harira, 4, 111, 113
Hassan II, 169
Healers, 63

Health, 165
Herbal remedies, 20–21,
  50, 57, 80, 87–89, 152
Herboristerie Palais El
  Badia, 57, 80, 88
Hideous Kinky (film), 38, 53
High Atlas, 34, 161
High Atlas dancers, 160
Hiking, 157
Historical sites
    Ali Ben Youssef Med-
      ersa, 3–4, 8, 46,
      67–68, 145, 168
    Bab Agnaou, 13, 43,
      57, 168
    Bab Doukkala
      mosque, 71
    Borj el-Berod, 153
    Chouf Fountain, 46, 69
    Dar Chérifa, 32
    Dar Si Said, 55
    Koubba Ba'adyin, 8, 45,
      46, 68
    Koubba Fatima
      Zohra, 61
    ramparts, 43, 62,
      151–152
    ramparts at Essaouira,
      151–152
    Saâdian Tombs, 12,
      43–44, 58, 168
Hivernage neighborhood,
  4, 16, 78, 101
Holidays, 165–166
Homosexuality, 165
Horse-drawn carriages,
  102, 163–164
Horse riding, 98
Hot-air balloon flights, 98
Hôtel de Ville (City Hall), 77
Hotel Les Jardins de la
  Koutoubia, 134
Hotels. *See* Lodging

I
Île de Mogador, 149, 150
Imilchil Marriage Festival,
  161
Immunizations, 165
Independence Day, 166
Institut Français, 134
Insurance, 166
Intensité Nomade, 75,
  80, 91
Internet access, 166
Islamic Art Museum, 15,
  26, 74
Islamic faith, 46, 102, 169,
  170
Islamic New Year, 166

J
Jad Mahal (supper club),
  128
Jamade (store), 28, 55, 93
Jardin'Art (festival), 160
Jardin el Harti, 76
Jardin Majorelle, 4, 15, 26,
  40, 74, 101, 102
Jbel Attar, 158
Jbel Toukal, 157
Jellabahs, 7, 28, 89, 90, 91,
  144
Jemaa el Fna, 3, 8–9
  dining in, 4, 63, 118
  entertainment in,
    21, 134
  festivals in, 160, 161
  lodging in, 144, 146
  map, 63
  walking around in,
    60–63, 164
Jewelry, 28, 29, 39, 50, 51,
  80, 93, 152
Jewelry Souk, at Essaouira,
  152
Jewish quarter (Mellah
  neighborhood), 54,
  56–57, 59, 168
Jnane Tamsna, 102
Jones, Robert Trent, 97
Juice carts, in Jemaa
  el Fna, 63

K
Kasbah Mosque, 57–58
Kasbah neighborhood, 54,
  57–59, 144, 164, 168
Kechmara (lounge), 114,
  120, 124
Kefta, 113
Kessa, 170
Khalid Art Gallery, 38, 70,
  80, 86
Khamsa, 46
Khettara, 102
Kingdom of Heaven (film),
  38, 152
King Mohammed's Birthday,
  166
Kite-surfing, 99, 151
Koran, 102
Kosybar, 3, 13, 120,
  124–125, 134
Koubba, 8, 68
Koubba Ba'adyin, 8, 45,
  46, 68
Koubba Fatima Zohra, 61
Koutoubia, 3, 7, 21, 43, 61,
  77, 168
Koutoubia Gardens, 7, 32,
  61, 101

L

Labor Day, 166
La Casa (bar), 125
Ladeuil, Cyril, 154
La Maison Arabe, 16, 38, 134
La Maison du Kaftan Marocain, 38, 91
La Mamounia (hotel), 40, 62, 78
La Mamounia Casino, 133
La Plage Rouge, 4, 40, 120, 128
La Qoubba Galerie, 69, 80, 86
La Sultana Spa, 3, 33
Late Rooms (website), 142
Laurent, Yves Saint, 4, 15, 26, 40, 74, 101
Lawrence, Kati, 90
Lawrence Bar, 125
Lazama Synagogue, 56
Leather goods, 51, 66
Le Chesterfield (bar), 125
Le Comptoir Darna (supper club), 4, 16, 23, 78, 120, 128
Leroy, Christophe, 115
Les Bains de Marrakech, 22
L'Escale (bar), 125
Le Tanjia (supper club), 120, 128
Le Théâtro (club), 78
Lippini, Allessandra, 39, 86
Live music venues, 114, 133–134
Lodging. See also Accommodations Index
    best bets, 136
    booking, 142
    in Essaouira, 154
    maps, 137–139
L'Orientaliste, 75, 93
Lost property, 166
Lounges, 124–125
Low season, 142

M

Maâlems, 52, 92
Mafid, Kharbibi Moulay, 29
Magical Marrakech tour, 18–23
Magic festivals, 23, 160
Magic Fun Afrika, 151
Mail, 166
Maimoune, Ali, 152
Maison Rouge, 75, 91, 93
Maison Tiskiwin, 27, 55
Majorelle, Jacques, 15, 74
Malay Abdullah, 168

Manifesto of Independence, 166
The Man Who Knew Too Much (film), 40, 41
Marabouts, 69
Marathons, 161
Marché Central, 75
Markets, 75. See also Souks
Marrakech
    culture of, 169–170
    favorite moments in, 3–4
    history of, 168–169
    maps, 2
    as The Red City, 43
"Marrakech Express" (song), 41
Marrakech International Film Festival, 39, 161
Marrakech International Magic Festival, 23, 160
Marrakech Marathon, 161
Marrakech Popular Arts Festival, 160
Mashrabiyya, 45
Matisse Art Gallery, 76, 86
Mawlid al-Nabi, 166
Mechoui, 49, 113
Mechoui Street, 49
Medersa, 168
Medina, at Essaouira, 152
Meknès, 168
Méléhi, Youssef, 77
Mellah neighborhood, 44, 56–57, 59, 168
Menara Airport, 162
Menara Gardens, 12, 34, 101, 168
Merenids, 168
Merlons, 46
Miâara, 33, 56
Mihrab, 45
Minbar, 74
Ministerio del Gusto, 38, 39
Mint, 49
Mint tea, 53
Mnebhi, Mehdi, 8
Mobile phones, 161–162
Mogador. See Essaouira
Mohammed V, 169
Mohammed VI, 59, 169
Money, 166–167
Monkeys, 63
Montecristo (club), 120, 126
Montreaux Jazz Festival Morocco, 160
Moroccan cuisine, 113
Morocco (film), 40
Mosques, 57–58, 67, 68, 71, 170
Mouassine Fountain, 53

Mouassine neighborhood, 4, 64, 70–71, 144, 164
Mouhalabieh, 110–111
Moulay Bouzerktoun, 151
Moulay Hassan, 101, 168
Moulay Ismail, 58, 168
Moulay Yazid, 168
Muqarnas, 44, 45
Musée de Marrakech, 8, 29, 32, 45, 68–69
Museums, 27, 55. See also Art galleries and museums
Music
    festivals, 152, 160
    venues for live, 114, 133–134
Musical instruments, 40, 52, 80, 94
Musicians, Gnaoua, 62, 63
Mustapha Blaoui (store), 71

N

Narongsak, Khun, 110
Nectarome, 156
Neighborhood walks, 48–78
    central souks, 48–53
    Jemaa el Fna, 60–63
    Kasbah and Mellah, 54–59
    north of souks and Mouassine, 64–71
    Ville Nouvelle, 72–78
New Feeling (club), 120, 126
New Year's Day, 166
Niam, Barakat, 12
Nigella oil, 88
Nightlife, 120–128
    bars, cafés, and lounges, 124–125
    beach parties, 128
    best bets, 120
    clubs, 125–127
    maps, 121–123
    supper clubs, 127–128
Nikki Beach, 4, 34–35, 128
Nomade Quad, 98

O

Oasiria water park, 99
Oasis. See Palmeraie oasis
Off-road rallies, 160, 161
Olives, 49
Olivier, Pierre, 111, 140
ONMT tourist office, 167
Open-air circus. See Jemaa el Fna
Orange oil, 88
Oriental Spa, 41

Index

Oukaïmeden, 99, 156, 158
Ourika Valley, 34, 156–158, 160
Ourzaz, Said, 152
Outdoor activities, 96–102
    Green Marrakech, 100–102
    and sports, 96–99

P

Pacha (club), 4, 78, 116, 120, 126, 161
Palaces
    Badi Palace, 33, 57, 160, 168
    Bahia Palace, 4, 11–12, 44, 55, 160, 168
    Dar el Bacha Palace, 70, 112
    Dar M'Nebhi Palace, 29
    Dar Si Said, 11, 27–28, 32–33, 44, 45, 55, 145
    Palais Rhoul, 114
    Royal Palace, 58, 59
Palais des Congrès, 39
Palais Rhoul, 114
Palmeraie, 4, 22, 23
Palmeraie Golf Course, 97, 102
Palmeraie Golf Palace, 98
Palmeraie oasis, 97, 102, 140, 144
Paradise Club, 126–127
Parks
    Cyber Park, 16, 26, 77, 78, 101, 160, 166
    Toubkal National Park, 157
Passports, 167
Pastillas, 4, 29, 110, 112–115, 117
Patisseries, 15, 50, 62, 75, 155
Perez, Lynn, 144
Performing arts, 130–134
Personal shoppers, 90
Petit taxis, 13, 164
Pharmacies, 167
Photography, 170
Pisé, 101
Place de Foucauld, 61
Place des Ferblantiers (Tinsmith's Square), 13, 21–22, 26–27, 56–57
Place du 16 Novembre, 75–76
Place Moulay El Hassan, 150
Place Orson Welles, 150

Police, 167
Port, at Essaouira, 150
Postage, 166
Poste Maroc, 166
Poste restante, 166
Priceline (website), 142
Prophet's Birthday, 166
Public toilets, 167
Puro Desert Lounge, 161

Q

Quad biking, 98
Qu'est-ce que vous cherchez?, 13

R

Rabat, 169
Rahba Qedima, 20–21, 50
Raï, 126
Raid Buggy, 98
Ramadan, 166, 170
Ramparts
    at Essaouira, 151–152
    of Marrakech, 43, 62
Recontres Musicales de Marrakech, 160
Recycled materials, crafts from, 92
The Red City, Marrakech as, 43
Religious sites
    Ali Ben Youssef Medersa, 3–4, 8, 46, 67–68, 145, 168
    Ali Ben Youssef Mosque, 67, 68
    Bab Doukkala mosque, 71
    Église des Saints-Martyrs, 78
    Kasbah Mosque, 57–58
    Lazama Synagogue, 56
    Zaouia Sidi Abdel Aziz el Harar, 69
Restaurants. See Restaurant Index
Rhassoul, 16, 20, 38, 67, 87–89, 170
Riad Enija, 35
Riads, 4, 35, 140–146
    amenities of, 144
    in Essaouira, 154
    renting, 142, 164–165
Riad Zitoun el-Jedid, 11, 28, 55
Riad Zitoun el-Kedim, 28, 92
Royal Palace, 58, 59
Royal Tennis Club, 99
Rue Dar el-Bacha, 70–71
Rue de Bab Agnaou, 62

Rue de Bab Debbagh, 66
Rue de Bab Doukkala, 71
Rue de la Liberté, 15, 75

S

Saâdian Tombs, 12, 43–44, 58, 168
Sabra Mode, 50, 93
Safety, 167
Sahara Expedition, 158
Sanchez, Roger, 126
Savon noir, 16, 33, 67, 88, 89, 170
Setti Fatma, 34, 156, 157
Shoppers, personal, 90
Shopping, 80–94. See also Souks
    antiques and art, 80, 86–87
    best bets, 80
    carpets, 71, 75, 80, 87. See Crafts
    in Essaouira, 149, 152
    fashion, 38, 39, 50, 75, 80, 89–91, 160
    at foundouks, 20, 70
    gifts, 28, 71, 80, 91–93, 152
    in Guéliz, 15
    herbal remedies, 20–21, 50, 57, 80, 87–89, 152
    jewelry, 28, 29, 39, 50, 51, 80, 93, 152
    maps, 81–85
Shopping hours, 165
Sidi Abdel Aziz el Harar, 69
Sidi Kaouki, 151
Sidi Mohammed III, 168
Si Moussa, 11, 55, 168
Skala de la Ville, 152
Skala du Port, 149, 150
Skiing, 99, 158
Slipper Souk (Souk des Babouches), 20
Snake-charmers, 63
Social graces, 169
Souks, 3, 8–9, 12. See also specific souks, e.g.: Spice Souk
    business hours of, 165
    central, 48–53
    at Essaouira, 152
    haggling at, 28
    in Tnine Ourika, 157
Souk Belaarif, 51–52
Souk Cherratine, 51
Souk des Babouches (Slipper Souk), 20
Souk Haddadine, 28, 52
Souk Kchacha (Fruit and Nut Souk), 49

Souk Kimakhine, 52
Souk Sebbaghine (Dyer's Souk), 7–8, 52–53, 87
Souk Semmarine, 7, 28, 49–50
Souk Siyyaghin, 51
Souk Smata, 28, 51
Spas, 142. *See also* Hammams
    in hotels, 141, 142, 144
    La Sultana Spa, 3, 33
    Les Bains de Marrakech, 22
    Oriental Spa, 41
Special events, 160–161
Special interest tours, 18–46
    architectural elements, 42–46
    arts and crafts, 24–29
    celebrity Marrakech, 36–41
    magical Marrakech, 18–23
    urban escape acts, 30–35
Spice Souk, 12, 55–56, 152
Sports, 96–99
Storks, 3, 117, 141
Storytellers, 63
Street entertainment. *See* Jemaa el Fna
Summer of Love, 169
Supper clubs, 4, 16, 23, 78, 120, 127–128
Supratours, 153
Surfing, 99, 151

T
Tadelakt, 28, 89, 91, 113
Tafilalet, 39, 50, 80, 94
Tagine, 113
Tanjia, 23, 112, 113, 115, 117, 128
Tanneries, 66
Tap water, 165
Taranne, Florence, 91
Taros Café, 155
Taxes, 165
Taxis, 13, 162, 164, 167
Tayebas, 33, 170
Tea, mint, 53
Telephones, 167
Temperatures, 161
Tennis, 99
Terrasse des Épices, 120, 125
Thami el-Glaoui, 71, 169
Théâtre Royal, 76, 134, 160
Théâtro (club), 4, 120, 127
Thuya, 29

Tinsmith's Square (Place des Ferblantiers), 13, 21–22, 26–27, 56–57
Tipping, 9, 167
Tnine Ourika, 157
Toilets, 167
Toll-free numbers, 173
Toubkal National Park, 157
Tourist information, 160, 167
Tours, guided, 156, 157
Trains, 77, 163
Treks, at Setti Fatma, 157
Trouillet, Laetitia, 90

U
UNESCO World Heritage sites
    Chouf Fountain, 46, 69
    Jemaa el Fna, 9
    medina at Essaouira, 152
Urban escape acts tour, 30–35

V
VAT taxes, 165
Ville Nouvelle neighborhood, 4, 72–78, 144, 169
VIP (club), 127
Visas, 167

W
Walking around, 164. *See also* Neighborhood walks
    in Jemaa el Fna, 60–63, 164
    near Bab Hmar, 97
Water, drinking, 118, 165
Waterfalls, at Setti Fatma, 34, 157
Water parks, 99
Weather, 161
Websites, useful, 162, 173
Welles, Orson, 150
White Room (club), 127
Willis, Bill, 113
Windsurfing, 99, 151

Y
Yacoub el-Mansour, 7, 43, 168
Youssef ben Tachfine, 168

Z
Zaouia, 69
Zaouia Sidi Abdel Aziz el Harar, 69
Zellij, 4, 26, 45
Zohra, Fatima, 61
Zouak, 11, 44, 45, 146

Accommodations Index
Caravanserai, 35, 136, 140
Casa Lalla, 35, 140
Dar Charkia, 136, 140
Dar Donab, 136, 140–141
Dar Les Cigognes, 136, 141
Dar Liouba, 154
Dar Ness, 154
Dar Sholmes, 136, 141
Es Saadi Gardens & Resort, 41, 136, 141
Grand Hotel Tazi, 124
Hotel Les Jardins de la Koutoubia, 134
Jnane Mogador, 136, 141
Jnane Tamsna, 136, 141, 142
La Maison Arabe, 134, 136, 142
La Mamounia, 40, 78
La Sultana, 136, 142
Le Caspien, 136, 142
L'Heure d'Été, 142
Madada Mogador, 154
Maison des Artistes, 154
Moroccan House Hotel, 143
Red House, 146
Riad 72, 136, 143
Riad Baladin, 154
Riad Dar Attajmil, 143
Riad Davia, 136, 143
Riad Eden, 143
Riad el Mansour, 144
Riad Enija, 35, 136, 144
Riad Farnatchi, 35, 136, 144
Riad Hotel Assia, 144
Riad L'Orangerie, 136, 145
Riad Mabrouka, 136, 145
Riad Meriem, 145
Riad Miski, 145
Riad Taghazoute, 146
Riyad El Cadi, 35, 136, 146
Villa des Orangers, 146
Villa Flore, 16, 136, 146

Restaurant Index
Adamo, 104
After Five, 155
Al Ahbab, 9
Al Fassia, 104, 110
Amanjena Thai, 110
Aqua, 110
Beyrouth, 110–111
Bougainvillea Café, 39
Café 16, 76
Café Arabe, 111
Café Argana, 61
Café des Arts, 28
Café des Épices, 21, 104
Café du Livre, 74–75, 104

Cantanzaro, 111
Casa Lalla, 104, 111, 140
Chez Bahia, 111
Chez Chegrouni, 63, 104, 112
Chez Pascal, 104, 112
Chez Sam, 155
Crêperie Mogador, 155
Dar Belkabir, 112
Dar Donab, 35, 70, 104, 112
Dar Es Salam, 41
Dar Marjana, 112
Dar Moha, 112–113
Dar Yacout, 104, 113
Dar Zellij, 113, 114
Earth Café, 12, 44, 104
Grand Café de la Poste, 104, 114
Ice Legend, 7, 104

Jardins de la Medina, 114
Jnane Tamsna, 102
Katsura, 114
Kechmara, 114, 124
L'Abyssin, 114
La Maison Arabe, 71, 104, 115, 142
La Sultana, 104, 115
La Table du Marché, 104, 115
La Taverne, 115
La Trattoria di Giancarlo, 115–116
L'Avenue, 115
Le Bis, 104, 116
Le Blokk, 116
Le Crystal, 116
Le Foundouk, 67, 104
Le Jacaranda, 117

Le Marrakchi, 63, 104, 117
Le Tanjia, 23
Le Tobsil, 29, 104, 117
Lotus Privilege, 104, 117
Maison Arabe, 46
Musée de Marrakech Café, 69
Narwama, 104, 117
Nid' Cigogne, 104, 117
Pâtisserie Driss, 155
Raja, 145
Silvestro, 155
Taros Café, 155
Tatchibana, 59
Terrasse des Épices, 32, 53
Terrasses de L'Alhambra, 63, 117–118
Villa Flore, 16, 104, 118

Photo **Credits**

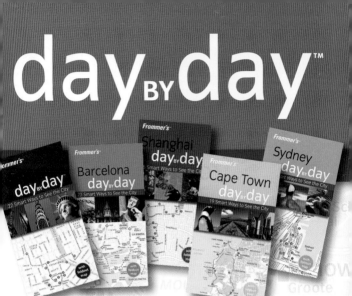

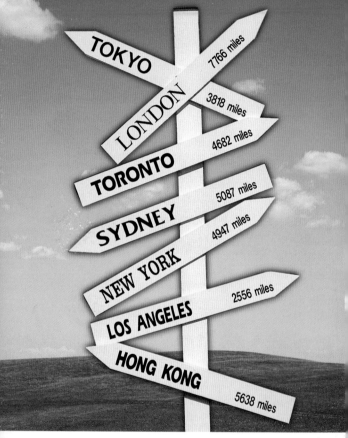

Explore over 3,500 destinations.

TOKYO — 7766 miles
LONDON — 3818 miles
TORONTO — 4682 miles
SYDNEY — 5087 miles
NEW YORK — 4947 miles
LOS ANGELES — 2556 miles
HONG KONG — 5638 miles

Frommers.com makes it easy.

Find a destination. ✓ Book a trip. ✓ Get hot travel deals.
Buy a guidebook. ✓ Enter to win vacations. ✓ Listen to podcasts.
Check out the latest travel news. ✓ Share trip photos and memories.
And much more.

Frommers.com